A Life of Azikiwe

K. A. B. Jones-Quartey was born in Accra in 1913.
After a missionary school education he worked under
Azikiwe as a reporter on the *African Morning Post* from
1934–37. He then went to America to continue his
education and graduated in Government from the
Universities of Lincoln and Columbia. By 1950 he was
back in Ghana, attached to the Department of
Extra-Mural Studies in the University College of Ghana,
of which he became Assistant Director in 1952. He is now
an Associate Professor in the Institute of African Studies,
University of Ghana. 'Soas' Jones-Quartey, as he is
known, has travelled widely in many parts of the world;
he is married with four sons.

A Life of Azikiwe

K. A. B. Jones-Quartey

 Penguin Books

Penguin Books Ltd, Harmondsworth,
Middlesex, England
Penguin Books Inc., 3300 Clipper Mill Road,
Baltimore 11, Md, U.S.A.
Penguin Books Pty Ltd, Ringwood
Victoria, Australia

First published 1965

Made and printed in Great Britain by
C. Nicholls & Company Ltd
Set in Monotype Times

Contents

Before Anything Else

It seems to be necessary, before anything else, for me to say something here about this book, a precaution which may save readers some impatience.

First of all, it is a *general*, not a *political*, biography. Students interested solely in political analysis are advised to go to James Coleman, Kenneth Post, Richard Sklar, and Babatunde Williams (see below) who have written mostly on this aspect of the life of Azikiwe, Awolowo, and the rest. Secondly, space limitations have made necessary certain exclusions which some will notice but none, I hope, will consider fatal: for instance, the absence of full accounts of the roles of the late Adegokeh Adelabu and Mazi Mbonu Ojike ... So much for general points; now to more specific ones.

In Part I, I have simply introduced my subject, giving but few details and hardly spelling out any themes, philosophies, or developments. Readers should therefore not expect to learn all about any particular subject or theme the first time they encounter it. Part II is relatively complete in the treatment of its subjects, but Part III, again, holds many questions over into Part IV and even later.

The reason for all this is simply the way of development and fruition of ideas, as of plans, in Dr Azikiwe's story. These follow their own pattern of progress in both time and space. A particular line of thought, for instance, starting with Zik at home is developed in America, and does not start functioning – or is not finally stated as a workable idea or working principle – until he returns to Africa. It seemed to me pointless to deal fully and finally with such a subject in an early chapter of the book, instead of following it through the whole narrative, if necessary, as it developed and moved about with its host. This may conceivably create in some readers a feeling of fragmentation; I hope it will not also give them an impression of disunity or incoherence.

In the Appendixes I have included a collection of letters, mostly from Dr Azikiwe's American period. They seem to me to be an important addition to the subject, partly for their honest imperfections and enthusiastic exaggerations in language, but principally for their disclosure of early virtue in social and political directions whose continuity remained unbroken till the 'end'. Because of this I feel a special sense of gratitude to Dr Azikiwe's young niece, Miss Elizabeth Arinze, for having informed me of the existence of these letters when I saw the family at Onitsha, although it was through Dr Azikiwe himself that I finally got hold of them.

It had been my intention to include in the Appendixes other material which considerations of space have eventually kept out, material such as the letter from Sir Eric Ashby to Dr Azikiwe in 1962, in which Sir Eric commented upon the University of Nigeria at Nsukka, after his visit and inspection there. Then there was Zik's own letter to the publisher of the *New York Times* in the same year, protesting vigorously against what he considered the bad-mannered treatment of the new African states and their leaders in the *Times* and in the American press generally.* Thirdly, and surprisingly, there was the section in an early book by Frank Laubach, the 'Each One Teach One' literacy education pioneer, entitled *Wake Up or Blow Up*, in which Laubach warned America about Communism and included 'Communist Zik' in a lurid catalogue of alarm. Indeed, however he came by the impression, Dr Laubach's commentary on Dr Azikiwe carried this astonishing passage (p. 80):

In Nigeria the British Government is torn between the desire to help the people read and the fear that it will help Communist Zik with his chain of Communist newspapers to win more Nigerians to his side. He claims half of Nigeria now. [1951]

Dr Laubach said he told 'the governor of Nigeria and Lord Healey',† who had invited him 'to a conference on their baffling dilemma': 'If you try to suppress literacy, you prove that Zik is right, and you will have to fight a bloody revolution. If you encourage literacy, . . .' etc., etc.

* A similar protest of Dr Azikiwe's did get published in the world press at about the same time.
† Lord Hailey.

There is also in my hands a friendly letter from Gene Tunney, undefeated heavyweight boxing champion of the world in the Twenties, to Zik the ex-boxer and still ecstatic boxing fan. There are congratulatory addresses, press clippings, and other relevant material, all of which have had to be excluded.

And now the time has come for me to cower before a task which moral duty as well as common courtesy places upon me: acknowledging the gratitude I owe to so many who in one way or another were involved in the production of this book. The number is indeed large and I can only hope that those who don't get mentioned by name here – if that should really happen – will understand and forgive.

First, I should like to thank my august subject himself, President Azikiwe – my old 'boss' – for the amount of time he gave me and the large range of facilities he put at my disposal. I do not expect him to be entirely satisfied or pleased with all the results his generosity has made possible, but I hope that nothing I have said or suggested about him in this book will be found by him to be unfounded, unwarranted, indelicate, or unfair.

Next, there are, as far as my text itself is concerned, the writers, historians, biographers, and analysts on whose books I have relied so much. They are: the Sardauna of Sokoto, Vincent Ikeotuonye, Professor James Coleman, Vice-Chancellor Kenneth Dike, Chiefs Obafemi Awolowo and H. O. Davies, Drs Saburi Biobaku, T. O. Elias, J. F. Ade Ajayi, Kalu Ezera, and Babatunde Williams; and Messrs Michael Crowder and Kenneth Post, with the latter of whom I also discussed a particular chapter personally in London. But the overriding usefulness to me of Ikeotuonye, Coleman, Chief Awolowo, and Williams should be acknowledged separately here. R. L. Sklar's minutely detailed study of *Nigerian Political Parties* was published a little too late to have helped me as much as it obviously would have done.

Apart from the authors there are the libraries and archives where their books, and my other vital sources, were found and used. I am grateful for the services and courtesy of the following: Mr Donald Simpson and his staff at the library of the Royal Commonwealth Society, London; Mr Allen and the staff of the

British Museum Newspaper Library at Colindale, where they have been serving up huge tomes to me for years; Hans Panofsky at the African Library at Northwestern University in Evanston, Illinois (here I found microfilms of the *West African Pilot* and, therefore, my principal primary source for Zik's early years: the series entitled 'My Odyssey'); the Law Library of the University of Chicago (for the loan of Babatunde Williams's dissertation cited in the book); Mrs Towun Ogunsheye, of Africana Library at the University of Ibadan; and finally the librarian of the Lagos Municipal Library, for the use of their copy of the fast-disappearing *Renascent Africa*, as well as, I believe, Orizu's *Without Bitterness*.

Of the friends and critics who helped me directly with the text I am grateful above all to four: Christopher Fyfe, author of our most detailed historical studies of Sierra Leone to date; Akin Mabogunje, geographer at the University of Ibadan, Nigeria; Miss Gloria Marshall, young anthropologist of African ancestry at New York University; and St Clair Drake, American cousin and friend of Africa. Of these four, Christopher Fyfe read several chapters, made 'a radical suggestion' on one and a fearful attack on another, both gestures producing the salutary effects intended! He also volunteered help with the page proofs. Dr Mabogunje – indirectly during a general discussion in America, and even at this writing entirely unbeknown to himself – suggested a new approach and thus added a new chapter to the book; and Professor St Clair Drake (like Fyfe) called many historical as well as contemporary facts to my attention, both in correction of error and in addition to my material. To Dr Gloria Marshall I owe perhaps my greatest debt on the text, for her perceptive, quick-witted, and extensive critiques, and her sheer hard work. She even acted for a bit, once, as my super-scale typist!

Others who read parts of the manuscript and made suggestions or gave early encouragement include my late colleagues on the Committee for the Comparative Study of New Nations at the University of Chicago, especially Professors Aristide Zolberg and Robert LeVine, and Dr Wilton Dillon, until recently of the Phelps-Stokes Fund. None of these kind people can be blamed for the defects remaining and the opinions expressed in *A Life of*

Azikiwe, in addition to the gaps I have already notified.

Mention of academic connexions reminds me here that it was the generosity of my own University of Ghana, and of the Executive Committee of the African and American Program, that enabled me to write this book. In these connexions I must also acknowledge the initial roles of Mr Michael Josselson at Geneva, and Professor Edward Shils of Chicago and Cambridge. Through Miss Marion Bieber's generosity I met Derrick Sington in London. To both, my thanks.

The other acknowledgements I have to make are for different but essential services without which it would not have been possible for me to collect my material at all. I refer to hospitality, domestic care, and the provision of transport facilities. On my many trips into and through Nigeria, I have always enjoyed the hospitality of my life-long friends the Adeniyi-Jones brothers, and many members of their families both in Lagos and Ibadan. On this occasion they gave me comfort as well as transport facilities to and from some of my sources of information on Dr Azikiwe.

So did Mr Modjabeng Dowuona, the Ghanaian Registrar of the Ahmadu Bello University at Zaria, and his wife Catherine. It was 'Modj' who at short notice made it possible for me to do the long journey by road to see Zik's birthplace at Zungeru. Two other friends were also invaluable in this respect: Mr Hugh Clarke, of UNICEF, Lagos, who took me along on his trip by road through parts of Northern Nigeria; and another old school-days friend, Professor Cox-George, then head of economics at Nsukka. 'Cox' let me take his car and drive myself to Onitsha to see Zik's family, staying away several days. Nor must I forget my three drivers: Odebode, Joseph Ladega, and David Itseko.

A Life of Azikiwe was to have been produced in a special Penguin West African series, and the original invitation to me to write it came from Tom Hopkinson, author and journalist well known to the contemporary Africanist public. He received suggestions on authorship for a proposed new series, including the Zik volume, from Miss Lalage Bown, formerly a colleague of mine in the old Institute of Extra-Mural Studies at the University of Ghana. I gratefully acknowledge here their key role at the beginning.

Miss Bown's present Director – she is herself Deputy Director – of Extra-Mural Studies at Ibadan, my friend Ayo Ogunsheye, at the last moment and at short notice arranged a small discussion for me in his house, from which I learnt much. Besides himself there were Father James O'Connell, Billy Dudley, Dr Essien-Udom, and Dr Sklar, all of them in political science at Ibadan; and in addition our old friend Akin Mabogunje, who needs no further introduction. My thanks to them for enlightenment on obscure points.

The Secretary to President Azikiwe, my ex-college mate, A. K. Disu, rendered more than formal service to me on numerous occasions; and the President's personal Orderly, Jacob, was always there with a smile of welcome. I wish to thank them both here.

My wife Pearl, finally, deserves my gratitude for carrying alone the burden of looking after four boys during my long and frequent absences from home.

J.-Q.

University of Chicago
February 1964

Part One

THE MAKING OF A MAN

And I realized what was meant by the expression:
'There is plenty room at the top.'

Yes, there is plenty [of] room at the top because very few people care to travel beyond the average route. And so most of us seem satisfied to remain within the confines of mediocrity.

*

And I began to dream dreams and to see visions.

From *My Odyssey*, No. 5

Prologue

Did Nnamdi Azikiwe, in the bargaining that followed the General Election of 1959, lose the golden opportunity of his life, after all? Had he, by accepting the Governor-Generalship thrown away the chance of taking something even more important to Nigeria for him, *Azikiwe*, to have at that moment in its history, namely the Prime Ministership? If he had, then the next question is: did he *know* he was doing so, or was he misled, either by his advisers or by himself, into accepting a compromise which has already been falsified, or is likely to be falsified, by history?

Or we could approach the matter from its more dynamic aspect and ask: *Could* Dr Azikiwe have got the Prime Ministership if he had played his advantages to that end? If so, on what grounds and at what cost: (a) to himself, (b) to the requirements of political equilibrium at that critical date, and, therefore (c) to the country itself? Would it have *cost* anything, or gained everything merely by its own potential? Are his critics reckoning without Zik's 'host' at the time, Alhaji Sir Abubakar Tafawa Balewa, or not? What were these supposed advantages Zik had?

The main question before us does not exhaust itself even by these many *sequiturs*. For instance: If Zik had not been 'misled' but *knew* what he was doing – and he says he did know – was he wiser perhaps than both his 'friendliest foes and deadliest friends' in choosing the role he did, rather than its alternative? Did he, in other words, recognize more hidden powers in a constitutional headship of state assumed under those conditions than appeared possible even to the revolutionaries themselves? Perhaps it was not so much a question of perceiving hidden possibilities if he accepted the Governor-Generalship as it was one of sensing hidden dangers if he *tried to take* the Prime Ministership. Was it, or was Zik merely seizing a practical politician's opportunistic chance of hanging up, at last, a self-portrait he had been

painting for thirty years, and which was captioned: 'I TOLD YOU
I HAD NO POLITICAL AMBITIONS, DIDN'T I?'

These are taxing problems, some of the solutions to which will
be found to be implicit in the story which this biography sets out
to tell. The main question is answered – adequately, I hope – in
one of the closing chapters of this book, but, to arrive at a
satisfying view of the whole Zik phenomenon at all, we must try
to observe *all* the facts most carefully. The succeeding paragraphs
of this Prologue, for instance, give details of some of the consequences of Zik's 1959 choice.

At the beginning of February 1963, I had the great opportunity
and privilege of travelling through Nigeria by train with Dr
Azikiwe, in further pursuit of original material for this biography.
He was then Governor-General and was returning to his seat of
government, Lagos, after one of his frequent retreats to his
intellectual home. His intellectual home is Nsukka, in Eastern
Nigeria, near Onitsha. There he has a great estate, his library,
and one of his dreams-come-to-life, the University of Nigeria.
And there he spends as much time as he can find away from
State duties in Lagos or on tour, reads, writes, entertains a little,
and attends to the ramifications of his numerous and large
interests. He also, of course, receives officials, ministers, and
politicians from the East Region, and any foreign visitors to
whom he must extend official or private courtesy.

The estate is really a vast complex, part of which is 'public'.
That part consists of the only 'Catering Rest House' in the area –
a good one – where visitors to Nsukka may stay and eat at
reasonable cost; a hostel for students of the University, just a
mile or two away; and the library, which Zik is building up as a
specialist (mostly *Africana*) supplement to the University
Library. A little further away there is also a new cinema, and
when I was at Nsukka a whole housing project was going up,
consisting in the main of semi-detached dwellings built on
modern lines. They now form part of Zik's Nsukka empire.

Empire? The term bears unpleasant associations, especially for
one of the outstanding anti-imperialists of the age. Zik would
react with bristling anger if anyone, ignorantly or with malice
aforethought, used that term in his hearing to describe his

Nsukka holdings. For this is, at least in his own view, a fulfilment of the Zikist* philosophy that without an economic foundation no amelioration of poor social conditions is possible. At Nsukka, Zik is steadily approaching the day when he can write 'finis' to his programme of using his talents for the benefit of a good many people.

An 'escape' from income taxation; the enjoyment of economic power; the making, and even more the leaving, of a good name – these are charges of 'hidden motive' which can be and have been brought against those, like Zik, who under capitalism build up large personal fortunes and then indulge in philanthropy. The complaints are understandable, and in many cases irrelevant. Wherever socialism, or African communalism, has organized or can organize economic society in such a way as to obviate the unlimited accumulation of personal wealth and achieve fair distribution of national resources, *together with other conditions of happiness* – such, for instance, as the elimination of the abuse of other forms of power – there, truly, is something of human goodwill and ingenuity, worthy of praise. Meanwhile, it is absurd to expect a gifted and well-intentioned man to sit on his talents, waiting to distribute these, at suitable notice, to people who then can neither eat, wear, nor sleep under them. . . .

Zik is protected – as anyone else in his position ought to be – by an elaborate system of communication lines and security checkpoints which often cancel one another out completely and leaves the anxious would-be visitor in face of a great void that is teeming with futuristic hopes and immense possibilities! If he does not know his own mind, or his business is a vague mission of goodwill, such a seeker is quickly cut up in that intricate machinery of exclusion, and the Big Chief is saved from one more interview. But with luck or perseverance a visitor is as likely as any friend to receive, at sight, an instantaneous and gracious invitation to dinner or lunch from the great man himself. If any arrangements go wrong, or his wishes get crossed, Zik passes rapidly into a state of barely-controlled fury. No genteel, centuries-old façade of politeness, he.

The journey from Nsukka by road to Enugu, the Eastern

* 'Zikist' here, and in some other parts of the book, is a direct adjective only and does not refer to the 'Zikist Vanguard' movement.

capital, and by rail from Enugu to the Northern capital, Kaduna, then south through Zungeru (his birthplace), Jebba, Ilorin, Offa, Oshogbo, Ibadan (capital of the West Region), and Abeokuta, to Lagos, was a long procession of personal triumphs for Zik. It gave me, along with those among the fifty million Nigerians who are at all conscious of their political identity and social environment, the opportunity of assessing the standing of this man who came closest to being a national symbol.

Enthusiasm for the person of Zik was most voluminous in the East, his own home region, and in the West, his long-time political stomping-ground. In both areas the million-throated *Zeeeeek*, which had become the people's own, almost mystical, greeting for him, rumbled forth on a hundred occasions. They danced for him and sang for him, emptying his private travelling exchequer.* In the North, where the people are shy of politics and their traditional rulers are formal and gravely correct, the greeting almost everywhere was more official and businesslike than enthusiastic. However, it was not lacking in warmth and cordiality, on the part of the Northern Governor, many of his Ministers, and other officials.

At the other two regional capitals, Enugu in the East and Ibadan in the West, the ceremonies at the arrival and departure of the distinguished visitor were more informal and hearty. Sir Francis Ibiam, Governor of the East, twinkling and felt-hatted as usual, and with him Dr Okpara, the Premier, did the honours at the Enugu railway station and at the very palatial new residence of the Governor. At Ibadan, the 'G.-G.' was met by the Governor, Chief Fadahunsi, the Premier, Chief S. L. Akintola, and the Ghanaian who had the honour of being Chief Justice of Western Nigeria until only recently, Sir Samuel Okai Quashie-Idun.† At each of these centres there was a huge welcoming party which included many Ministers and a complete cross-

---

* At one point I quickly offered to pool present resources with him, so that yet another dancing group could get their 'dash'. Zik accepted immediately with a grin, and we conducted the manipulations in a few seconds, 'under the table'.

† Sir Samuel was a magistrate in Accra in 1936 when Zik was tried in the sedition case, and was reported to have counselled caution in the interpretation and application of the procedural aspects of the law by the law officers and the police.

section of the community. They crushed and crowded one another in that characteristic African anonymity out of which éliteness is often seen finally extricating itself only with great difficulty, sometimes even with diffidence.

It was in the centre of such gatherings that Zik was most at home, at the same time most outstanding. He was Head of State, and also six-foot tall. He knew most of these people intimately, and had some personal word or private joke to share with many of them individually. And when the occasion demanded it he put his hand to his mouth in a characteristic mannerism and laughed through his teeth until he was almost out of breath. At the Lagos Terminus the crowd was thickest of all. But before he was enveloped in it, way had to be made and sufficient time allowed for Mrs Azikiwe to welcome her husband back and for the Federal Prime Minister, the unobtrusive-looking but dignified Alhaji Sir Abubakar Tafawa Balewa, to offer his friendly greetings and pay his official respects. After that followed the short, vociferous drive to State House, where the high spirits of friends, ex-colleagues, ministers, visitors, and gatecrashers were at their highest. . . .

A number of people have often wondered why 'His Excellency' insists on travelling by train on these long and mostly hot, dusty, dreary journeys. Surely, travelling long-distance by rail in West Africa, even in the comparative luxury of a Governor-General's special train, is a test of physical tolerance and endurance to which an overburdened Chief of State should not be subjected more than once in a while? The question is reasonable. . . . Why then does Zik do it? I asked him this, and his answer was not too immediate nor too decisive. Why should it have been? He knows that he does not like flying: 'Why should one rush about so much, and is this necessary for a whole life-time?' He knows that he likes best to go by ship: isn't that just the opposite of flying? . . .

The reason for preferring the train to the plane is the same as the reason for preferring the ship: but to say so is somewhat embarrassing, because everyone knows that the train, in West Africa, gives you torture along with time. Don't we all repeat with relish, at the expense both of our governments and of the British colonials who built our railways, that you can get off a moving 'Express' in West Africa, do some shopping in the bush, and jump on again without the slightest trouble?

The truth is that Zik sticks to it because the train keeps him in touch with the land and with the people. The vastness of Nigeria and the number and variety of its inhabitants demands constant reminding and repeated personal contact. Zik sees the people, and they see him. It is good for both him and them. This was not simply the old campaigner's love for the crowds and their votes, though there is, no doubt, some residual nostalgia in him for that too. This was more a case of the constitutional 'Father of his People' running a knitting thread through them, taking very seriously to heart the need for drawing this complex amalgam together into a oneness. It is a good way, too, of looking closely at the woods, the forests, the red earth; the parched, thirsty soil; the rich areas, the poor areas; the clothed and the naked; the immense tasks ahead. . . .

Police Deputy-Superintendent Adewusi kept the buffer-state clear between his Chief and all-comers, except at the proper times; and Miss Dorothy Emery, an English secretary, carried out what duties were necessary or possible during the four-days long trip. At lunch and dinner we joined the 'G.-G.' in his white-and-gold lounge for drinks, then followed him a little later into the dining car. Here, where everything and everybody was nearer, the atmosphere was quite relaxed. By the end of the meal it was more likely than not that Zik would be regaling us with some tale or other of old political exploits, laughing infectiously from the back of his teeth and rocking from side to side as he warmed up to the good but simple food and the occasional sip of table wine.

For years, well into his later political career, Zik did not smoke and touched no alcohol. But he is no Gandhi or Stafford Cripps, no prophet of abstinence on spiritual or moral grounds. It was with him largely a matter of physical and intellectual disinclination. But years of political rough and tumble, of standing among the crowd and also being of them, finally taught him to take a little for the party's sake. This has yielded rich dividends for those fortunate enough to be in intimate social 'business' with Zik. In that kind of small setting he is fascinating to watch, as he savours his bit of sherry, or quaffs his occasional mug of stout, or sips at surprisingly large quantities of after-dinner cordials.

However, it is a good cigar that obviously gives Zik the most fun. He lights it and licks it round and round and turns it upside-down, sucking on it, pointing with it, waving it back and forth, as he talks volumes on any chosen subject. In his enthusiasm for talk Zik sometimes forgets the cigar; but quite often it is the cigar that forgets Zik and goes out. After one or two efforts to re-light it, he would suddenly turn it around and look it full in the face for a few moments, then put it down and say, abruptly: 'Well, Lady and Gentle-Men ...' The uniformed steward pulls back his chair, and we all get up and wish 'His Excellency' a very good night.

Today, at sixty, he is 'The President', which Zik likes much better. It is more in line with modern ways. It has enabled him to shed the uncomfortable trappings of a British-style pro-consul gracefully, and to carry readily the status of constitutional head of a member-state of a commonwealth of political equals.

Chapter 1

The Man

As for me, my stiffest earthly assignment is ended and my major life's work is done. My country is now free, and I have been honoured to be its first indigenous Head of State. What more could one desire in life?

The speaker was His Excellency the Right Honourable Dr Nnamdi Azikiwe, giving his Inaugural as first Nigerian Governor-General and Head of State of the new Dominion. He was addressing an international, multi-racial concourse of people at once massive and, in large part, distinguished. The date, Wednesday, 16 November 1960, was for him doubly significant, for it was also his fifty-sixth birthday anniversary. 'Zik' – as he is known to millions in many parts of the world – had, on that memorable day, arrived at the apex of a long, turbulent, and dazzling public career.

Today, over four years later, he is still Head of State in his country, but now as President of the Independent Republic of Nigeria. Nor had there been a single doubt anywhere that when the day of republicanism came, the first Nigerian Governor-General would, by some universally approved formula, automatically become the first President of the Republic. For it would be the same man, 'Zik'. Thus, in his own opinion at least, he had converted himself from a politician – the title he had so long rejected – into a statesman of continuing importance to his country, a role and a description more in tune with his sense of destiny.

'What more,' then, 'could one desire in life' indeed, than that at the splendid age of fifty-six years – not young, not old – a man should have become head of state in his 'new', large, populous, and promising country, being also many other things besides? For he is six-foot tall and handsome, the husband of a beautiful woman and the father of four fine children; a recognized patriot, nationalist, and leader largely responsible for the ushering in of the last phase of the African independence movement exactly thirty years ago; a former athlete, a lively scholar, an author, and an orator.

The outstanding Nigerian of his day and one of Africa's foremost personalities of any age, Nnamdi Azikiwe had, on that sunny day in Lagos – scene of many of his greatest triumphs as well as defeats – achieved the ultimate in personal progress. He had become, as much as any Nigerian could ever have become, the national symbol of his country's aspirations.

The climb to this pinnacle had been long and laborious, but the influences behind the effort had been equally strong. First, Azikiwe had had his own personality to draw upon: athletic physique, tough character, great gifts of mind. Add to these, secondly, the challenging family influences of his childhood, and, thirdly, the fortunate appearance and the choice of his first heroes and life models: Dr J. E. K. Aggrey, a Ghanaian resident in America, James A. Garfield, the twentieth President of the United States; and Marcus Garvey, prophet of the 'Back to Africa' movement. These three encounters with the ideal were quickly followed, fourthly, by Azikiwe's practical experiences in America and Britain. Finally, the fires of African nationalism, to which he himself eventually added many a flame, burned and fashioned his ideas on African emancipation into an effective, fruitful programme.

At the confluence of such fateful roads as these there could be nothing less awaiting a man of Azikiwe's calibre than the prize he collected on his birthday that day in 1960, to the acclamation of a vast concourse of his admirers.

Chapter 2

The Models

Azikiwe's formative years were influenced most by his family and his three early heroes. The first of these, J. E. Kwegyir Aggrey, was soon to be called, in biography, 'Aggrey of Africa': he died shortly after Zik saw him.* The second, General Garfield, came out of American frontier lore; and the third, Marcus Garvey, was a catalyst whose power to inspire his audience was equal to Aggrey's but wholly different. It is the importance of these three men for Zik's early life that we shall consider in this chapter.

James Emman Kwegyir Aggrey (1875–1927) was a Ghanaian (Gold Coast) African of Fanti origin. He had gone to America for higher education as a young man and had returned in middle-age covered with honours as a great Christian and religious leader, a preacher, scholar, educator, teacher, orator, and African patriot of infectious appeal. When Aggrey toured West and East Africa late in 1920 and 1924, under the auspices of an American foundation (the Phelps-Stokes Fund), Azikiwe was in Lagos, capital of Nigeria, where he had been first a secondary schoolboy and then a young recruit in the civil service.

Aggrey had been sent out to Africa to survey, in company with a group of white Americans, the educational needs of both the east and the west coasts. Overflowing with his own peculiarly expansive brand of Christian love for all mankind, but also acutely conscious of the shortcomings of his people, Dr Aggrey mounted a personal campaign of exhortation and encouragement among the Africans he was visiting, such as no one before him had had the opportunity, or indeed been qualified, to attempt.

The message Aggrey delivered was everywhere an adroit review of the educational, economic, and political conditions of Africa, set, as he saw them, in a matrix of race relations which he

* *Aggrey of Africa*, by the Rev. Edwin W. Smith (London, Student Christian Mission Press, 1929), was the first and is still the fullest account of Aggrey's life.

acknowledged to be bad in many ways but would not himself worsen by malicious exploitation. Indeed Aggrey was totally incapable of malice. On the contrary, he urged his countrymen to the persuasion that only cooperation between black and white – like the harmony from the keys of a piano – could produce economic and social improvement for the blacks. But most of all Dr Aggrey played on the self-respect, the pride, the then relatively dormant ambitions of his people. He said that nothing but the best was good enough for them. He urged them to fly high as the eagles they were, and not to be content with the low fortunes and mean pickings of chickens: 'My people of Africa!', he cried,

'we were created in the image of God, but men have made us think that we are chickens, and we still think we are. But we are eagles. Stretch forth your wings and fly! Don't be content with the food of chickens!'

Here was the living complex, the composite ideal, on which Nnamdi Azikiwe was to base much of his own Grand Design of life: through personal preparation and achievement, to the emancipation of his country and people.

From Log-Cabin to White House sounds immediately like the summation, familiar to everyone, of the life of America's great national saint, Abraham Lincoln; in fact it is the biography of General James A. Garfield, twentieth President of the United States of America. It had been written by a William M. Thayer for the youth of his and President Garfield's country, but a copy fell into the hands of an African youngster too, some three thousand miles away. The book received from Benjamin Azikiwe – as he then was – a reaction to the Garfield story that was as direct and positive as it ever got from any of those for whom it was originally written. Nor was this surprising. Presented at the proper, psychological moment, the biography of James A. Garfield, at least as Thayer wrote it, could not fail to have on an ambitious and earnest boy in his teens much the same undifferentiated impact as that of Lincoln would have done. For there was a similarity in the two lives that went far beyond the simple outline of 'log-cabin to White House' which applied to both, and the extreme impressiveness of each record was equally exciting. Indeed, biography can show nowhere a more astonishing parallel than that formed by the main facts and fortunes of the lives of these two men.

Born in log-cabins built by their fathers in the wilderness of the American frontier, in the same degree of total poverty; bereft of one parent each in very early life; both powerfully endowed mentally and physically and obliged to manage their own self-education at prodigious cost in labour and privation, their lives followed the same pattern. Each in his day* worked on farms, chopped wood, served on river-boats, and did odd jobs of all kinds to maintain himself and help his family to make ends meet. Each gave his every spare moment to study and learning, by voracious reading of any material he could find, developing himself so well and so early that he could teach others among his backwoods fellow-citizens as soon as he himself knew enough to do so. Each proceeded to the study of law while trying to earn a living, Lincoln as a surveyor and Garfield as a teacher.

Being and doing all these things, the two men would have been thought to have resembled each other closely enough. But still there was more to the likeness than that. Lincoln had begun his public career by entering the legislature of his native State, Illinois, before he was thirty years of age; much later, Garfield did the same in Ohio. Lincoln fought as a soldier in a war and later became the youngest army officer in his day; Garfield in his generation and about the same age achieved an exact copy of this record.† Lincoln's talents as debater and orator were so compelling that, allied to his proved abilities in other respects, these valuable gifts eventually and almost inevitably took him through Congress and into the White House; the same was true in every detail for Garfield. Moreover, neither man was a candidate for the honour, at the national party Convention which eventually nominated him. Finally, tragic and most surprising of all, both President Lincoln and General Garfield died in office by the assassin's bullet.‡

* Lincoln, 1809–65; Garfield, 1831–81.

† Lincoln fought in the 'Blackhawk War' and Garfield in the 'War of the Rebellion'.

‡ The fourth assassination of an American president in office took place soon after this chapter was completed. President John F. Kennedy was shot and killed in Dallas, Texas, on 22 November 1963.

'History', concludes Garfield's biographer, 'has no parallel for this amazing fact. We search in vain the annals of all countries for a kindred record. ...' It is only that that last ten per cent of supreme genius and humanity distinguishes Lincoln from Garfield, inevitably, and makes him tower over most other historical figures as well, a distinction which young Ben could not have made at the time and which was thus quite irrelevant to the question of inspiration.

Thayer's book on Garfield's life, as told in his deliberately adolescent style in *From Log-Cabin to White House*, was presented in December 1920 to Azikiwe as a school prize. Coming so soon after his personal encounter with Aggrey just a month before, its impact was immense. It convinced the youngster, burning with ambition, that his secret yearnings were not futile day-dreams. If a poor boy, without a father and starting right there in the American equivalent of the African 'bush', could have done that much for himself and risen to such heights, so – Benjamin Azikiwe told himself – so can I! All I need is the determination to work hard. ... It was a meeting of points in the dreamer which renewed those stirrings of fate first set in motion by the force of the Aggrey revelation.

We come, lastly, to Marcus Garvey. But this is not because Garvey was third in time to the other two major influences – that is, apart from his family – of Azikiwe's formative years. In fact he was first (by a few months), for it was while Zik was at the well-known secondary school, the Hope Waddell Institute at Calabar, in the earlier part of 1920, that he was introduced to the legend of Marcus Garvey. It will be remembered that he encountered Aggrey and received the Garfield biography in Lagos only later that year.

The reason for presenting Marcus Garvey last is the great contrast between him and the other two. For that matter we can, without disadvantage, leave out Garfield at this point and draw the contrast between Aggrey and Garvey alone. Aggrey's philosophy, as we have seen, was a plea for love and cooperation among races. It had a religious base which was Christian-Protestant and whose symbols were the accepted symbols of Christianity, as propagated throughout the world by its originally white proselytes. Its whole motif for Africa, as for the rest of humanity, was salvation through redemption by Christian (or God-directed) means.

Marcus Garvey, for his part, believed in God too, and, like Aggrey, held 'the Creator' up to his fellow blacks. But his was a revolutionary God, a black God, a God to fight for the black man against the white. Garvey's was essentially a counsel of war, not of peace; of withdrawal, not of *rapport*; of challenge to the white man, not cooperation with him. Addressing his people, Garvey cried: 'You must forget the White Gods! Erase the White Gods from your hearts. We must go back to the native church, to our own true God!' The late George Padmore, whose own revolutionary career started in America under these influences, has given many accounts of the 'Garvey Movement' – as 'Garveyites' to this day refer to it; he did so particularly in his *Pan-Africanism or Communism?* Padmore, and other chroniclers too, have described how Garvey suited the action to the word and established, among others, the African Orthodox Church, with its ideological symbolism of the black Christ and black Madonna. . . . And so on.

Benjamin Azikiwe's first contact with the Garvey philosophy was when one of his school friends told him of a Negro who was said to be coming from America to redeem Africa. Benjamin 'spoofed the idea', but later was shown an old, tattered copy of *The Negro World*, carrying the weekly letter of Marcus Garvey. Garvey was identified as 'Provisional President of Africa' in the paper, and the motto of the organization – 'One God, One Aim, One Destiny' – was also prominent. But most of all the youngster was impressed with the fiery message of Garvey to the whole black world. He copied down the passage he liked most, which said:

God Almighty created each and every one of us for a place in the world, and for the least of us to think that we are created only to be what we are, and not what we can make [of] ourselves, is to impute an improper motive to the Creator for creating us.

For a long time after that, Benjamin and his schoolmates debated the issues raised by the Garvey message. Always the precocious one, he 'was able to convince [his] friends that if

Garvey was a great man, which his admirers claimed him to be, then we were not "Hopeless, Worthless Idiots", unless we chose to be. On the contrary, I suggested that we could make ourselves "Hopeful, Worthy Individuals" who were capable of appreciating the benefits of Western civilization and adjusting ourselves to make life worthwhile.' (It should be explained here that 'Hopeless, Worthless Idiots' was the sardonic filling-out of the initials of the name of the school: *H*ope *W*addell *I*nstitute, for the specific purpose of torturing defenceless 'freshers'. Benjamin Azikiwe's fertile mind quickly made an advantageous play on words out of this tradition, as soon as the occasion offered.)

Then he talked to his father about Garvey, but there was no encouragement there! 'Father told me that Garvey was too noisy and too crude', and that if he (Benjamin) was caught with any of Garvey's writings he would be arrested. Garvey, said Azikiwe Senior, was '*persona non grata* with the authorities'. But this discouragement did not stop the young man;

Nevertheless, the motto of Garveyism appealed to me – 'One God, One Aim, One Destiny' – and I resolved to formulate my philosophy of life, as far as practicable, towards the evangelization of Universal Fatherhood, Universal Brotherhood, and Universal Happiness.

That was the direct effect of Garveyism on Benjamin Azikiwe. Of the direct effect of 'Aggreyism' Zik has also given us a fuller record:

One day I listened to a sermon which saturated my spirit so much that I became electrified and it dawned upon me that life had a meaning and I had a mission to realize and it was my task to make life worthwhile for my fellow man and be a friend to struggling humanity.

From that day I became a new man, and my ideas of life changed in so much that I lived in daydreams, day after day, hoping against hope, for the time when it would be possible for me to be like Aggrey.

By this evidence, therefore, both men – the man of Christian peace, with his plea for racial harmony and cooperation, and the man of war, with his challenge for separate and competitive existence – both men made a profound impression on young Ben. The obvious reason was the common denominator of the theme of Black, African emancipation. But at a deeper level lurked the real heart of the matter: the rejection by both men of *the philosophy of the static* in respect of their people.

Aggrey said Africans were made in the image of God but men had fooled them into the belief that they were mere chickens. *They should not accept this lowly status. They were not chickens; they were eagles:* 'Stretch forth your wings and FLY!' he cried. And Garvey, even earlier, had said exactly the same thing, though in a different way: If even the lowliest among us thought he was created *to be only what he is now and not what he could make of himself*, he blasphemed the motives of the Creator.

This was the level from which both men called to the youngster.

Chapter 3

The Moulding

The thirteen years that followed Zik's meeting with Aggrey, his study of Garfield's life, and his first look at Garveyism, saw the completion of his labour of preparation. It meant the finding of more heroes and the setting up of more models for examination and study. It involved for a long time the inevitable eclectic exercises among current political and economic theories and faiths. It included a period, too, of race-consciousness and 'anti-imperialism' sparked off chiefly by the Negro 'protest' literature of vintage 1920s.

The process also involved three distinctive sub-periods, falling between 1925 and '31 inclusive, and all spent in America. From 1925 to '28 the mental horizon of the young tyro was thick with American heroes and their political and social turmoils. In the two years – roughly – between 1928 and '29, the initiate was shifting his emphasis from politics to economics, through the introduction of European economic theory into the second phase of his studies. Then, from 1929 to '31, the seeker was finding a synthesis reasonable for his own political and economic ideas for Africa. The time, that is to say, between 1925 and '31, was Azikiwe's period of quest.

Before leaving home for the United States he had lots of time to think, and a lot to think about:

'NOTHING but the best is good enough for the African.' I kept musing within myself the above statement of Dr Aggrey until I became infatuated with the idea which surged right through my head and made me experience a brain-wave.

And I looked round the various sections of West Africa. And I saw the leaders of the various trades and professions. And I noticed that very few of them measured up with the best in their calling, when compared with the rest of the outside world.

And I marvelled at this example of arrested mental development in man's Odyssey on earth.

Then I began to ponder why some people were born to rule others and why some people were born to be ruled by others.

And I realized what was meant by the expression: 'There is plenty room at the top.'

Yes, there is plenty room at the top because very few people care to travel beyond the average route. And so most of us seem satisfied to remain within the confines of mediocrity.

... and I began to be intellectually curious and I made up my mind that if Providence willed it, then I would proceed to America, and realize my dreams, and if I could not be the best in my chosen field, then I would try to be numbered among the best, because only the best was good enough for Africa.

Then I became interested in the biography of Dr Aggrey. And I wanted to learn more about him in order that his experiences might be a beacon to me, if and when I was sufficiently prepared to embark upon the great adventure.

There was also the parallel line of thought occasioned by the Garvey themes: 'One God, One Aim, One Destiny', 'Back to Africa', 'Africa for the Africans'. ... Thus, with Aggrey and Garvey as foundation and background, Benjamin Azikiwe proceeded to America in 1925. There he built upon it with the stirring chronicle of John Brown, his anti-slavery passions, his martyrdom, his body in the grave and his soul still on the campaign march. This was further bolstered by the poetry of J. G. Whittier, much of which was on the same theme; and to it he added Longfellow, for beauty and simplicity but also because Longfellow was then popular. Awaiting him impatiently at the next remove were two groups of interveners that were to shake the young student to both his intellectual and psychological foundations: the Negro vanguard of protest, and the great American political and social theorists, most of whom were also men of action.

Alain Locke, the Negro philosopher of Howard University, small, immaculate in appearance and thought and speech; and with him W. E. B. du Bois, aristocratic, intellectually proud, and even more significant – these were, in their different ways, setting the moral and intellectual tone of the Negro protest movement. It was Alain Locke's book, *The New Negro* (an anthology), that gave Zik his idea of 'the New Africa', the emotive slogan with which he opened his campaign in Accra years later.

Opposed to du Bois was the figure of Booker T. Washington, and, opposed to both, that of Marcus Garvey, ominously preparing for the physical evacuation of all Negroes in the western world back to Africa. Around them all were the disturbing poems of Langston Hughes and Countee Cullen, the latter of whom was singing:

> These men were Kings, albeit they were black,
> Christophe and Dessalines and L'Ouverture;
> Their majesty has made me turn my back
> Upon a plaint I once shaped to endure.
> These men were black, I say, but they were crowned
> And purple-clad, however brief their time.
> Stifle your agony; let grief be drowned;
> We know joy had a day once and a clime.

To make matters a little worse for the stranger from Africa, there, with his powerful stand on internationalism, was William Jennings Bryan; and, going much further back, were the scientist-inventor-thinker-administrator, Benjamin Franklin, and Thomas Paine, throwing his intellectual and religious radicalism across the Atlantic to both old and new worlds. There also was Thomas Jefferson himself, a profound ruler profoundly distrustful of rulers, and declaring sovereignty to be the supreme prerogative of the people: 'The will of the people is the only legitimate foundation of any government', as he put it in his letter to W. Waring in 1801.

When Azikiwe broke temporarily from the hold of these 'priests, poets, and politicians', he fell into the grip of the economic theorists: the Utopian-Marxists, the Guild-Socialists, the Fabians. Attention to these economic studies, as a necessary phase in the education of a man, removed for the time being the emphasis from the theory and practice of political freedom to those of economic freedom. Now Zik looked with intense, concentrated interest at the ideas of Passfield, Snowden, Bernard Shaw, and Ramsay MacDonald, comparing them meticulously with those of Marx and the various Utopians. ... He was at the turn of the decade by now, and had been in America going on for six years. Time was passing, and his ideas, for their part, were gradually approaching a focal point. Two more years – 1931 to '33 – at the University of Pennsylvania, and it was practically all over. Zik had made up his mind how he was going to tackle the development problems of his Africa. He was ready to return, and did so in 1934.

In the four years after Aggrey's visit to Nigeria in 1920, and in the following nine years spent in the United States of America, Zik had pursued his ambition through a bewildering complex of experiences. He had been pupil-prizeman, student-worker, and university instructor. He had made a name in college sports, been driven to the point of attempted suicide by food hunger in its absolute, had earned several degrees, written a scholarly book, and seen something both of England and of America.

When he returned to West Africa in October 1934, Nnamdi Azikiwe was not only ready but also possessed of a personality that was to draw millions to him as a magnet draws metal chips to itself. In the process he also repelled many, to an almost equal degree. He repelled them by his *hauteur*, his irritability under pressure, his impatience with situations not of his own ordering; by the outstanding contradiction in the man who, throughout his thirty-year public career, had always declared in public, in private, and in print : 'I have no political ambitions', but who had, of all Nigerian politicians, been often the most skilful (his enemies would predictably say often the most ruthless) and had certainly been the most successful in his generation. More, he repelled them by his on-and-off advocacy of socialism, this man who, they point out, has become now one of his country's richest 'capitalists'. . . .

But surely the man who rose from the obscurity of backward early twentieth-century West Africa to the world-eminence he enjoys today could not possibly also have been 'consistent' in all things? What is consistency anyway? 'Do I contradict myself?' asked the saintly Gandhi himself once. 'Consistency', he answered his own question, 'is a hobgoblin.'

If Zik had been a blameless angel, perhaps his biography would not have been worth writing, for serious people to read.

Part Two

PREPARATION

I started, like other human beings, at a very early age, to be curious.

My maternal grandmother told me that I was so curious in my attempt to find out the constituents of fire, that I was almost roasted alive, had she not been present to save me.

*

One day, I asked her why were the people of Onitsha so named. . . .

Then I asked her why we despised others. . . .

I insisted that she should explain to me what was this historical background. . . .

I continued to belabour my grandmother to tell me more regarding the history of the Onitsha people.

*

Then grandmother stopped. But I insisted that she should tell me more about Chuma and what happened to him.

*

And as grandma continued I dozed away in her arms and fell into a deep slumber, mentally wearied at the exploits of man. . . .

From *My Odyssey*, No. 3

*

And I began to dream dreams and to see visions.

And I said to myself that if Garvey could dream of 'One God, One Aim, One Destiny' in America, and influence his contemporaries; and if Aggrey could also dream that nothing but the best was good enough for the African, by being educated in America, then not even death would stop me from reaching America in order to make my dreams come true.

From *My Odyssey*, No. 5

Chapter 4

Azikiwe's Nigeria

All the various tribes of the Yoruba nation trace their origin from Oduduwa and the city Ile Ife. In fact Ile Ife is fabled as the spot where God created man, white and black, and from whence they dispersed all over the earth.

That is the central belief in the mythology of one of the three major divisions of people in Azikiwe's Nigeria. The words are to be found in the Reverend Samuel Johnson's *History of the Yorubas*, but their import is to be sought in the dynamic pulse of life among the people whose ancestry nurtured itself on so towering a degree of exaltation. And yet that is only one-third of the story, so to speak, to which we shall return in due course. Immediately, it is necessary to enquire into the remaining two-thirds. Who are the other major peoples of Azikiwe's Nigeria, and what are *their* claims about themselves or the dominant themes in their tradition?

By far the largest of the three main divisions of people in Nigeria is the northern population: the Hausa and their rulers, the Fulani conquerors – together with many smaller ethnic groups. *Conquerors* – that is the key word. More than a century and a half ago a Fulani religious leader, the Shehu Usuman dan Fodio, started a rebellion and launched a military campaign against the Hausa among whom he and his scattered people had been living. In thirteen years dan Fodio's *jihad* (holy war) had resulted in conquest and in the establishment of an Islamic empire and a Fulani dynasty in the north. The Hausa who had eventually succumbed to this religious zeal had themselves been established in the region long before dan Fodio's birth in 1744 in the Hausa Kingdom of Gobir, nor had they given in easily to the Fulani onslaught. A good idea of the situation towards the end of the campaign can be gleaned from the words of the present Sardauna of Sokoto and Premier of Northern Nigeria, Sir Ahmadu Bello, a direct descendant of dan Fodio, in the abbreviated account he gives in his 1962 autobiography, *My Life:*

The main difficulties of the Eastern Empire were revolts by the suppressed peoples of Gobir and Zamfara who had been brought under Sokoto, but other revolts broke out at intervals all over the Empire. All these took much time and energy and patience to suppress and in spite of all efforts were constantly breaking out again and again. Much trouble came from the old Hausa rulers who had taken refuge in Damagaram which is now part of the Republic of the Niger.

The difficulties were not with the Hausa alone. At Ilorin, in the south-western, previously all-Yoruba domain of Oyo, the Fulani and the Yoruba clashed too, and remained in 'an almost continuous state of war' for a long time. But 'these wars', in Ahmadu Bello's words, 'had reached no conclusion or proper settlement when they were interrupted . . . by British intervention from the coast and Colonel Lugard's activities on the Niger. . . .' So Ilorin became in the end, and remains to this day, a fusion of Fulani-Hausa and Yoruba cultures and peoples. Mohammadu Bello, dan Fodio's son and first Sultan of Sokoto under the Shehu's 'will', thus became the progenitor of a long line of Sultans of Sokoto. The present ruler (1963) is the ninth, in his direct succession, on the throne of this 'western empire' which includes Ilorin.

The combination among any one people of the elements of ancient ethnic existence, religious as well as secular wars and conquests, and the establishment of long-lasting dynasties, occurs often enough in world history, but as often as it occurs bespeaks the same reality: a dynamism that cannot be ignored. Kingdoms, dynasties, even a virile people, do not necessarily last for ever, but while they last they command serious interest and attention. In the same way it may be added that though wars and massacres are not a pleasure to remember or record, yet as a dynamic of human history their incidence in the records of any people marks them out as a people of note. In African history such were the Zulus, the Benins, the Oyos, the Dahomians,*

* The story is told of a King of Dahomey who informed an English visitor in 1822 that the Dahomians recognized only three great powers: first, the King of Dahomey, second, God Almighty, and third, the English. In vain the Englishman tried to convince him of his error; he was 'tenacious of his *precedence*'.

and the Ashanti. And such a people are the Hausa and their princely Fulani rulers.

What of the third of our three major divisions of people in Azikiwe's Nigeria? To answer that question is to deal with Zik's own group itself: the Ibos of the East. The Ibos form the largest and most important ethnic group in Eastern Nigeria, among a number which includes the Ijaws, Ibibios, Itsekiris, and Efiks. It was among the Ibos – numerous and land-hungry, ambitious, far-ranging, crafty, and able – that a theocratic myth developed, similar in the boldness of its claims to that of the Yorubas but completely dissimilar in the uses to which it was put by its chief votaries. Kenneth Diké (the Ibo historian who is Vice-Chancellor of the University of Ibadan), says in his book on *Trade and Politics in the Niger Delta*, 1830–1885:

Two types of trading organization operated in the hinterland [that is, as distinct from the Delta]. The first, centred upon the Aros, obtained mainly in the period of the slave trade. Their influence was based on the Aro Chuku Oracle which was universally respected and feared throughout Ibo-land, and in fact by every tribe in eastern Nigeria. This oracle was supposed to reside in the territory of the Aros, a section of the Ibo tribe. In 1854 Baikie wrote of the 'noted City of Aro where there is the celebrated shrine of Tsuku [God], to which pilgrimages are made, not only from all parts of Igbo proper, but from Old Calabar, and from the tribes along the coast, and from Oru and Nembe. The town is always mentioned with great respect, almost, at times, with a degree of veneration, and the people say "Tsuku ab yama", "God lives there".' Aro people (whom the Ibos call 'Umu-Chukwu' – the Children of God) exploited this belief in their oracle to dominate the life of the region economically, and they made themselves the sole middlemen of the hinterland trade. ...

Diké shows how this was done by the establishment of Aro colonies along the trade routes of the hinterland, in effect in the name of Chuku; and he draws a parallel between this Ibo device and the course of Greece's colonization expeditions, which were largely directed by the priests of the Delphic oracle.

Acting as mediators between God and the clans, [the account continues] and assuming themselves to be the spokesmen of the Almighty, they [the Aros] held a privileged position throughout the land, erecting what amounted to a theocratic state over eastern Nigeria. ...

This privilege lay in their immense wealth, acquired through the studied exploitation of the dreaded myth of Chuku the God-Oracle. 'And with wealth,' the narrative ends, 'came great political influence.'

The second, better-known, and far more important tradition of Ibo life is what has been called 'Ibo democracy'. Ibo democracy has in turn been described in various ways: Ibo individualism, the kindred or 'village-group' system of political authority, 'the Ibos [who] make no Kings', ... It simply means that, with the exception of the historical 'accidents' of Onitsha and one or two other communities which have a kingship system said to derive from Benin origins, the social tradition of the Ibos never had any room in it for central government.

The basic political unit was a village, or a group of villages, whose members regarded themselves as kindred and formed their own structure of government, recognizing no power outside their community, no over-all sovereign at a distance, no king, 'Kingship is not and never was a feature of the Ibo constitution,' wrote C. K. Meek in *Law and Authority in a Nigerian Tribe*. And Awolowo, making his case for federalism in 1946, said: 'The Ibos ... are essentially individualistic. ... The Ibos or Ibibios cannot tolerate anyone assuming the authority of a chieftain among them. ...' The Aro-Chuku phenomenon is the more interesting, therefore, as a deviation from the norm by which an outsider group, for their own materialistic ends, successfully penetrated these kindreds and cleverly exploited their superstitious fears. It must be observed, however, that the myth, or the use to which it was put, developed in much later times as a by-product of slavery and of the eastern trade Dr Diké describes, and secondly that the 'loyalty' exacted was to a superstition, not to a concrete form of authority.

If economic exploitation, proceeding indirectly from a theocratic ideal, was the means to political power developed by an élite class of the Ibos, imperial spheres of influence, acquired and expanded through military action, seem to have been the principal interest of the Ile Ife theocracy of the Yoruba, to whom we now return. It was with the Yoruba, as with the Fulani *jihad*, a case of the religious sword in the hands of the prophet-founder (Oduduwa), being employed to destroy unbelievers and lesser breeds or to convert them to the true religion and subdue their lands under God through the prophet-militant-in-His-name. (Christians destroyed 'the heathens', and Romans destroyed Christians, in the same bursts of fervour though not necessarily with the same ends in view or with similar results.) The Reverend Mr Samuel Johnson continues his account of the Yoruba tradition:

In fact we may also take it as proved that as Oranyan [son and successor of Oduduwa] and his army, as well as his brothers, pushed on their conquest in every direction, the princes and the war-lords were stationed in various parts to hold the country, and from them sprang the many provincial Kings of various ranks and grades now existing.

Nor was this 'Yoruba sway' confined to within the borders of Nigeria. Quite the contrary. 'This also accounts for the tradition,' continues *The History of the Yorubas*,

that the Yoruba sway once extended as far as Ashanti [in present-day Ghana] and included the Gas of Accra [capital of Ghana], for the Gas say that their ancestors came from Ile Ife; ... And, certainly, until comparatively recent times the Popos and Dahomians paid tribute regularly to Oyo as their feudal head; it is certain, therefore, that the generals and war-lords of Oranyan pushed on far beyond the limits of the Yoruba country as now known. ...

However, by the time of the dan Fodio revolution of 1804 the *gloria mundi* had already passed away for the Yorubas. The great Oyo kingdom and empire had completely disintegrated, as much from its own internal troubles as from external causes. Oyo had been, in the words of J. D. Fage's *History of West Africa*, 'from almost every point of view, the greatest of the four great forest states' of West Africa, of which Benin, Dahomey, and Ashanti were the other three. But for over ninety years during the nineteenth century Oyo was torn by, and eventually collapsed partly as a result of, endless civil war. The other part of the reason for its disintegration – Fulani incursions as a prolonged extension of the *jihad* – was in fact also partly a result of the first, the civil strife among the various Yoruba kings and factions: a house divided could not withstand the inroads of acquisitive neighbours. Says Johnson (page 203):

The power of the Fulanis was now very great, and they aimed at nothing short of the subversion of the whole Yoruba country, and the short-sighted Yoruba war-chiefs were playing the game for them by their mutual jealousy of one another. One expedition followed after another and the result was the devastation and depopulation of the country. Far-seeing men had predicted all this, if the various Yoruba families did not unite and expel the foreigners; but jealousy and rivalry among the chiefs prevented unity of purpose. Allegiance was no longer paid to the King, not even in the capital. Intestine wars not only weakened the country, but offered it as easy prey to the common enemy.

Nevertheless, Oyo and the Yorubas had undoubtedly had their day and their glory.

Thus, whether one looks north, east, or west, one finds in Azikiwe's Nigeria a virile people capable of producing not only great myths but also great men and heroes; who have in fact produced many of the latter too: Oduduwa and Usuman dan Fodio, through Jaja of Opobo to Nnamdi Azikiwe. It is true, as Saburi Biobaku has said in *The Origins of the Yoruba* ('Lugard Lectures', Nigerian Broadcasting Service, 1955), that 'too many gods, giants and heroines stalk the pages of traditional accounts', and that 'as the past recedes, events get overlaid with romantic inventions, heroes become gods and the impossible is often said to have happened'. Dr Biobaku's deflating observation is applicable, however, more to the mythology of Ile Ife itself as 'the cradle of mankind' than to the real-life 'giants and heroines' that stalk Nigerian history.

So Nigeria also is a country with a past, a past different only in degree from that of others. But, for a long time this was a history of largely separate ethnic and political groups engaged in going each its own way. However, by the end of the nineteenth century and the time of Azikiwe's birth in 1904, the picture had been altered radically, and when in 1914 Lugard brought north and south together under one political administration, the modern history of Nigeria became, principally, a history of 'exercises in unification'. To understand this in explicit as well as concise terms we shall adopt the outline once given by Professor J. F. Ade Ajayi, the Nigerian historian at the University of Ibadan. But we shall do this in our last chapter.

Chapter 5

Early Life in Three Idioms

The year 1904 was exactly one century from the beginning of Shehu dan Fodio's Islamic revolution, in the north of what later became Nigeria. The north was important not only because of the unification movement first staged there, but also because the area became the base of operations for Lugard. And it was Lugard who, as we saw in the last chapter, united north and south in 1914 under one central administration.

A Northern Nigerian headquarters was first established at Lokoja, then moved to Jebba. In 1902 it was again moved, this time to a place called Zungeru, slightly more than 200 miles from Lagos as the plane flies today. To Zungeru therefore went such officers, clerks, overseers, and other classes of civil servants as could then be recruited both from England and from the south of the country itself. Among the earliest of the Nigerian civil servants to go north to Lokoja and Zungeru was Obededom Chukwuemeka Azikiwe. He went north as a clerk to the army, and it was at his second station there, Zungeru, that his first child and first son, Benjamin Nnamdi, was born in 1904. This event, insignificant at the time, has thus added more history to the centenary of dan Fodio's *jihad*.

Today Zungeru is nothing to look at: just one more of West Africa's hundreds of untidy little towns waiting endlessly for development. It is hardly more than a railway stop, its three or four thousand inhabitants happy in their rustic simplicity, wise and wily in a thousand unexpected ways. The sheep, chickens, and goats mix maddeningly as usual with both the people and such wheeled traffic as is resident, or as comes through on the flying business call or official visit. The Hausas tend their herds of oxen and sheep, the southern Ibos and others mind their little shops, or teach. But generally life rushes uncaringly past Zungeru towards the northern capital, Kaduna, or south to Lagos, capital of the whole Federation.

It was not always so, though, with Zungeru, and the ruins of bygone days of glory are there to testify to its past importance.* Within an area of five acres it is possible to espy today the remains of what were once the Commissioner's residence, the court-house, the police post, prisons, and one or two other ruins claiming to have been this or that. Most of all, a grand old man, the local oracle as well as talking library, will lead you to a spot where he will point out a crumbled base as that of the small house in which Zik was born. His gestures become more and more evocative as he distinguishes bath-house from kitchen and bedroom from everything else, and as he tells a tale or two about the event. But Zik himself, who goes through Zungeru by train quite often, and stops off sometimes in the interest of visiting V.I.P.s, of friends and relatives, or, perhaps, of a biographer, laughs quietly behind a discreetly cupped hand at the old man's stories. Later, out of ear-shot, he will confide to his visitor, between loud guffaws, that he himself could have only an approximate conviction of the truth of these allegations. The more so since the old man manages to sound or look as if he had witnessed the great events personally.

When a man is just born, nobody really knows he is, or will become, great, unless he is born a king, or very rich, or the son of a famous father; in any such case the undiscriminating may call the child great. But it is when a man proves his greatness in later life that the romantics, awe-struck parents, and sycophants remember, very appropriately, the wonderful things that happened at the birth, or the extraordinary, prophetic behaviour of the infant itself.

None of the dozen or so of hero-worshipping but completely valueless little pamphlet biographies of Azikiwe bother to ascribe any miraculous phenomena to the incident of his birth; but neither is the chronicle altogether free from claims of unusualness. The only full-scale, serious study of Zik's life to date, Vincent Ikeotuonye's *Zik of New Africa*, records the 'prophesies of greatness and good fortune' which accompanied the feast of ram flesh

---

* 'Zungeru became the headquarters of Northern Nigeria in 1902. In 1917 the headquarters of the Northern Provinces of Nigeria were moved to Kaduna, and Zungeru was practically abandoned.' (Sir Alan Burns, in *History of Nigeria*, Allen and Unwin, 1929, p. 197n.)

following the safe delivery. But Ikeotuonye points out in great gravity that these are mentioned 'only because in Zik's life they [the prophesies] were destined to be fulfilled.' In point of fact the occasion of Zik's birth was not remarkable for any signs, omens, or auguries, except such as hindsight would love to create as fit company for the other facts of so remarkable a life.

Azikiwe has himself supplied very full accounts of the basic details of that life, at various times and in many forms. There is one in the 'Odyssey', a newspaper series; there is another in the appendix* to the printed version of his great Inaugural Address: 'Respect for Human Dignity'; and so on. The best and most appropriate for quotation is from the 'Odyssey':

I was informed that on the paternal side, we belonged to the Royal Family. In fact, the present Obi of Onitsha, His Highness Okosi II, is related to us and we are bound by blood to worship in the same pantheon, and our penates are thus intra-related.

My paternal grandfather was supposed to be the Spokesman of our Village Council and he ranked high in the military organizations of the Ogbeobu administrative unit of the Onitsha State.

My paternal grandmother was the daughter of one of the oldest Chiefs to live in Onitsha. She was the older sister of the late Honourable Chief Isaac Okechuku Mba (formerly Owele of Onitsha) who incidentally trained and brought up my father.

On the maternal side, my mother was the daughter of one of the members of the Cabinet of Obi Okosi I. Through my maternal grandmother, I found myself bound by blood to Chief Samuel Chukuemeka Obianwu (the Owele of Onitsha) who was a former Member of the Legislative Council.

His mother, Rachel, was also the great-granddaughter of Obi Udogwu, that King Udogwu of Onitsha whose son and successor, Obi Akazua, signed a treaty of commerce with Great Britain in 1863. Azikiwe's father, Obededom, was born in November 1879, to Azikiwe Chukwude, of the Onitsha houses of Molokwu and Mbidokwu, both being of the Ogbeobu Quarter. Obededom went to school at Onitsha and at nearby Asaba on the Onitsha River, then went north in 1902 as a civil servant with the army. The union with Rachel produced two more children besides their

* Flora Azikiwe points out in much amusement that in this summary, her (otherwise meticulous) husband erred by a month here and a month there in stating her own birthdate as well as that of her only daughter, Obiozo.

first, but the second boy died in infancy and only the one sister, Cecelia Arinze, survives with Zik. She still lives in Onitsha, a widow with children of her own.

The whole family belonged to the Anglican communion of the protestant Church Missionary Society, and the oldest child was baptized Benjamin Nnamdi. He was thus known as Ben Azikiwe for some time, acquiring the nick-name 'Zik' in America later. But in 1934, when he returned to London from America full of pride and enthusiasm for many things, he received a rude shock to which he reacted with resentment and which saw the end of 'Ben Azikiwe'. On the grounds of the technicality that Nigeria as such did not have a team there, he was denied the right to compete as a runner in the British Empire Games of that year. Zik saw in this incident the ugly head of prejudice rising up again, especially as in those days racial harmony just did not exist and was not encouraged in the Empire. In 'retaliation' Zik excised the 'Benjamin' from his name. 'Why should I bear a so-called "Christian"* name,' he asked himself, 'in the face of such un-Christian behaviour on the part of those who gave it to me?' He has been plain 'Nnamdi Azikiwe' ever since.

Benjamin did not grow up in Zungeru, or in the north as such, but since he was born there and did not leave for the south until he was seven years old his first contacts with many kinds of reality were *northern* as well as *Ibo*. The Ibo part of it was merely such as he experienced at home between father and mother and sister; the northern was everything else. This formed indeed that beginning of almost-thorough acculturation into the major idioms of Nigeria which has remained so enviable a part of the equipment of one of the most-nearly complete Nigerians of his day. Let us have it in his own words:

Up to the year 1912, I was practically living in the North of Nigeria with my parents. In fact, I was a Hausa boy then, and I was able to speak that language very fluently. My father was so apprehensive lest I should lose my mother tongue that I had to return to Onitsha in order to be trained by my maternal grandmother.

* Purists invariably point out that Benjamin is Jewish, not Christian. It makes no difference. Under foreign rule most colonials took – that is, were given – 'Christian' names at baptism, and these could have been Jewish, Christian, Biblical, etc.

Northern Nigeria in the 1900s was very trying for a southern family with few of their kind in the whole community; for a Christian couple among Muslims it was an even greater spiritual hardship; for an African civil servant among his English *superiors* it was bitterly cold-shouldered; and, lastly, for an educated father with a young son soon to require schooling, its prospects were indeed bleak. Naturally, when the time came for it, something had to be done: Zik's father, with the help of a tutor, managed to teach him to begin to read and to do simple arithmetic. As Zik put it himself: 'A Sierra Leone gentleman by name of Ray was my [first] teacher. I think I was told that he put the finishing touches to my ABC studies.'

The meagre resources at their disposal in those stringent days had to suffice for all, and little Benjamin had little enough of anything to fall back on. But he had a strong father to look up to, and his mother was a beautiful woman – 'my own lovely mother', as he called her in a letter once – at whose knee her son learnt many a lesson of childhood, apart from the language of his ancestors. By the time he was leaving for Onitsha he had had a good grounding in both Ibo and Hausa (although today he apologetically confesses his Hausa is no longer perfect),* he could read and write well enough to be ready to enter regular school at Onitsha, and he had benefited sufficiently from parental love and care to have a firm foundation in psychological stability.

The love, so to speak, was supplied by Zik's mother, the care by the father. Obededom Azikiwe was a man both of strength and sensitivity, who did not leave small but important items of business to chance. He had been trained as a teacher himself in the fold of the Church Missionary Society, hence his early concern with his son's education. In fact he was a contemporary of an Assistant Bishop of the Niger Delta (the Rt Rev. A. C. Onyeabo), and might have become a cleric himself but for his sensitive reactions to some of the 'challenging situations' of the day. In other words, Obed Azikiwe could not take kindly to the attitude

* In his 'My Odyssey' Zik said again (1938) that in 1917 when he went back for a holiday with his family, the northerners on the train regarded him as one of themselves, 'since I spoke Hausa fluently'. The *apologia* is thus a matter of almost fifty years later.

of some European missionaries, whom he could accuse of racial prejudice and partiality. Indeed he felt strongly enough about these anomalies to sever his connexion with the mission and retire permanently into the position of a nominal Christian, no more. It was at this point that he joined the civil service, first to go on an historic trek with Major A. G. Leonard to the Niger regions, and then to be posted with the army at Lokoja, then to Zungeru, where Zik was born. Ironically enough, Obededom Azikiwe met with race prejudice in secular life too, as he had in religious. Indeed he was once insulted at point-blank range by a twenty-five-year-old English newcomer. (See Chapter 6, below.)

In spite of the misalliance with the C. M. S., however, Obed again reacted sharply, later, to a prospect that didn't please him, namely, that of his son joining the Roman Catholic Church. This was when, on his being dispatched home to Onitsha for proper schooling at the age of seven or eight, little Benjamin was 'made to attend the Roman Catholic Mission School' with his mulatto cousin, Andrew MacIntosh. The senior Azikiwe was still a Protestant Christian at heart, and wanted his son, in spite of everything, to be raised in the same faith. He therefore issued peremptory instructions to Benjamin's Onitsha guardian – to wit, his grandmother – for the immediate transfer of the boy to the C M.S.

Before he was twenty years old, Benjamin Azikiwe was to go much wider and deeper in religious travel than his father had ever dreamt of. Instead of the old man's abrupt withdrawal and self-exile, in a physical sense, from the church, his son went through – that is, put himself through – the incredible routine of examining and 'trying out' practically every known form of Protestantism. In addition, at one period or another in his life, he has found time to test the dogmas of other faiths or religious beliefs, such as Islam, Buddhism, and Confucianism.

'... At the threshold of my twentieth birthday, I became a rebel and decided to think of the world that was, instead of the world that was to come,' wrote Zik years afterwards. His grandfather, he said, had had cause to question some of the values of Western civilization. His father, in his turn, had had reason to worry about 'the problems raised by the impact of Western cultures on an African environment', and had tried in a humble way to find a synthesis between the practical life of the world and the ethical teachings of the Bible. Eventually, he had become a practical instead of a merely precept-ual Christian. When it came to his turn – the third generation – Zik was

... a Roman Catholic at the tender age of nine. At the age of ten, I became an Anglican. At the age of twelve, I was a Wesleyan Methodist. At sixteen I became a Presbyterian. At ... eighteen I was a soldier of the Lord (Hallelujah!) in the Salvation Army. At nineteen I left the emotional side of Christianity for the intellectual. ... I became a Student Bible Expositor under ... Russellism (now Jehovah's Witnesses). At twenty-one, Baptist. ... Twenty-four, Congregationalist. ... Twenty-five, re-affirmed Presbyterian. ... Thirty, returned to the Methodist faith....

It may be added here, to close the matter as it were, that Zik did oblige his readers with an equally detailed and frank catalogue of the reasons for this wild religious careering. But it would be too much to give that here too. Suffice it to say, old Obededom Azikiwe would have wanted nothing to do with it.

Zik lived with his grandmother at Onitsha until 1915, when he was eleven. Then he joined his parents in Lagos, his father having been transferred there from the north. Let us here complete the account of young Benjamin's movements at this stage of his life, and get that much into perspective before continuing the narrative. He spent the years 1915 to '18 in further elementary schooling in Lagos, returned to Onitsha in the latter year to finish elementary school, then until March 1920 was a pupil-teacher at two different schools there. The next month Benjamin entered the well-known missionary secondary school at Calabar, the Hope Waddell Training Institute. But he remained there only until August of that year, when he went back to Yoruba-speaking Lagos and entered the Methodist Boys' High School until September 1921. By this time he was just under seventeen years of age, but that was all the formal schooling he was ever to get in his native Nigeria. It was not until he was in his twenty-first year, and in America, that he was able to complete his secondary education, 1925-6. So that, from age seven to seventeen, Benjamin spent his life at 'home' between his paternal grandmother and his parents, and at school between Onitsha (also Calabar) and Lagos.

His sister, Cecelia Eziamaka Arinze,* the only other survivor of the primary family, retains vivid memories of what life with Zik was like, on the occasions when they lived together with the parents or other relatives. Her now famous brother, she remembers in matter-of-fact tones, was 'very clever' both at home and at school, even as a small boy. He was rather serious, and apt to want to be left alone. But he was also an ideal 'mama's little helper', washing and sweeping and even helping with the cooking. His non-domestic activities, though, were something of a mystery to his mother and a surprise to the father – not, in his case, unmixed with considerable pride and a certain controlled sense of anticipation. For the young man saved up all his pennies to buy such books as there were both for himself and, often, to help schoolmates who couldn't have any; he spent long periods hidden away in his little corner of the house absorbed in his reading; sometimes he collected his companions together and 'lectured' them on various subjects from his reading books, and in other ways demonstrated an unmistakable 'differentness' in personality and interests. He was often reticent to the point of being anti-social.

One source of profound unhappiness for the youngster must be narrated here, and perhaps best of all in Zik's own words. This was the unexpected and shattering conversion of his family from a monogamous into a polygamous one. He had not felt anything until he went north to spend a school vacation with his family. Zik takes up the story:

On arrival at Kaduna South, I found my parents waiting for me at the platform. It was a grand reunion for I saw my mother and my sister and my father once more. I also had the opportunity of renewing acquaintance with the new wife of my father.

At the tender age of thirteen, I was privileged to study the part played by polygamy, as an African marital institution, in the family of the African.

The new wife was known to me when I lived with my paternal grandmother at Onitsha. . . .

I found everything pleasant at first, but later I discovered that what my father had always advised others was true.

* Cecelia had been baptized 'Lily', but had been re-christened on entering the Roman Church at marriage.

You see, whenever people asked him about polygamy, he neither denounced it nor praised it. He would simply answer in words like these: 'One wife, one trouble; two wives, two troubles.'

By having a new wife, not only did he incur the displeasure of my mother but he also invited tragedy in[to] his home, because day in and day out, either the two wives quarrelled or he and one of them would quarrel, so that he had no peace of mind.

Judged from this angle, my young mind revolted against polygamy. I saw my mother exchange blows with my father for no other reason than jealousy. And I saw my mother and the new wife exchange blows for the same reason.

These conditions became unbearable and so my father and my mother agreed to disagree, after seventeen years of connubial life. How this estrangement affected my life and my way of thinking . . . is reserved for the following chapters.

The immediate results of this misalliance were unfortunate in the extreme for the youngster. His father tried to get him on his side, but the mother, who had by then returned home to Onitsha, recaptured the boy's loyalty instead. The inevitable reaction set in, and Benjamin wrote impulsively to his old man accusing him of ill-treating his mother: 'Somehow, I nursed a grudge against my father and so I wrote to him and condemned his action. . . .'

But the denouement to the whole episode was as shattering as its previous effect on young Benjamin Azikiwe:

. . . I told him that he should have taken into consideration the fact that this woman had perpetuated his seed through two of us and that he could have been less drastic.

And he understood that I was being influenced by my mother, so he wrote and told me not to pass judgement on him until I had had the opportunity of becoming a husband in order to appreciate women.

For which I thank him, because I have been gaining the necessary experience and I might, like other men, feel the same way about women. They are mysterious creatures, you see! [Original not in italics.]

And then, a little later, the closing passage on this extraordinary subject:

My stepmother was kindly disposed towards me and she made me to appreciate her as a member of the family. Although she is no longer with my father, after fifteen years of married life with him, yet I still hold her in high esteem.

Still, the Azikiwe household, or wherever brother and sister happened to be living, was not always cheerless. Benjamin and Cecelia Eziamaka had a lot of fun. But of course there were also the little quarrels and fights that children cannot avoid among themselves. And when these got to the point of real battle the two antagonists knew exactly how to attack each other. Benjamin hated the smell of raw onions, and Cecelia loathed that of tobacco, especially in a stale pipe. The rest can be imagined – and sometimes only the intervention of the senior folk and the threat of sticks and stripes could get these two-man riots quelled. Finally, Cecelia Eziamaka remembers that her brother was called, during his school-days at Onitsha, *Olobommanebuluokwu*, which term – despite its own controversial appearance – meant 'a good-looking youngster'.

Chapter 6

On the Trail

Benjamin was now determined to go to America, but where was the way and where the means? Did someone say once that a strong will could find both? Then it had to be so in this case, for the young man certainly had the will.

A great deal had happened to him since his return to Lagos in September 1920. Entering the Methodist Boys' High School there, he had had enough time to settle down before his encounter with Aggrey. That was the beginning of his new day. Azikiwe has given us the record of this himself in his 'Odyssey', the series he published in the *West African Pilot*. The revelation took place, appropriately enough, in church on a Sunday in November 1920. He (Benjamin) was in the boarding house of his school, and sang in the choir of the Methodist church in town, at what is still one of the busiest centres of Lagos, Tinubu.

Aggrey was the preacher that morning,* as he often was on those Phelps-Stokes tours in Africa. And, as always, he moved everyone under his voice with his unfailing power to elate and elevate. As his biographer relates it, his texts, and the lessons he drew from them, were always apropos, and his humility, sincerity, learning, and eloquence left everywhere a profound and lasting impression. On that morning his 'soft and melodious' voice struck Benjamin's soul, as he told the story long afterwards, 'with the force of a supernatural wand', and Aggrey's message found his heart 'a ready soul for the dreams of a new social order'. To this initial and moving experience was added the delirium of meeting the great man later in person at his school, and, what was more, receiving a book from him. The book was *Negro Education: A Study of the Private and Higher Schools for Coloured People in the United States*. Azikiwe says that, on the purely practical aspect of the matter, it was to this book that he owed his higher education. It was through it, that is to say, that

* This was the sermon already mentioned in Chapter 2.

he first made the contacts in the Negro universities that finally took him to the United States and his college education there.

About a month after the meeting with Aggrey, Benjamin received his second shock of inspiration, the biography of James Garfield. This, with Aggrey, and the book on American Negro colleges, formed the firm foundation of the youngster's 'supreme and irrevocable decision [to] proceed abroad for higher education ere I die'.

But the time was not yet. He remained at the Boys' High School until the following September, then left school and took a job. He entered the Civil Service in Lagos as a clerk in the Treasury Department. The conditions of employment in the Colonial Civil Service in those days were grim enough for the expatriate* staff, who were also automatically senior; for the Africans they were paralysing. The overseas civil servant had to do without most of the amenities of his civilization and culture, and was in addition exposed to many and serious health hazards against which in the 1920s there was little help on the spot and less protection. But at any rate he was paid a comparatively princely salary, and on the average enjoyed a status and a standard of living quite out of his reach in his own home. The African, for his part, received a contemptible pittance, and was economically, socially, and otherwise so inferior in status as to be nearly hopeless. From this lowliness proceeded the condition that was even more unbearable: the constantly present hazard of indignity, insult, or even brutalization.†

Most youngsters of Benjamin's age going into service with the Colonial governments then would have been rather innocent about the nature of their disabilities, and therefore also completely harmless to the régime. But a few had the insight which high intelligence bestows, and the rebelliousness normally characteristic of the leader, the genius, the creative ones. Such a youngster was Benjamin Azikiwe; such, from the record, was

* They were never called 'expatriate' but 'European' staff, until very recently.

† There were recurrent court cases of assault and battery brought against Europeans by their African subordinates, and this reporter still remembers vividly once seeing the picture, in *West Africa*, of a white man resting one foot on a timber log and the other on the shoulder of his African workman, in the forest.

Obededom Azikiwe before his son. Benjamin chafed under the shackling tediousness of the routine, the dull uniformity and conformity, the drudgery, the bleak look of the future. The more he saw of it the less he liked it. In addition to the discomfort of the implications of race, colour, and the colonial status, all of which tormented him, he also had to contend with the 'internal' problems of tribalism and nepotism, among other evils of life with his own people. His people were no more than human; therefore the young man saw among them, early, the failings which were to strengthen his own resolve to do and be better. Living beyond your means already at seventeen, and having to cope at the same time with the enervating effects of favouritism and corruption in various forms, did not strike Benjamin Azikiwe as a way of fulfilment for a young man with an elevated sense of mission.

Therefore he returned to his guide-book, the one on Negro education, and studied it again. He picked out Howard University in Washington, D.C., and wrote to the President, as American Vice-Chancellors and some college principals are generally called. He asked for financial aid, stating his great ambition for himself and Africa. President J. Stanley Durkee's reply (written to another aspirant, S. N. Adibuah, for both of them) was an encouragement as well as a challenge, stated in these explicit terms:

... I have no available funds [at Howard] with which to help you. I can however put this up to you as a challenge.

If you could secure about twenty pounds in money and work your way from Africa to England on the ships, and then to America, I could secure you entrance at a splendid school – Storer College, Harpers Ferry, West Virginia. ...

I will help in all I can and shall be glad to seek funds later with which possibly I can aid just such worthy boys as you to gain the education you so much need.

Dr Durkee mentioned three young Gold Coasters who had also written to him. They were: J. E. Thompson, J. T. Marbell, and C. O. Robertson, all writing from the same Accra Post Office box number.

Benjamin's elation at the sight of this communication can well be imagined. He next wrote immediately to the President of

Storer, whose reply – again to Adibuah for both – was even more exciting:

... I am now writing you to say that we shall be glad to do all we can for you here at Storer College.

I think that the suggestion of Dr Durkee of Howard University, as to the amount of money you should have when you reach this country, would be entirely adequate for your needs in this institution.

There were more lines to the letter of Dr Henry T. McDonald. They gave Benjamin additional encouragement, promised scholarship assistance, offered summer vacation jobs. His mind became obsessed with the project, which he kept to himself while turning over in his mind the permutations of fortune: what were all the possible ways of accepting the challenge of the two American university heads, who had said to him, in effect, 'Just find your way over here and we shall do the rest for you'? That Benjamin did not once think of passing his problem over to his father was illustrative of many facts. In those days, going abroad for education – or anything else – was the romantic prerogative of but a few Africans; for the majority of those – themselves a minority, really – who were at all interested in education and higher standards of life, an overseas experience was the material of dreams and hallucinations. Secondly, going to America for education was then, and for long years afterwards, even more ludicrous than hallucinations. Dr Aggrey himself could do nothing to change a traditional attitude of contempt – which this was – in a few years, though all acknowledged that he personally was incomparable. In addition, Benjamin knew that his father hadn't the money to finance such a project in any case. Therefore, especially if he had to work his way in a ship all the way to America, it had to be a secret operation. He would have to 'stow-'way'!

His life was now more than full: he was preoccupied, excited, and anxious. Since he left school and started work he had paid a good deal of attention to public affairs, in particular to the activities and contentions of the National Congress of British West Africa. This, the first Pan-African gesture on African soil, had been spearheaded by J. E. Casely Hayford in the Gold Coast, and in Nigeria had drawn Herbert Macaulay into its movement for constitutional reform. Herbert Macaulay was then the foremost political figure in Nigeria, and naturally commanded Benjamin's attention and admiration. The National Congress movement in West Africa had part of its ideological and emotional foundations in both the Pan-African beginnings in London (around the turn of the century) and Paris (1919), and in the Indian Congress movement.

The key figure in the Pan-African movement was W. E. B. du Bois, and these two (the man and the movement), as has been noted in Chapter 3, were the exact opposite in aims and methods of Marcus Garvey and his own movement, 'Back to Africa'. But Marcus Garvey's appeal was equally understandable and acceptable, emotionally, to Africans of the nationalist and potentially-nationalist type. At widely separated intervals (1938 and 1957), both Nnamdi Azikiwe and Kwame Nkrumah, for example, acknowledged this influence. Zik summed it up again in the 'Odyssey': 'Dr Kwegyir Aggrey's sermon made me to become intellectually curious. And Marcus Garvey's epigram made me ambitious to be of service to Africa.' In the context of his growing interest in wider issues and greater problems, therefore, the smaller irritations of incompetence, unambition, and meanness in some of those around him made him the more miserable, the more impatient to be rid of them. He began to save money. He made friends with a number of young fellows. He began the unheard-of habit of seeking company among seamen on the water-front. And all the time he practised 'elimination by substitution', one of Aggrey's favourite formulas for successful planning.

Eventually Benjamin settled upon two young men, Sidney Brown and John Anyaso, as fellow-adventurers. They too wanted to get away, to better themselves; so together the three made their plans for the great adventure, in league with a number of seamen on the ships themselves. One night in June 1924, they met at the appointed spot on the Marina, Lagos, boarded their canoe, rowed to the side of the good ship *Appam* (of the long-established West African line of Elder Dempster), and were helped aboard by their seamen accomplices. They had few things and little money. They paid £15 (£5 each) out of their meagre funds to the seamen, for the hazardous privilege of being hidden and protected and fed from Lagos to Liverpool.

The first stage of the journey was Lagos to Accra. The three adventurers were shown to their bunk for the night: the inside of a lifeboat. For dinner they had been given something or other from the sailors' mess. And soon they were face-to-face, or rather body-to-body, with the immense reality of their venture into the unknown. John Anyaso was reckless, compared with the other two; Benjamin Azikiwe was resolute; but Sidney Brown proved a shambles, both morally and physically, before the adventure had seen its first dawn. The unaccustomed sea and its uncaring waves; the cold night with its whistling winds pouring into the boat; a tired body, anxious mind, and nauseous stomach, these factors combined early to create a nightmare for Sidney, though his companions suffered enough on their part. He retched and groaned and cried.

The ship reached and left Accra, to make a stop at Sekondi. Sidney Brown got worse instead of better, and presented Benjamin with his first big test of character. By now he too was in tears, out of sympathy with Sidney, and so was John Anyaso. But John, to Benjamin's horror, called the latter aside 'and suggested to me in low tones that, since Sidney seemed destined to be the fly in the ointment of our ambition, we should dump him into the sea, in the dead of night, so as to continue our voyage and mission without hindrance'.

From the composure and security of third parties and over forty years later, this extraordinary invitation to murder, in such cold blood, sounds more foolish than ferocious. It is difficult to see how a young man's share of the instinct to do violence could have been provoked into eruption by so intrinsically mild a situation. But the Zik of later years told this story seriously enough to earn credence for it. On that fateful occasion, said Zik, he convinced John Anyaso of the inhumanity of his suggestion, and they then 'agreed to bear with Sidney and to suffer together, in silence, hoping for better luck'.

The result of it all was that when the *Appam* anchored at Sekondi the three mis-adventurers disembarked, for Sidney's sake. And that was the end of Benjamin Azikiwe's first attempt to travel to America. A twice-sad end it was too. Their seamen accessories-to-the-fact refused point-blank to return their £15, so they were that much the poorer, being also stowaways stranded in a strange country. The sea-sickness had of course disappeared,. and with the return of physical fitness came also the awareness of acute hunger. While they were engaged in devouring a meal of *kenki and fried fish* – the Gold Coast equivalent of the Nigerian *garri and beans* or the English *fish and chips* – an Ibo man, one David Okeke, heard them and helped them over their immediate difficulties.

But the long-term problems were another matter altogether. They were settled, eventually, according to each man's individuality and outlook. John Anyaso, being a printer by training and not being in favour of further adventures, got into that trade and settled in the Gold Coast. Sidney Brown spent only as much time there as was necessary to find domestic accommodation with a female of the species. Benjamin, the only one of the three with a secondary school education of any sort, found it impossible to get into employment, 'after three weeks' stay in Sekondi'. 'One could appreciate my dilemma,' he has written.

At this point both his pride and his policy of secrecy suffered severely from the pitiless realities of indigence and loneliness. He had not written to his father until he arrived at Sekondi. The latter, meanwhile, along with his mother and other relatives, had been distracted beyond words by the sudden vanishing of their boy. Benjamin did not expect his father to do any more than perhaps send him some financial relief, and in the meantime his luck, too, changed. He was taken into the Gold Coast Police Force and transferred to Accra, the capital. But there his mother, after much trouble, found him, for his old man had taken decisive action. Benjamin returned home with her, and thus the Gold Coast Police lost a promising recruit. What course Nigeria's political history would have taken had he been persuaded – as a British Police Officer tried to do – by the prospect of rapid advancement to adopt this career and abandon his other ambitions, it is futile to try to imagine. Futile as well as impossible.

Chastened, contrite, but also disappointed and dissatisfied, he returned to his father, who was now working in Calabar. Benjamin explained his case to his dad, citing his correspondence with the American college presidents. Azikiwe senior was interested but 'not fully convinced that I would be successful without having sufficient money'. And since he didn't have that full confidence or conviction in this overseas project, he did his best to get his son back into the civil service as the only present means of economic security. The old man failed in his efforts, as a result of which Benjamin took a job with a Scottish lawyer practising at Calabar at the time, Mr (later Justice) G. Graham Paul. Here he not only learnt some of the forms of the legal profession but developed that interest in law itself which he was later to pursue in America. He was also tremendously impressed with the Scotsman's urbanity and deep humanity. The rest of this story is best told by Zik himself:

How father became convinced that it would be better for me to go abroad instead of remaining in Africa is the theme which follows hereon.

Among the early pioneers of the Nigerian Civil Service was my father.

It was the wish of his mother that he should be trained for ... Holy Orders and it was the wish of his father that he should be a clerk.

He became a clerk and served for about twenty-three years before he retired on pension, on grounds of ill health. Prior to his retirement something happened which affected me greatly.

Aged forty-six and the senior member of the African staff it was the task of my father to put new officials, European and African, through the routine of the duties of the Staff Officer's office.

Through this, he inspired some Africans to aim higher in life. For example, five years of contact with him were sufficient to inspire the late Mr D—, Barrister-at-Law, to leave the Civil Service and proceed to England to become the first lawyer of Calabar descent. I think he was Efik.

One day, a young military Officer openly insulted father in the office. He called him names and threatened to kick him.

In view of the fact that this chap was just a boy of about twenty-five and considering that since his arrival in Africa he had been tutored by father, it was more than a shock for him.

He told the Officer that he was old enough to be his father and that outside his colour and lack of opportunity he could match him. ...

The Officer made some challenging remarks about the affinity of father's race with Simiidae.

As soon as father reached home, he told me that I was right after all. There was no need to remain a clerk for ever. If one could develop oneself intellectually one could boss even one's father.

Father could not bear to remain in the Civil Service longer. Moreover, his health had been bad. He was nauseated. He could not work.

All day long, he recollected his twenty-three years of service which were chequered, at times, with insults of variegated nature, and he felt that after all, an African clerk was just a clerk, no matter whether he was ranked in the seniority class or not.

He developed some kind of delirium and became feverish. After some treatment, the Medical Department at Calabar recommended, at his request, that he should be invalided.

This was very welcome, for father's mental outlook completely changed as soon as he left the environment where he had answered 'Yes sir' for so long that it almost became his second habit, even in his sleep.

Then my father told me that he had saved some money during his twenty-three years of service in the Nigerian Civil Service.

He told me that if I was sure that £300 would meet all the preliminary expenses, then he would make the same available to me so I could proceed to America forthwith.

As soon as he was about to retire on pension, he called me and presented me with the sum of £300 and he spoke to me in these words:

'Son, I have slaved day and night in order to earn an honest livelihood. I have saved money in order to introduce my father and myself into the Aristocratic Order of Ozo, at Onitsha, according to custom.

'I have not much money left in the world. If I had had, I would have given you more than this. Here you are, son, this is only £300. It is part of all my life's savings.

'If, as you say, it will be a good foundation to improve your mind in America, then take it, and go to America and realize your dreams.

'You will succeed. God knows that Africa needs more Aggreys.'

And my soul was suffused with the spark of inspiration and aspiration to make a man out of myself in the world. And I knelt down and thanked my father for his sacrifice.

And he blessed me and said to me: 'Go and bring back the Golden Fleece, my boy.'

Chapter 7

'God's Own Country' in the Mid-Twenties

When Zik reached America in August 1925, 'God's own Country' was in a rather ungodlike condition, at any rate for its Negro population. It was in the middle of the first post-war period, about which Gunnar Myrdal and his experts gave the world such a detailed picture in 1944. Myrdal's book, *An American Dilemma*, painted the definitive picture of the economic, social, and political position of the Negro in the United States, in particular his experiences during and since the first Great War. It was a gruesome picture. Yet the decade after the War was also one of the most important for the Negroes, for alongside their increased persecution they increased significantly the volume of their protest against it. Also, not only the volume but the nature of the protest changed.

The conditions of the post-war period for the Negro began to take shape even before the war. Myrdal's book described, as two principal causes of intensified unrest among these people, the 'upheaval in Southern agriculture' and the waves of mass migrations from rural communities to cities, and from the south to the north. The war itself simply completed the cycle of disequilibrium. The Negroes had been eager, in spite of everything, to get into the war too and fight for their country. Eventually, 400,000 of them were drafted, and something like half of that number went over to France. But everywhere and in everything, both at home and overseas, they met with discrimination and ill-use. Specifically, they 'found themselves segregated in labour camps or as servants'. Nevertheless, those who went to Europe 'got a view of the larger world'.

When they returned, however, they again faced suspicion and fear on the part of the southern whites, and anxious, belligerent competition for jobs in the north. The Myrdal team found that during the war the whites had felt themselves pressed 'to place a higher value on democracy as "the American Way of Life"', and there was talk at home of eliminating the abuses which nullified this idea. Such sentiments had created a feeling of hopefulness, though vague, in the Negro population generally. It had been stimulated, moreover, by any small gains in Negro achievement, reported, with appropriate exaggeration, from the overseas war theatres. But not only were these hopes not fulfilled after the war; in addition, there was a new wave of terror against the southern Negroes, including lynchings in markedly increased numbers. In the north, too, a series of bloody race riots developed, in excess of previous experience.

Meanwhile, at many points there was at the same time a development of new forms of protest and a stiffening of old ones. On the occasion of the Paris Peace Conference in 1919, W. E. B. du Bois had been sent by the Negro movement in the United States to go and study the records and put together a history of the Negro war effort in Europe. This mission developed into – or at least came to be combined with – du Bois's first Pan-African Congress, through which he and his co-protesters presented a case for the improvement of the black man's general condition around the world. An indirect effect of the Congress idea was the calling, significantly enough, of the National Congress of British West Africa in 1920, of which young schoolboy Benjamin Azikiwe had been so aware during his employment in Lagos.

A man du Bois had met in Jamaica, West Indies, in 1915 now burst on the American Negro scene. Marcus Aurelius Garvey, whom we have met before in this book, had for his part also started operations based upon the American Negro discontent soon after the end of the war. By the turn of the decade his movement, the first on a mass scale in American Negro history, was at its peak. The burden of his message was that the brutalized and deprived Americans of African descent should return physically to their ancestral home, there to capture, or recapture, their lost heritage. Garvey's was a combative and potent personality, whose persuasiveness brought the Negroes flocking to his standard by the million. Under his drive they supported the organization of cooperative enterprises, including hotels, restaurants, grocery stores, laundries and printing plants. He also established a journal, *The Negro World*. All of these activities took place under what Garvey named the Universal Negro Improvement Association (the famous 'UNIA'), which was the main organization. Garvey made a great appeal to the masses, denounced all other Negro leadership in the States, mismanaged the various aspects of his own movement, was deported from the United States, and eventually died in London in 1940, 'poor and forgotten'. But he had, in his time, shaken the American Negro world and its great white suppressors to their foundations. And but for his own intense intolerance of other people's ideas, and his fanatic extremism, Marcus Garvey might have accomplished, forty years earlier, some of the aims of the 'Great March' on Washington of 28 August 1963.

Two American Negroes, each an enemy of Garvey's methods as well as of each other's, were also involved in the protest movement of post-1918. Booker T. Washington, founder of Tuskegee, had compromised with the *status quo* of White-Negro relations in the south, and had become, on that account, much favoured by the whites. With a large following of supporters fearfully hopeful of winning, and keeping, further toleration from the whites, Booker T. Washington had long established an unquestioned leadership of his people – long before, that is, the end of the last century, before the Great War, du Bois, and Marcus Garvey.

But du Bois soon challenged this leadership. And around him, progressively from the early 1900s, gathered a body of Negro intellectuals strenuously committed against 'the Tuskegee Compromise'. By the mid-1920s Booker T. Washington and W. E. B. du Bois were each leading a different school of thought among their people. The du Bois school developed their protest along intellectual lines, but also founded organizations and organs of direct action, like the National Association for the Advancement of Coloured People, and the magazines *The Crisis*, which du Bois edited, and *Opportunity*, edited by Charles S. Johnson. They had already established in 1915 the *Journal of Negro History*, which the leading Negro historian, Carter G. Woodson, edited until his death in 1950. In addition, there was the one-volume anthology, *The New Negro*, edited by Alain Locke in 1925, which broke new ground in accomplishing what it set out to do:

This volume aims to document the New Negro culturally and socially, to register the transformations of the inner and outer life of the Negro in America that have so significantly taken place in the last few years. . . .

Dr Locke also wrote in his Foreword about 'the galvanizing shocks and reactions' of recent years which were 'making by subtle processes of internal reorganization a race out of its own disunited and apathetic elements. A race experience penetrated in this way invariably flowers. . . .'

The Negro flowering was in all forms and embraced all themes, not alone those of suffering, bitterness, death, and despair. Of these, though, there were volumes, washing over the stricken people like turbulent waves over shipwrecked sailors. But mostly it was mixed, as Alain Locke's collection showed; mixed, and vibrant, and eroding in its humour and its pathos. Like the opening to Rudolph Fisher's 'Harlem Sketches':

Ezekiel Taylor, preacher of the gospel of Jesus Christ, walked slowly along One Hundred and Thirty-third street, conspicuously alien. He was little and old and bent. A short, bushy white beard framed his shiny black face and his tieless celluloid collar. A long, greasy, green-black Prince Albert, with lapels frayed and buttons worn through to their metal hung loosely from his shoulders. His trousers were big and baggy and limp, yet not enough so to hide the dejected bend of his knees.

A little boy noted the beard and gibed, 'Hey, Santa Claus! 'Tain't Chris'mas yet!' And the little boy's playmates chorused, 'Haw, haw! Lookit the coloured Santa Claus!'

'For of such is the kingdom of heaven,' mused Ezekiel Taylor. No. The Kingdom of Harlem. Children turned into mockers. Satan in the hearts of infants. Harlem – city of the devil – outpost of hell.

Or like Claude McKay's 'White Houses', dark and bitter, matching memory with experience, retching inwardly at both:

> Your door is shut against my tightened face,
> And I am sharp as steel with discontent;
> But I possess the courage and the grace
> To bear my anger proudly and unbent.
> The pavement slabs burn loose beneath my feet,
> A chafing savage, down the decent street,
> And passion rends my vitals as I pass,
> Where boldly shines your shuttered door of glass.

Oh, I must search for wisdom every hour,
Deep in my wrathful bosom sore and raw,
And find in it the superhuman power
To hold me to the letter of your law!
Oh I must keep my heart inviolate
Against the potent poison of your hate.

Langston Hughes, in whom ancestral nostalgia and realism
have struggled for co-existence for more than a generation, and
who of all the modern school of Negro poets and writers has best
united 'darkness' and 'light', summed up the contrast in his
people's lives in a characteristic poem, 'Our Land':

We should have a land of sun,
Of gorgeous sun,
And a land of fragrant water
Where the twilight is a soft bandanna handkerchief
Of rose and gold,
And not this land
Where life is cold.

We should have a land of trees,
Of tall, thick trees,
Bowed down with chattering parrots
Brilliant as the day,
And not this land where birds are grey.

Ah, we should have a land of joy,
Of love and joy and wine and song,
And not this land where joy is wrong.

'God's own country' in the 1920s presented problems of
different kinds and varying dimensions to its white citizens
too: President Lyndon Johnson, who succeeded his martyred
chief, John F. Kennedy, in 1963, has reported that in the 1920s
he could find no work in his native Texas and had to move
thousands of miles from home to the western frontier. But at
least for him and for millions of other white Americans there
were and have always been the limitless American frontier-
world; for them there is still the limitless frontier-world today.
For American Negroes it was never that easy – then or now.

In 1928, writing to his cousin C. O. Anazonwu, Zik described his own findings, in language which was remarkable in more ways than one:

The United States so far is a good country but with the complex material civilization that has encroached upon its manhood, she is materially inclined and less spiritual from the philosophic standpoint. She is the home of billionaires, yet the worst type of crime, (viz. – lynching, a most brutal crime yet perpetrated on mankind, savage in its ideal and barbaric in its operation) is being committed daily. . . .

I am not at all harbouring in my mind a juridical enquiry into the ethical conception of the United States as a sovereign state worthy of the respect accorded [a] foreign nation according to International Law and usages, but I think that the Negro today in the United States is worse off there than anywhere else. *I say this with knowledge of the South African fiasco**. . . . Let us hope that the time will come when the precepts of Christianity that is being unethically and unmorally imposed on the already religious African, will be practised wholeheartedly to the letter of the Decalogue. The United States, once more I say, is the place for the socio-economically minded person and not the usual humanic [*sic*] type of the average African; everything here is business. Here is an arithmetical country. The language is interpreted in dollars and cents. . . .

* Italics are the present author's, meant to call attention to the fact that this observation on the South African phenomenon, still so fresh today, was made more than thirty-six years ago.

Part Three

THE QUEST

The first step towards my escape from becoming a
perennial wage-earner was to be mentally equipped. ....
Then I planned to reach the United States of
America and be re-educated from my mis-education. ....

From *My Odyssey*, No. 4

Chapter 8

Starting Afresh in America

Ben Azikiwe's secondary education had not been completed in Nigeria. If he wanted to do university work this gap had to be closed. Storer College, a small Negro school* at Harpers Ferry† in West Virginia, offered both to prepare him for college and at least start him on his university studies. American education, being designed primarily to benefit as many as have the desire for it, offers an unlimited range not only of subjects and courses but of possibilities. Thus in the rural south, especially, with its fewer and lesser facilities, an institution like Storer would make it possible for a young man with uncompleted secondary schooling to go on to his next stage instead of bringing his education to an abrupt end by default.

So Benjamin was accepted into a preparatory section at Storer, in which he remained from 1925 to 1926. He spent a further year at this institution as a beginner in undergraduate studies. Academically, this was not a very important period, except in the sense that it was the beginning for Benjamin: he was here already getting into contact with that somewhat mysterious horizon of the mind whose mere contemplation brought so much exhilaration to him. But something more there was at Storer to give him immense satisfaction and even a sense

* 'School', in American education, is a term used habitually in its widest sense. One can be in 'grade school', 'high school', 'med. school', 'law school', or even 'in school at Harvard' (the same as 'in college at Harvard').

† Harpers Ferry is a highly emotive symbol in the history of American humanism, especially for the Negro. It was here that John Brown staged his desperate and – for himself – fatal raid to free a number of captive slaves; and it was here that he was hanged for that act. Generations later, W. E. B. du Bois chose this spot for the opening of his famous 'Niagara Movement', which was the beginning of his own life-long campaign for Negro, indeed African, freedom. As a symbolic act of reverence and dedication, du Bois walked – with a group of his recruits – barefoot on a short pilgrimage to the grave of John Brown, on the occasion of the launching of the movement.

of fulfilment. Benjamin had always been keen on sports and games, and at Storer he had the opportunity of developing his abilities in them. At the Wesleyan Boys' High School in Lagos he had been given a school-leaving certificate which said he had 'played regularly for Kingswood House and for School football team'. At Storer he developed rapidly into a long-distance runner, specializing in the mile and the popular cross-country.

Benjamin Azikiwe was certainly not that first runner in history who heralded the four-minute mile; nor did he set any world records. But he ran fast enough in those days to be nicknamed 'Flying Zik' and 'the African Eagle'; moreover, he represented Storer College at many athletic meets and was often the first-prize winner in his favourite distances. He also boxed and played American football. Says Zik in a personal memoir: 'In American Football my record was a bashed nose on many occasions. . . .' Ben Azikiwe in fact considered that sport played a very important part in his life then, and he has put down some of the reasons for this:

I am mentioning these [various sports and games] because they affected my philosophy of life a great deal.

From the experiences gained by me during my various athletic activities, I have been able to adjust myself to life's variegated problems and surprises.

From American Football, I was able to learn that until the referee's whistle was blown, the battle must continue. . . . The Coach warned me that in football I must be always on the alert and I should always fight the other fellow until the game was ended. The Coach did not have to emphasize that point. The goal post did!

In athletics, I learnt some of the bitterest lessons in my life. . . . I was last in that race. And for over two weeks I had to spend my time in bed convalescing from sheer exhaustion. Here I learnt that unless one is well-prepared in any work of life, no matter how latent may be the brilliance of that fellow, the talent will never reach its highest peak of development.

From athletics I learnt how to suffer in silence. [And] I learnt how to let the other fellow suffer with me as soon as I decided to apply the pressure. I learnt how to act as if I was helpless even though I was as powerful as an ox. I learnt how to make the other fellow keep guessing how I would make my defence after he had made his offence.

It was at Storer that Benjamin Nnamdi Azikiwe became the

widely known 'Zik' of today. His college mates in the first place objected to 'Benjamin' because it was not African. 'Azikiwe' had possibilities, if broken up and carefully examined. When so treated, the different parts soon yielded a choice morsel of a nickname for Yankee auditory tastes, and 'Zik' it was from then on.

He soon became popular with the students for many good reasons. He was physically handsome and an athlete; mentally, he kept ahead of most of them. This combination of gifts made him an attractive character to both sexes, and Zik is not averse to confessing to the many temptations thrown across his path by the female population. Also, since he could type and handle papers and documents, from his days at Mr Graham Paul's office in Calabar, he was soon offering his secretarial skills at 'Zik's Type-Writing Bureau'. Here he accepted and typed student manuscripts at one cent a page. But, less publicly, he also made money off the lazy and the unable students, by doing their written-work assignments for them; where there were no requirements for the defence of theses, so to speak, this was quite easy. Lastly, in quest of further funds to augment his meagre 'bank account' Zik began yet another line of business, if possible more desperate than the previous ones: a pawnbroker's – 'Zik's Pawn Shop'.

'... I loaned the students from wealthier homes, who were always in need of money, sums ranging from twenty-five cents [one shilling] to one dollar [4/2d.], with interest varying from a nickel [threepence] to a dime [sixpence] per month.'

This was in augmentation of Zik's total funds, made up of what was left from the £300 his father had given him to go to America with, and what he made from the usual jobs on an American university campus. Soon after his arrival he had been summoned by the Dean of the College and given the job of a fireman, after the following conversation chronicled by Zik himself:

Dean: We want to help you work your way through college. Tell me what type of work you can do.
Zik: As a clerk, Sir, I can typewrite.
Dean: Oh yes, that's a good job for women. What else can you do?

Zik: I was once a lawyer's clerk and I am familiar with the making of affidavits, conveyancing and agreements.

Dean: These are very helpful in other circumstances. Tell me this: have you ever been a fireman in your life?

Zik: A fireman? To carry coal! No, Sir.

Dean: We are getting on well. What hard work have you done in your life?

Zik: Scholarship and office work, Sir.

Dean: There, young student, your education is wrong. At your age and with your excellent form and health, you should be a good farmer. Leave typing and conveyancing to weaker beings. Come along and make a real man of yourself.

At first the experience of his initiation into the honourable profession of physical labour nearly finished Zik off psychologically, such is the contrast between the British – indeed European – system of education and the American. This type of heavy work for schoolboys or college students is not known in Europe or in its African colonies and ex-colonies, even now; the 'dignity of labour' is still, for this group on this side of the Atlantic, just a vaguely interesting theory, very little more. However, after much chagrin and head-shaking Zik settled down to his first job; indeed he performed so well that soon he was elevated from fireman to college janitor! Now he was sweeping and carrying away rubbish in the sight of all, especially the young 'co-eds'. But he soon learnt that in America these were honourable, if onerous, ways of making money to 'help yourself through school', as everyone did or said it every day.

Worse was to follow, however. At the end of his preparatory year, Zik was offered work on the college farm for the equivalent of £2 1s. 8d. (10 dollars) per week. But he was persuaded into trying for better than that in the city of Baltimore in Maryland, not far north of Washington, D.C. The job he got in a steel mill was so tough that Zik became ill and had to return to Storer before he would do himself more harm. The President and the Dean put him under medical care immediately, and with rest and good nourishment he rapidly recovered. There was always, of course, his naturally strong, though lanky, physique to count upon.

He joined the farm staff as soon as he was well enough to work again, and throughout his second year supplemented his funds that way. With his incurable love of series and of particularization, Zik later described his work as a farmhand: he had, he said, 'to feed the hogs, the cows, the horses, the chickens, etc.'; he 'learnt to plough, to furrow, to weed, to harrow, to seed, to harvest, etc.', with machines as well as with animals. 'It was probably one of the most delightful experiences in my life', Zik has recorded, namely, to use the plough and talk to the horse in the accepted language.

Chapter 9

The Student Makes Progress

To the most illustrious of my former students, the Honourable Nnamdi Azikiwe, Governor-General of Nigeria, and the one (a) who perceived most clearly the greatness of Africa's past, (b) who demonstrated best the great potentialities of the African present.

This was part of a tribute paid to Zik in 1960 on the occasion of his elevation to the Governor-Generalship. It was from one of his old American teachers, Professor William Leo Hansberry, of Howard University, the archaeologist and historian of ancient Africa.* The piece was apt, and not merely for the factualness of the first part. As a student Zik was concerned with *the story of Africa* above everything else. For this reason he pursued studies, and aspects of studies, into African life and history which went deeper than and beyond the normal interests of African students anywhere. It is, even so, more profitable to study Zik the nationalist-politician, statesman, and prophet, than to try to study Azikiwe the thinker or writer; but it is a fact that he had put his heart and soul into his studies. His naturally brilliant mind had kept him well in front of most of his college mates.

When he left Storer in the summer of 1927 Zik proceeded straight north to the city of Pittsburgh, in the great coal and steel centre of Pennsylvania. There he was still dogged by hunger and lack of funds. As a result of unemployment he had a rough brush with his first landlady; moved his lodgings to a Y.M.C.A. hostel; acted as sparring partner to professional boxers just long enough to be knocked out of the game for good; and then, when all hope seemed lost and hunger had reduced him to utter dejection, Zik tried to end it all by taking his own life.

Around midnight he made his way towards his intended rendezvous with tragedy. He chose a quiet, dark part of town as venue, and the tramways as his means of self-destruction. He was

* Leo Hansberry is now at the University of Nigeria at Nsukka, in the east – 'Azikiwe's university'.

going to lie across the rail lines and be crushed by the first available tram. To make sure of success, he selected a part of the track which showed a gradient, so that the tram-driver would find it difficult to apply his brakes effectively and in time. Soon after a half hour past midnight, the noisy monster came charging down the track towards the hapless young African, prostrate across the rails and quivering with a thousand nameless sensations. ....

But suddenly, as if from nowhere, came the hand of a stranger. It dragged him, with one desperate movement, away from the approaching tram, while he struggled feebly against this interference with his freedom to commit suicide in a free country. Later, he was thankful for his salvation, while the history of Nigeria breathed a long sigh of relief.

After this Zik washed dishes in a restaurant; then, for six weeks, he worked in a coal mine in the capacity of that most hated of all classes in a strike situation: the class of strike breakers, 'scabs' – the men who, temporarily, are persuaded or induced to take the place of the regular employees at the moment on strike. Zik made nearly five hundred dollars mining anthracite coal at this job, but in the end nearly got shot – some of the other 'scabs' did get killed – by the strikers. So he gave it up, collected 497 dollars-plus, and moved on to other jobs. It was necessary for him to make enough money, as well to keep himself in health and strength as to enable him to return to college. Among the terrible pressures he had to remove from himself during this period was that of the Immigration Service. According to the regulations of the 1924 U.S. Immigration Act a foreign student in the United States had to be either attending full and regular courses during the academic year or on his way back home.

To avoid going back home prematurely and – intolerable thought – without even a first degree to show for his strong-willed adventure, was now his sole preoccupation. If he wasn't in college again by the following January he would surely be deported. Zik and a West African friend in the same position, Bankole Wright, then took a quick-order car-washing course, and went to work in a garage doing just that. But they were also expected to be able to drive the cars about the garage, into and out of position. This they bribed their Irish colleague to do for them whenever necessary. But the Irishman got drunk one day and damned the boss to hell. He was promptly given the sack. His two African protégés were now alone and unprotected, and, when the test came, readily proved that they neither of them knew a gear-lever from a light switch. Upon which they, too, were fired without argument.

His financial position was immeasurably better now than when it had driven Zik to the extremity of attempted suicide, but still it was not good enough to take him back to college. Yet the re-opening was very near. Zik therefore took a decision that seemed to him the most reasonable in the circumstances: he would forget other ambitions for the time being and proceed to the famous Tuskegee Institute in Alabama, there to learn the trade of printing. On the way he stopped in Washington, as he must, where he was re-united with an old friend, the West Indian Cyril Ollivierre.* But Cyril was distressed to learn of Zik's financial difficulties, whose consequences were this decision to do a vocational course at Tuskegee: the position was so contrary to Zik's previous idea of coming to Howard University, there in Washington, as the next stage of the American student-career he had planned so earnestly back in Nigeria.

Through the fortunate intervention of Cyril Ollivierre Zik met and was engaged (at 25 dollars a month) as private-secretary *pro tem* and part-time by the distinguished Dr Alain Locke, first American Negro Rhodes Scholar to Oxford, Professor of Philosophy at Howard, author, pamphleteer, and one of the early intellectual leaders of the Negro protest movement in this century. Under the quiet inspiration and guidance of Alain Locke – as refined and unobtrusive a revolutionary as ever was – Zik began his first real acquaintance with great thought; he made here his first strenuous intellectual efforts, and began also his identification with the momentous issues of the American world. For the momentous issues of the American world were more

---

* Ollivierre became a medical doctor eventually and later an eye-specialist. He has a flourishing practice in Harlem, New York. He, like many others of Zik's American friends, contemporaries, and teachers, was invited to both the Nigerian Independence celebrations in October, 1960, and to Zik's installation ceremonies the following month. For almost forty years since Zik, Cyril Ollivierre has remained a friend and benefactor to succeeding generations of African students in America.

than American for Zik: they were the issues confronting other segments of humanity at large. Were not the problems of democratic government, which had engaged the best American minds for so long, and so tragically in many instances, also the problems of England? Was not the position of the American Negro in many ways the position of the African colonial? Capital versus labour, socialism versus capitalism; the domination of the rich, the submergence of the poor; the great obvious need to alter human society for the better, the more equitable; these problems, some long established and other ominously incipient on the American scene, all bore a universality of touch which no seeker after knowledge and truth could escape from realizing. Benjamin Nnamdi Azikiwe was a seeker after knowledge and truth, therefore he could not escape the contemplation of them.

But Zik was still at the beginning, for all that. He was seeing truth, for the time-being, only through a glass, darkly. There was much more ahead. During the one academic year he spent at Howard, he studied as much as possible the historical background of the Negro race, of the African. He read Dr Locke's *New Negro* and got ideas; he received guidance from this philosopher in the exciting and crucial field of research. He looked at Negro achievement in antiquity through the eyes of Leo Hansberry as recorded in classical literature and in the histories of ancient Greece and Rome. At the same time he read other histories, especially American and English, and studied the subject with Ralph Bunche (Nobel Prize winner) of the United Nations. Zik had lost a year between Storer and Howard, during which time he had gone through the tortures of hell itself, fighting desperately to save both his life and his career. But in the two 'outer' years of that critical period he had devoted his main concentration to the task of acquiring a basic academic preparedness. In those two years – one each at Storer and Howard – whether in lectures or in extra-curricular reading, he had made good acquaintance with the fundamental bodies of knowledge and of ideas, and had also contemplated the implications of the emotional content of all social movements.

Chapter 10

The Great Issues

We mentioned in the introduction to the Zik story (Chapter 3) the main characters and philosophies which influenced him most during these years of his academic career and ideological development. It is now necessary to expand this subject.

Zik had read snatches here and there, from the meagre offerings of his school text books, about the lives and works of historical figures of America like John Brown, Abraham Lincoln, Booker T. Washington, Jefferson, and Benjamin Franklin. Naturally, these biographical snippets had been of the simplest in form and content. In Lagos during his last years in school and his first in employment Zik had been able to advance his understanding of these men and their historic position to a considerable degree. This was the more commendable in view of the pitifully small volume of literature available, even in Lagos, at that time. In his two years at Storer College he read full accounts of these heroes of revolution and reform.

He was enthralled. John Brown's last speech in defence of himself and of the rightness of his action in interfering 'on behalf of (God's) despised poor', for instance, moved him profoundly:

This court acknowledges, as I suppose, the validity of the law of God. I see a book kissed here which I suppose to be the Bible, or at least the New Testament. That teaches me that all things whatsoever I would that men should do to me, I should do even so to them. It teaches me, further, to 'remember them that are in bonds, as bound with them'. I endeavoured to act up to that instruction. I say, I am yet too young to understand that God is any respector of persons. I believe that to have interfered as I have done – as I have always freely admitted I have done – on behalf of His despised poor, was not wrong, but right. Now, if it is deemed necessary that I should forfeit my life for the furtherance of the ends of justice, and mingle my blood further with the blood of my children and with the blood of the millions in this slave country whose rights are disregarded by wicked, cruel, and unjust enactments – I submit; so let it be.

Of the mass of anti-slavery literature available for study, of which the John Brown tragedy was only a small though highly charged fraction, Zik had time and attention for only just a little more. Among this was the poetry of J. G. Whittier, of which the following is a representative sample of his brand of opposition to slavery:

> Our fellow-countrymen in chains!
>   Slaves – in a land of light and law!
> Slaves – crouching on the very plains
>   Where rolled the storm of Freedom's war!
> A groan from Eutaw's haunted wood, –
>   A wail where Camden's martyrs fell, –
> By every shrine of patriot blood,
>   From Moultrie's wall and Jasper's well!
>
> *
>
> The groan of breaking hearts is there, –
>   The falling lash, – the fetter's clank!
> *Slaves*, – SLAVES are breathing in that air,
>   Which old De Kalb and Sumter drank!

One wonderful feature of the effects of this literature on Zik must be mentioned. This was the fact that while it made him bitterly vengeful towards the perpetrators of these crimes against his own people, it also led him to a boundless admiration of American liberalism and philanthropy. It was the other side of the coin. Hence his feelings towards the fallen heroes of the war of liberation: John Brown and, by extension, liberals like William Jennings Bryan, Thomas Paine, and the great Thomas Jefferson himself. Jefferson, especially, represented for Zik a critical central point in the consideration of the problems of American democracy.* Here was a great principle, propounded by a great democrat and progressive: *the people are everything*; they are the only legitimate foundation of all true state power and all constituted government; their good sense will in the end triumph over the dangers of popular error and the corruptibility of rulers. . . . And so on. But was there any polity on earth or in history in

* Many will know that Jefferson – scientist, intellectual, and learned man though he was – had long allowed himself to be misled by the racial prejudices of his time, but had later made full confession of his error and recanted. (See *Jefferson and Henri Gregoire*.)

which the people had demonstrated these qualities successfully, permanently?

Here, for instance, for all to comprehend, was the history of slavery in the south, and, after slavery, the unregenerate intransigence of the slave-holders at heart. Here, culminating from two generations of protest, was the literature of protest at its plaintive and angry best. But are *the people* doing anything about the Negro problem, in their good sense and legitimate purpose? Well, in the 1920s it might have been agreed that the southerners certainly were doing something, but *to* the Negroes, not *for* them: they were lynching them at a greatly increased rate, and neither Jefferson's mistrusted rulers nor his trusted *people* were any help to the 'motherless children of Africa, a long ways from home'. All of which of course immediately led back to Africa, where, if not slavery, then colonialism had created conditions for the Africans in their native land not much better than their American 'cousins' were suffering in their enforced home. *A contemplation of post-Emancipation slavery, on the spot in the American south, definitely led to a tightening feeling of antagonism against British colonialism.* Freedom from political thraldom – thraldom whether in the form of American slavery or European imperialism – became a challenge to Benjamin Azikiwe, that is, more than ever before.

But the question, 'What do you do about political freedom?' now had to be shelved for a while, for the political cannot be solved apart from the economic problems of man (though in practice they may best be tackled earlier in certain cases). Zik's introduction to economic ideas and practice had to begin now, therefore, in order to bring him into line with this basic fact. The same Howard University, where he had extended his acquaintance with problems of government, was the scene of the new initiations.

It was here that he learnt of the theories of the German Jew who had turned the economic – and political – world upside down; of the theoretical 'perfectionists' in economic organization who had both preceded and succeeded Marx; of the Guild socialists, who would remove political passion and ideological loyalties out of the business of government, leaving a chaste, almost mechanical structure in the hands of economic interests which would be bound by no emotional ties; of the Fabians, who believed in curbing capitalism and introducing socialism of a limited kind at gradualist pace, according to the methods of their patron-saint, Fabius Maximus. . . .

After one year at Howard University (1928–9) however, Zik was obliged to transfer these new interests to Lincoln University, in Pennsylvania, his third institution. He was doing well at Howard: his 'class'-work was very satisfactory; his labours in the library were rewarding to him personally; he was still a popular student, even if he did not cut quite the swathe, here in this highly sophisticated urban centre, that he did in the rural south; that is to say, a fair proportion of boys and girls – or 'men' and 'co-eds' – were friendly enough to make social existence supportable. But one enemy still kept at his heels, as always since his arrival in the country: poverty. In spite of his steady, pleasant, and profitable part-time employment with Professor Alain Locke, it was quite clear that he could not carry on financially any longer at this rate and would not be able to return to Howard the next year. Since there were no prospects of a substantial change in these conditions Zik decided to make the change himself in another direction. He applied to Lincoln University, in Chester County, Pennsylvania, for admission into the Junior (3rd year) class.

Zik seems to have heard of Lincoln rather late. Had he been more fortunate or more inquisitive, earlier, he would have applied and transferred to this institution at least two years before he did. For Lincoln is almost unique in time in its connexions with Africa, in its warmth of heart and generosity of hand, especially in view of the modesty of its establishment. Starting its life-history as the Ashmun Institute in 1854, Lincoln set out on the modest course of training missionaries for work in the vineyards of nineteenth-century Africa and Asia, later added other studies to its curriculum and was raised to the status of a university in 1890. It is a small institution, by any American standards, but makes up for this by the surprising proportion of its contribution to American – not merely American Negro – professional and educational life.

When the late President John F. Kennedy said that 'Lincoln University has produced some of our most distinguished

citizens' he was referring to a roster of Lincoln men which carried
the names of scientists, ambassadors, judges, founders, Congress-
men, college and university presidents, a great folk-poet, and
others. Among them could be numbered Thurgood Marshall, a
Federal Judge who for almost a generation had been the
national symbol of Negro rights fought through the courts,
above all the U.S. Supreme Court; Langston Hughes, world-
famous folk-poet and one of the most prolific and versatile of
contemporary writers; and Hildrus Poindexter, internationally-
known malariologist. Under the heading of 'General Statistics',
the Vice President of Lincoln, Dr Frank J. Dowd, Jr, sent in the
following additional information to the author:

Lincoln has probably given undergraduate education to more Negro
physicians than any other college. Over fifty Lincoln men have served
or are serving as college presidents. Over 60 per cent of Lincoln's
alumni have received or are working toward graduate degrees or are
engaged in such professions as medicine, law, the ministry, teaching
and social science.

Dr Dowd stated that this record was being sustained by a body
of living alumni, numbering, in 1964, no more than 4,200 –
whereas, it may be added, many of the great American universities
graduate more than that number in a single year.

Most touching of all, Lincoln was a haven for many African
students from both east and west (offering them scholarship help,
friendship, and opportunities for acquiring a well-rounded
education) at a time when the emergent continent was still largely
unknown in America. In return, the Africans that have graduated
from this small institution and have made good in life are vastly
disproportionate in number and importance to the products of
other universities, taking those same factors into consideration.
Moreover, they include both the men who eventually became
their countries' first African Heads of State: President Kwame
Nkrumah of Ghana (1957) and President Azikiwe of Nigeria
(1960). No institution of Lincoln's smallness can hope for a
greater 'reward'.

Zik was admitted at the beginning of the 1929–30 session and
here completed the first phase of his academic studies. At
'Commencement' (Convocation) in June 1931 he graduated B.A.

(*cum laude*),* one of the best in his class. 'On that never-to-be-forgotten day in the history of my life,' wrote Zik in his 'Odyssey', 'I found myself realizing my immediate dreams. . . . And as I put on my Gown and Hood . . . I was happy that all my toils at Storer College, all my sufferings in Pittsburgh, all my travails in the Coal Mines . . . and all my experiences at Howard University, etc., had not been in vain.'

As he received his B.A. Diploma, 'enscrolled in Latin', from Dr W. H. Johnson, President of Lincoln, 'a new light dawned on me', Zik recounts. 'Ah yes, it is Commencement, the beginning of a new era in my life.'

* In-term work is usually graded 'A', 'B', 'C', or 'D', corresponding to 'excellent', 'good', 'average', and 'poor' ('fail'). At graduation the diplomas are awarded for ordinary passes (these usually entail a wide range in performance), or for outstanding records denoted by the following ascending grades of excellence: *cum laude*, *magna cum laude*, and (very rare) *summa cum laude*. (Approximate translation: 'with distinction'; 'with great distinction'; 'with highest distinction'.)

Chapter 11

Zik and American Education

From his first, preparatory courses at Storer College in 1925 to his last well-earned degree at the University of Pennsylvania in 1933, Nnamdi Azikiwe spent eight years in study at five American university institutions, except for the session 1927–8. He specialized in political science, but paid great attention to history – especially 'Negro' history – economics, philosophy, and anthropology. He found time, in addition, to do a correspondence course in law from the Lasalle Extension University, Chicago, and, for three consecutive summers (1930, '31, and '32), to join the class in the theory and practice of journalism at Teachers College, Columbia University, New York.

Zik gained a Certificate in Law from his correspondence course in this subject, in 1927; he had concentrated on the principles of international law. At Lincoln he 'majored' in political science for his A.B., leaning heavily towards comparative government. Teachers College of Columbia University also gave him a Certificate in Journalism for his labours there, during which he had edited the *Columbia University Summer Session Times*, once during his three sessions. (At Lincoln and at both of his previous institutions he had already been very active in college journalism.) In 1932 Lincoln awarded him an M.A. degree with honours in religion and philosophy.* While teaching political science at Lincoln he registered for and did a course of studies in anthropology at nearby University of Pennsylvania, which awarded him a Master of Science degree in this subject in 1933. . . .

The ranging freedom which the American academic system

---

* It is to be noted that President Nkrumah of Ghana, graduating from Lincoln five years later in 1937, and from its Seminary in 1939, had taken almost the same subjects as Azikiwe, but with greater concentration on philosophy and religion for a longer period. President Nkrumah also took a Master's degree at Pennsylvania.

allows those who use it enabled Zik to exercise his mind and develop his intellectual abilities and academic interests in very much his own way. There are, undoubtedly, excesses in this 'permissiveness' in American education. It does throw up many a graduate of whom it can be said – as one New Zealander Professor at an African university did once say of a visiting American Junior-year student – 'he is well-informed but not learned'. All this is eminently true, while not denuding the system of its major virtues in the slightest.

This is no time and place to argue at length the merits and demerits of this or that system of education, as against some other. The movements, interactions, and confrontations within the international academic and intellectual community, during the last two decades especially, make argument unnecessary and undignified. Some basic points, however, may be made here with advantage to both the critic and the criticized. The first is that people sometimes forget that the United States of America is an *outsize* agglomeration of people, things, facts, relations, and standards; that these exist in huge proportions: the good, the bad, and the indifferent; and that this truth applies to universities and graduates as decisively as it does to anything else. Secondly, education is one of those things that states or nations try to work out for themselves, according to their own peculiar history and present conditions of life. That their national premises may be false and lead to conclusions or results utterly disastrous for the nation's short- or long-term future, is no invalidation of the principle.

American education seeks to fulfil the American *dream* of a democratic society in which nothing is too good for the citizen who can acquire and use it, be it economic, political, or social means. The American hope of realizing this dream is, in turn, based upon a convinced empiricist and pragmatic approach dictated by the demands of a scientific age spawned suddenly upon a new polity. America escaped the imperatives of an ancient classicism and the restrictions placed upon the popular approach by the medieval régime in Europe, and faced, in the New World, a new and different set of conditions. The frontiers could not have been pushed back, nor huge tracts of 'waste-land' reclaimed, with classical Greek or metaphysical indulgences. Rather, the ordered observation of natural phenomena just had to be the method of dealing with these, and the concrete result became necessarily the only test of truth. Such an outlook would make little provision, in a vitally formative period, for classicism and privileged minorities.

An authoritative summary of the idealism we are discussing is here presented in the words of James Bryant Conant, scientist, scholar, educator, and university-president-turned-diplomat during the Second World War:

This mixed-up, confused society of ours is something which I believe most Americans, when they view it objectively, view with pride – just as they take pride in the fact that America has been and still is the land of opportunity. Indeed, when I attempt to sum up for Europeans American education in terms of American idealism, I say the development of our schools and colleges has been motivated by our desire to move constantly towards two goals: equality of opportunity for all youth, equality of respect for all honest citizens.

Was it not this doctrine of equality of respect that was taken over by the academic profession in the United States a century ago when agricultural and mechanical arts colleges were founded and sustained? Has not the whole American educational tradition been the development of a tradition in which the equality of all useful labour is recognized?

To that formulation Robert Maynard Hutchins, *enfant terrible* of American academia a generation ago, adds: 'I believe that the doctrine of education for all is America's greatest contribution to the theory and practice of democracy.'

But, you may say, this is praise for America by Americans. To which the reply is that eminent non-Americans all over have often put the position in even more striking terms. Here, for instance, is Sir Eric Ashby, F.R.S., President of the British Association for the Advancement of Science, and currently an English oracle in things academic:

Let me put the figures into perspective in this way. Consider five children born in 1943: an American, a Canadian, an Australian, a Russian, and a British child. There is about a one-in-three chance that the American is now receiving a full-time higher education. The equivalent chance for the Canadian is one-in-six, for the Australian, one-in-nine, for the Russian, one-in-twelve, and for the British child –

but only if one includes all those taking sandwich courses – also one-in-twelve. No one supposes that these ratios represent differences in resources of ability between these countries. What, then, do they represent? They represent differences in policy for investing in man. ...

The American system and our own illustrate two fundamentally different approaches to investment in man. The Americans have an open door to higher education. ...*

These views on the spirit of American education must be held to be both correct and valid, theoretically. But this is not to say that they are necessarily always so in practice. Hutchins, for instance, in the book from which his brief quotation, above, is taken (*Some Observations on American Education*), was not writing in its praise at all, quite the contrary; he was mercilessly laying bare most of its well-established weaknesses. And we do know that very often the results of this university education don't live up to the promise of the beginning, either at graduation itself or later in life; that sometimes the system breaks down altogether, through liberal but false assumptions on the part of university authorities. And more.... To the system itself, however, this is not catastrophic, because the system is elastic, flexible, accommodating; it produces the ten per cent of quality required for performance at the highest national and international levels. The ratio of success to failure, therefore, does not matter all that much, among 4,000,000 and more would-be university graduates. Out of this mass the élite, whom we must have, emerges triumphant at the top, anyway, by the natural processes of selection, elimination, and survival: '... the best ones are free to reach the highest standard; the poor ones are encouraged to improve, to stagnate or to wither away', as Ikeotuonye puts it.

It is not on record that Azikiwe's worries included the question of how his American education would compare with that of European-educated countrymen and contemporaries later. It is doubtful whether the question ever occurred to him at all, or, if it did, whether it made any impression on him. The evidence in fact suggests that it did not. 'Diffuseness' is one of the charges brought against the American system: too many subjects over

* This was Sir Eric's Presidential Address to the British Association in August 1963 at Aberdeen, Scotland, and his topic was: 'Investment in Man'.

too-widely separated areas of knowledge in too short a time, and worse. Azikiwe seems to have pressed on with his interests, in complete oblivion or disregard of this prejudice. The humanistic approach of America, rather than the pronounced specialism of Europe, appealed, without argument or strain, to one already destined for political and social leadership. So Zik gave his greatest attention to political studies and economics, but in addition took all those courses in history, philosophy, education, law, religion, anthropology, and science that have been mentioned before.

Most of these were useful to him in the way always intended: they provided him with many ideas, they suggested both method and methodology, they added relevant facts and indirect information. They were, in short, the broad base of his educational and intellectual pyramid. It was at the top that he concentrated his real and abiding interests: politics, economics, and history, as these gave him knowledge of or insight into the past, the present, the future of the Negro peoples of the world. This was the general theme, the universalist view. But based upon it and drawn from it was the idea of an urgent need to mount a programme for the emancipation of Africans from European – and particularly British – political and economic domination.

In other words, Zik studied politics, economics, and history, informed and guided – not *limited*, which he could easily have been – by his Africanism. He saw truth in some of the basic teaching of Karl Marx: 'Even capitalism ... cannot refuse to accept the fundamentality of the theory of economic determination in society.' In *Renascent Africa* (page 126), Zik continued his observations on Marxist theory by declaring that:

Applying this thesis to life in Africa, it cannot be done away with peremptorily. As it was efficacious in the life of mankind in the other continents, so, too, it is destined to be efficacious in the African continent.

His peace with this theory was further restated:

Economic Determinism must be the basis of African economic thought. The quest for food, shelter, and clothing has been the primal motive in the establishment of society. It was responsible for the formulation of the social and political institutions of society. It is still the dominant factor in African contemporary history.

But he was also sympathetic with the Guild Socialists for thinking that society could remove contentious ideology out of politics and reduce it to a system purely of trade interests which would take care of their respective groups without passion and without prejudice. Zik was next immensely impressed by the Fabians, who proposed the application of brakes on revolutionary socialism. Not just their gradualism – which revolutionary socialists and modern nationalists call 'reactionary politics' – but their ideas for 'phasing' political-economic reform, for freeing or liberalizing the spirit of change from unnecessary rigidity and harshness, impressed Azikiwe as worthy of consideration too. Passfield, Philip Snowden, Bernard Shaw, Ramsay MacDonald, and the other founders and early theoreticians of the Fabian Society and the Labour Party shared equal attention with the Utopian-Marxists on Zik's time-table of discussions and paper-writing.

By about the time he had reached the middle of his graduate studies at Lincoln and Pennsylvania, Zik had formed his syntheses and taken his decisions. These syntheses, to have validity, had also to have a general master-principle as foundation, and Zik was now ready to formulate a simple one. He was to cling to it throughout his future career. '*I am an African*,' he said to himself then, as he still does today, '*and [must] always relate all theories, ideas, proposals, etc., to that fact.*'

From this it was easy enough to proceed with his synthesizing of the political and economic theories and practices of Europe and America, with his own ideas, so that it would be possible, later, to erect a programme of action upon them. On a 'political philosophy of Africa' Zik stated that the 'forces which were responsible for the birth, growth, and decay of Ethiopia, Egypt, Babylo-Assyria, Phoenicia, Greece, and Rome will determine the fate of the West, the East, and Africa'. Other canons of this philosophy have been stated or summarized below in Chapters 15 and 18, but Zik also wrote that 'the forces of nationalism are automatic, especially when factors leading to them are intelligently directed', and he thought that 'the right of self-determination is a phenomenon which defies human deviousness and manoeuvring.'

Zik's economic philosophy, later enlarged and propagated in

great detail, was at first intensely personal for the greater part. Rugged individualism, he affirmed, was opposed to the African way of life, which recognizes the principle of 'one for all and all for each'. 'The profit motive is nevertheless valid. It becomes bad only when overdone', that is, when it becomes an end in itself instead of a means for the betterment of others. Again, 'I believe in competition', he said, breaking with Marx, 'but not in monopoly', he added. He was later to put these economic compromises to such use personally as to cause his followers to wonder and admire, and his enemies to turn away in distaste as well as in frustration. But that was because the latter did not know their man and had not studied sufficiently his philosophy for public as well as private success. When he wrote in the *African Morning Post*, and later in *Renascent Africa*, that 'the Renascent African cannot create a new social order without an economic foundation', he was affirming a belief which he held as firmly for Nnamdi Azikiwe as for Africa. However, he liberalized this stand with more Marxist principles. He said: 'No longer must wealth be concentrated in the hands of the few', and, more personally important: 'no longer must the profit motive guide and control the aims in life of the African. ...' From this strictly limited, pragmatic viewpoint, the economic determination of history was perfectly acceptable to Nnamdi Azikiwe. There is little to show that he went much beyond this point in personal belief or acceptance, for instance with regard to the theory of the class struggle and the eventual establishment of a completely stateless society. But then a 'class-structured' society is meaningless in Africa in any case.

The last two to three years of Zik's career in America were among his most active, and certainly the most profitable and satisfying. While acting as an instructor in political science at Lincoln, he also wrote prolifically, producing a large collection of manuscripts on many related subjects, general as well as African: 'The Practice of Forced Labour' (1931), 'A Critique of Polygyny' (1932), and 'Theories on the Origins of the State', 'Mythology in Onitsha Society' (University of Pennsylvania thesis), 'Anthropology and the Problem of Race', 'Theories on the Origins of the State', 'Syllabus for African History', and 'Readings in Historiography', were all produced in 1933, the year before his departure from the States. The year of his departure was the best of them all, for it was in 1934 that he prepared at Lincoln and had published in London his outstanding major work to date: *'Liberia in World Politics'*.*

During most of his journey through his universities and colleges, Zik also managed to keep up his great interest in journalism – which was later to become his means of entry into public life back home in West Africa. He acted as a university correspondent for the Baltimore *Afro-American* from 1928 straight through to 1934, and as a general and sports correspondent to the Philadelphia *Tribune* (also a Negro publication) during the same period. In 1933 he took overseas membership in the Institute of Journalists, London, which he still holds. His membership of learned societies, also, was indicative of his wide academic and intellectual interests and activities: the American Anthropological Association (1932–4), American Society of International Law (1933–4), American Political Science Society (1933–4), American Ethnological Society (1933–4), Royal Anthropological Institute (1933, Life Fellow), and Royal Economic Society (1934, Life Fellow). Much later, in 1947, he became also a Life Member of the British Association for the Advancement of Science.

In 1924 Zik could have chosen to remain in the Gold Coast and work his way up from the ranks in the Police Force, perhaps to change his mind later, perhaps not. Under strong parental and circumstantial pressure, however, he had to reject that temptation quickly and return to Nigeria to prepare for a different adventure. In 1934 he was presented with a much more alluring prospect: that of remaining in academic life in America and rising to professorial fame, perhaps, with limitless opportunities and facilities for the production of learned works. 'My teaching is a success so far,' Zik wrote to a cousin in February 1933. 'If I did not swear that I shall return to serve my folks in Africa, I think that I have a better chance today to make a name in the world of scholarship.'

Zik chose to return home 'to serve his folks'.

* Stockwell. Now out of print. (See Chapter 12.)

Chapter 12

Liberia in World Politics

According to the date at the end of his Preface to this book, Zik finished writing *Liberia in World Politics* at Lincoln University in June 1934. The year coincides with Zik's entrance upon the public scene, and the time that has elapsed since that first publication is exactly the same as the entire period he has participated in the drama of African liberation and progress. *In those thirty years Nnamdi Azikiwe has not produced anything to equal this book* and until he retires from his present exalted position and from public life altogether, he is not likely to be able to do so. *Liberia* is not only his *magnum opus* to date but is unquestionably his finest effort of head and heart and hand so far. The scholarship is impressive, the writing straightforward and fine in the main.

This is not to belittle the quality of *Renascent Africa* or the best of the Zik speeches, particularly his magnificent Rhodes House (Oxford) paper on 'The Development of Political Parties in Nigeria' and his great Inaugural Address as Governor-General: 'Respect for Human Dignity'. But the speeches and some of the later publications are not of the same scope as *Liberia* and therefore not comparable, except perhaps for style; nor is a comparison on those lines called for here. As for *Renascent Africa*, it is undoubtedly comparable in size and scope generally, but in hardly anything else. Admittedly the two works are quite dissimilar: *Liberia*, concrete, factual, academic, and scholarly; *Renascent Africa*, ideological, emotional, and hortatory.* Moreover, *Africa* was more effective by far for its purpose than any response *Liberia*'s academic challenge ever received. Even so, no honest appraisal of pure merit would fail to give the palm to the latter book.

All this is not to suggest, however, that *Liberia in World*

* *Renascent Africa*, it must be pointed out, was in the main an edited collection of a large number of separate pieces from Zik's 'Inside Stuff' series in the *Morning Post*.

Politics is without fault. Far from it. As human beings we can only aim at perfection: that is the justification of human life and effort; but perfection is seldom attained, and thus we keep on striving. Certainly *Liberia in World Politics* is not perfect, but it is an eminently satisfying book.

The background to the undertaking of this significant work by Azikiwe provides one of the most engrossing and pertinent stories of the entire preparatory period to Zik's public career. It involves revealing, vital correspondence and self-examination which we shall presently reproduce (slightly edited) in part.

In his own words, it was during his short stay at the Calabar Hope Waddell Institute that Azikiwe 'first heard of a country whose administrative officials were black men. It was so unbelievable!' The 'Odyssey', continues the account:

A friend of mine (a member of the Kru tribe) was one of the students of the Institute. He used to tell us that in his country, the President and the Governors of the Counties were black men, and so were all the judges, the law officers, etc.

The next two paragraphs do not read like the greatest writing of the century, but are necessary for continuity in this account:

When I asked him why he came all the way to Nigeria where the reverse was the case, he told me that in Kru parlance, it was said that whenever dogs congregated they often mused philosophically that human beings who had been blessed by God, by being allowed to have buttocks instead of haunches which were allowed dogs, did not appreciate the divine gift.

In other words, his country had the opportunity, but instead of using the same to advantage, they gave impression to the outside world that they were like swines [*sic*] who had pearls and either knew not their value or could not make use of them.

'This revelation drew us closer together,' continued Zik, 'and I became very much interested in Liberian affairs.' Here was the first link in the chain. Years later, the chain was completed: 'My humble attempt to interpret Liberian Diplomacy, in book form, fourteen years later, has since received the approbation of competent students of international politics and diplomacy.'

But it appears from a part of what follows below that by

1927 in America Zik had forgotten the 'revelation' of 1920 at Calabar. And even when the subject was called to his attention again he seems not to have remembered the first awareness, for his 'Odyssey' account said in two separate places that it was in America in 1927 that he 'became interested in the Republic of Liberia'. Now we shall let Zik tell the story of his 'conversion' himself. He writes:

Some time in March 1927, I received a letter from a West Indian friend who was studying at Fisk University.

The letter is so challenging that I am reproducing it, in part.

Incidentally, this letter and my acquaintance with a Liberian student, who was also studying at Fisk, at that time, made me to become interested in the Republic of Liberia.

The letter from my West Indian friend reads as follows:

'Despite the fact that we are unacquainted with each other, I feel that I can take the liberty of addressing you, on the basis of our racial kinship, with respect to a matter that I feel is of mutual interest to us.

'Permit me, therefore, to offer to you my most sincere greetings and wish you well.

'I am writing to invite your fellowship and co-operation in a movement that I am hoping to work out along with Mr —, a student from Monrovia, Liberia.

'We are trying to lay plans to establish a political organization among foreign Negro students in American colleges and universities.

'The primary object will be to foster racial consciousness and a spirit of nationalism aiming at the protection of the sovereignty of Liberia.

'We anticipate that the organization will assume certain aspects similar to the Kuomintang Party, which was organized by Dr Sun Yat Sen and Chinese students who received their education in countries of the Western world.

'We do not expect the movement will meet with much support from the local students, who are not as a rule interested in the African continent.

'However, if there are any desirous of participating, provision will be made for their membership.

'It will, therefore, be a matter of most concern to us who are looking forward to going back to the fatherland.

'It is not easy to enter into lengthy details in an introductory letter, but I would like to draw your attention to the Firestone project in Liberia, which is only another manifestation of Imperialism.

'I do not think it inopportune to start a campaign of propaganda on our respective campuses, and elsewhere with the object of arousing public sentiment against such forms of Imperialism.

'If our ideas meet with your approval, I shall be exceedingly pleased to hear from you.

'We take this opportunity to invite suggestions, and shall in turn send you full details as to our tentative plans, as well as a copy of our manifesto.

'I have the honour to be your brother in a common cause.'

I replied to my friend and also to a friend of his, the Liberian student, who was well-known to me.

Whilst I agreed that the time had arrived for the intensification of the propaganda of African nationalism with a view to crystallizing racial consciousness, yet I was of opinion that the primary task was mental emancipation.

I believed in Sun Yat-Sen-ism, and was proud to read of the victories of Marshal Chiang Kai Shek in the attempt to unify China.

But I thought that an intellectual revolution was more potent as foundation for the superstructure that must be built inevitably.

To this, my Liberian friend replied as follows:

'Dear Friend and Countryman. Evidently, you have received a letter from Mr — because he said something about having an encouraging letter from you.

'Ben, he is acting on my advice, in fact he and I had planned to make this a working organization.

'I want you to feel that I am not [so] ignorant of the conditions of our country and its peoples that I do not know the difficult task of working with the many tribes, because I do.

'I know that Africa cannot be compared with China in the least, because that country (China) has had an unbroken history of 4,000 years with her ethical and philosophical background.

'Our purpose is not to start a revolutionary propaganda as the 'Nationalist' China, or the Kuomintang, but rather an educational propaganda.

'(a) To stimulate interest among African students that they may determine more, with a 'Dark Africa' ever before their minds.

'(b) To hasten the Renaissance and to do our part in preparing our people for the inevitable factors of history.

'Somebody must make a start and I think it is our duty, as students, who have the opportunity to observe the world's economic struggles and the motives of man.

'It is a fact, considering the country's condition, that we can't do much, but we can start the work for those who will follow to see it through. . . .'

Then I became interested in the Republic of Liberia and its position in world politics.

I was ashamed that even though I was an African, I knew less of the African continent generally speaking, and the Republic of Liberia particularly.

I found out that some Americans, black or white, were more familiar with the history of the Republic of Liberia than myself and most African students.

Then came my moment of self-realization.

I mused that if I was willing to become an Intellectual Revolutionist for the mental emancipation of Liberia and Africa, then there was no reason why I should not formulate a philosophy toward the crystallization of this dream of a New Africa.

But my training was limited and I knew less of Systematic Philosophy.

It took a course of lectures in the subject of Social Philosophy, under Professor Alain Leroy Locke, B. Litt. (Oxon.), Ph.D., to guide me towards constructive and systematic thinking. . . .

In 1931, after Zik had started attending the Columbia University Teachers College Summer School (through a Phelps-Stokes Fund grant) and had lectured at Lincoln as a Graduate Assistant in political science, he thought it was time for him to seek a permanent job, *in Africa*. By then the subject of Liberia was a psychological and patriotic obsession with him. He therefore wrote to President Edwin W. Barclay – then in office in Monrovia – offering himself for the foreign service of Liberia. Two months later came a courteous reply regretting the President's inability to employ Zik, mostly for final reasons but also raising the question of nationality. Whereupon Zik, in a fit of disappointment, swore to make himself such an authority on Liberia as would cause even the citizens themselves to 'sit up'.

Eventually Azikiwe began his study of Liberian history and government. By the end of 1931 he was well enough prepared on the subject to have read a paper in New York on the African republic to the annual conference of the Association for the Study of Negro History, a creation of the distinguished American Negro historian, Carter G. Woodson. Zik defended Liberia and condemned guilty western nations who were both guilty towards and at the same time censorious of that inexperienced little country. He also demonstrated his love of the comparative approach, in a passage which still has pertinence today. Zik said, in part:

The eyes of the world are on Liberia. Men without appreciation for the contribution of the Negro to modern statesmanship are content to criticize this African Republic without deep thought on the onerous duty of statecraft. Greedy nations are lurking and watching Liberia like hawks. . . .

Ladies and gentlemen, I submit that eighty-four years of political autonomy are not sufficient to pass a final judgment on the political incapacity of the Liberian Negro. Dr Woodson states that Liberia's first century compares favourably with that of the colony of Virginia. While Liberia encouraged education and social uplift, Governor William Berkeley [of Virginia] was narrow enough to 'thank God that there were no free schools or printing presses in the province'.

Let it be remembered also that it took Great Britain fourteen hundred years after the conquest of Boadicea to draft the Magna Carta. It took her several centuries more to pave the way for the English Revolution which established a constitutional democracy. It took France eighteen hundred years after Caesar's conquests in Gaul to dream up and effect the French Revolution, thereby founding a government of the people, for the people, by their accredited representatives. Even the United States of America spent one hundred and fifty-six years, after the landing of the Pilgrim Fathers, in political tutelage as a vassal of an alien colonial power. As Judge T. M. Stewart pointed out, the United States was heir to generations of civilization and experience in government. Her builders were fresh from the schools and universities of Europe. British brains and capital laid the foundation of the American commonwealth of nations.

In spite of this unequal handicap, Liberia is still keeping pace. Commander A. H. Foote states the case of Liberia more tersely: 'Let then the black men be judged fairly, and not presumed to have become all at once and by miracle, of a higher order than old historic nations through many generations of whom the political organization of the world has been slowly developing itself.' Even acknowledged authorities in the field of politics and government recognize the evolutional nature of modern democracies. Liberia should not, therefore, be hastily condemned.

Liberia in World Politics is primarily a meticulous examination and analysis of the history of that country in its relations with the principal world powers, from the founding in 1847 to the year or two preceding the publication of the book. Or, in the author's own words, it was 'an analysis of the backgrounds and contributing factors to the contemporary problems of the Republic of Liberia ... a critique of Liberian history and diplomacy'. And his stated aim was 'to present all the angles of the Liberian situation' – a worthy undertaking worthily executed.

Zik guides himself and his readers by dividing Liberian history into four periods. The first was the *Period of Colonization*, when the repatriating American Negroes came in 1822 to the various spots on the west coast of Africa which were eventually consti- tuted into the Republic. The American Colonization Society was the administering authority, and supplied the first agents and governors for the settlements. The *Period of Self-Determination* began only twenty-five years later, in 1847, when the settlers declared their independence, established a national existence, and began to seek ways of creating a viable polity.

Thirdly followed the *Period of Imperialism*, when 'Liberia lost about one-half of its territory through "big-stick" diplomacy' to England and France, and when later it came under American influence during the Presidency of Theodore Roosevelt, the 'big stick' philosopher himself. This was the period of the control of Liberia's economic life by alien powers, and therefore also the period of greatest threat to the sovereignty of the new and 'tiny' state. Lastly, we had the *Period of International Mediation*, which was still current when *Liberia in World Politics* was being written. During these years the Republic was under an intense world spotlight, particularly as a result of the circumstances leading to the appointment of the 1931 International Commission of enquiry into allegations of slavery and forced labour against the Government. The Commission's work was done under the auth- ority of the League of Nations, the world's first attempt at a universal supra-national body of sovereign states.

Azikiwe approached his task of examining and analysing Liberia's diplomatic history from a set of postulates: (1) that 'the foreign policy of the Republic of Liberia has been formulized in accordance with the exigencies of colonial politics'; (2) that the weakness of this new country as a small state, and the fact that it depended on certain western Powers for its finances, had 'subor- dinated its diplomacy to the forces of economic imperialism in tropical Africa'; (3) that Liberia's position as the sole republic on that continent had 'affected its international relations'; (4) that the 'Colonial powers, in their attempt to maintain their various spheres of influence, have employed coercive means to shape the economic and political destinies' of that Republic; therefore (5) that Liberian diplomacy was, inevitably, the obeisance paid to 'the dictates of colonial imperialism'.

The formulation of such postulates must naturally proceed *a posteriori*, and Zik's evidence in proof of these claims is overwhelming in the book; it was not with him a case of *a priori* prejudices. That the United States of America, Great Britain, France, Germany, Belgium, and other western powers played cat-and-mouse too often with the almost helpless young Republic between 1871 and 1926 is proved beyond doubt by the documentation. A living, participant witness and authority like the American, Raymond Leslie Buell (*The Native Problem in Africa*, 1928, 2 volumes), testified at the time to some of the more inexcusable activities of those involved, including American financiers and the Government itself. Wrote Buell:

The activities of the Departments of State and Commerce in promoting, in the midst of this secrecy, American enterprise in Liberia, and the disregard or lack of knowledge of the American Government of the effect of the entrance of such enterprise upon the people and Government of Liberia is disconcerting, not only because of this particular instance, but because it is symptomatic of what may happen on a large scale in the future. . . . It is important that the United States, the people of which do not wish to be associated in a territorial scramble or in the abusive exploitation of primitive peoples, should work out methods to direct foreign investments along intelligent and socially beneficial lines. (*The Native Problem in Africa*, 851–2.)

Yet in 1909 it was America that was offering to save Liberia from France, Great Britain, and Germany, who were accused, in the author's words, of 'designs to dismember the Republic'. But the same circumstances which had occasioned the American alarm over the intentions of the three European powers had just led one of them (France) to accuse another (England) of having an '. . . army of occupation' in Liberia – a case of the accused accusing the accused and a perfect analogy to the popular Sierra Leone creole saying: 'Tief tief, God laugh!' That is, the spectacle of a thief stealing from a thief is so amusing that even God laughs.

So the United States appointed an American Commission to investigate the condition of affairs in Liberia; the Secretary of State, Mr Elihu Root, told Congress that Liberia was a colony of the U.S., which was under high obligation to give 'assistance toward the maintenance of free, orderly and prosperous civil society' in the little Republic; and President Teddy Roosevelt himself joined his minister in urging 'an imperative duty' of help to Liberia.

All of which illustrates the ambivalence, the tortured official conscience, of the United States, as to its role in or responsibility for Liberia. It was very much – if Zik had wanted to draw the analogy – like the situation at Westminster during most of the first three-quarters of the nineteenth century, with respect to the 'West African Settlements' of the British connexion. Her Majesty's Government, Parliament, leaders of the Abolitionist movements, and concerned individuals of all types, now counselled Britain to withdraw from these primitive and profitless lands, now urged full Christian and 'civilized' responsibility for these territories. The Colonial Office shifted administrative headquarters constantly: now the Gold Coast under Sierra Leone, now Lagos Colony under Gold Coast and vice versa, now the Merchants' Association put in control, then a representative of the Crown, then back to the Merchants. . . .

But ambivalence and erosion of conscience were not diseases endemic only to Washington or Westminster. Azikiwe gives evidence also of a love-hate complex in Monrovia itself, where 'contemporary politics is still divided. One group is anti-American,'

It . . . believes that the United States has used its good offices in many instances to effect a financial control which will eventually dictate the political and economic destinies of the country. On the other hand, there is another group which maintains that anti-Americanism is not consonant with the traditions of the country. 'If anyone should try to create the impression (of anti-Americanism) we assert right here that it is false. The masses of the people of Liberia are not opposed to American interest in the country. . . . Stand by Uncle Sam and Uncle Sam will stand by us.'

Nnamdi Azikiwe, in this powerful work of scholarship, was highly critical of the western powers, as we have seen, in their differential attitudes and activities in Liberia; in contrast he was very generous towards the Liberian authorities under his scrutiny. Taking the whole man into account, the burden of his life and thought, the background to the undertaking of the study, and the utter ferocity of some of the forces ranged against both him – as an African – and Liberia, it is not surprising that on the whole, and in spite, too, of much negative evidence against his 'principals', the Azikiwe stance should have been fiercely defensive, and even protective, of Liberia. Otherwise much of his special pleading would be unacceptable.

But this is not to suggest, therefore, that Azikiwe's eyes were completely shut against some of the failings and weaknesses of some of the pioneers. Almost from the beginning, these, Zik wrote, 'disfigured their historic achievement with a record which is now the basis of most political intrigues directed against the Republic'. He was here discussing one of the weaknesses: relations between the pioneer-settlers and the 'aboriginal Liberians', which made President Daniel B. Warner issue in 1866 a warning and an appeal to his fellow-members of the ruling class: '... These Chiefs and their subjects have, undoubtedly, certain rights, both natural and political, which should be highly respected by this Government and people.' It is recognized that today, even if all conditions are not satisfactory in Liberia, basic social and political attitudes are changing, on the part both of the Government and of individual citizens.

In a chapter on the need to 'reforge' Liberia, Azikiwe essayed to advise the authorities there on a number of changes that he considered should be made in the body politic, economic, and social of Liberia, if it was to overcome some of its paralysing disabilities. It was a bold gesture, but not made in a spirit of impudence. Indeed the author was humbly apologetic for his boldness, and craved the sympathetic indulgence of the very people he was out to help with his suggestions for reform:

It seems pedantic to find flaws in Liberian political organization. It is not intended to dictate what should be done. The opinions contained herein are respectfully submitted for consideration. They represent some of the tested and applied principles of politics and government which have worked out successfully in other parts of the civilized world. The political organization of man has been undergoing a series of changes from time immemorial. In this field of study nothing is static. . . .

The Republic of Liberia should seriously consider the suggestions made hereunder. . . .

But the question is, what Liberian authorities were seriously going to consider this unsought advice as anything more than an academic exercise in comparative ideas and institutions of government? It is not on record that any of them did. But whether they did or didn't, Azikiwe felt about Liberia in 1934 that 'this last vestige of hope for African nationality should be safeguarded and revitalized by every true son and daughter of African descent. . . .'

So *Liberia in World Politics*, with its slight over-ambition in scope and in reformist intent, and its inevitable semantic problems for the reader here and there, remains, if nothing else, an astonishing performance for a man of thirty whose higher education had started only seven to eight years previously. It is the brightest feather in Zik's academic-intellectual cap so far, and was an enviable prize with which to return home.

Part Four

THE RETURN

I returned to Nigeria at the end of 1934, but soon moved on to Accra, ... where I became editor of the Accra *African Morning Post*. In [1937] I returned to Nigeria, where I established the newspaper *West African Pilot*. After a period of political activity in the Nigerian Youth Movement, I combined with the late Herbert Macaulay to found the National Council of Nigeria and the Cameroons. From that time, through journalism and through political leadership, I have fought consistently for the greatness of Africa and for her citizens everywhere. In particular I have constantly striven for the freedom and unity of Nigeria. ...

From the Preface to *Zik – A Selection from the Speeches of Nnamdi Azikiwe*, C.U.P., 1961

Chapter 13

Ghana as a Starting Point

Ghana was, on each of two widely separated occasions, a kind of starting point for Azikiwe. The first time was when he landed at Sekondi in 1924 as both a runaway and a stowaway, and when he started work as a police recruit at Accra. This was his day of frustration and humiliation. The second occasion was ten years later, when, as 'Zik', he returned in triumph to become, over-night, West Africa's outstanding journalist-cum-public figure. The ten intervening years had made a radical difference both on the Gold Coast, as it then was, and on Azikiwe.

Economically, socially, and politically, the country had taken immense strides forward, as progress is measured under colonial-ism. In a few years, one of the most humane of colonial Gover-nors, Sir Gordon Guggisberg, had set up in the Gold Coast, practically single-handed, four comparatively impressive monu-ments to development, whether measured in terms of the colonial world of the 1920s and 30s, or even in terms of the present post-colonial situation – 'neo-colonial', as some in-sistently call it. He had built Takoradi Harbour, the Korle-Bu Hospital, and, dearest of all to his heart, Achimota School.* All of these were unprecedented in their size, cost, scope, and facili-ties, at the time. In addition, he had extended into the Gold Coast the 'revolutionary' practice of elective representation† of the people in the legislature, first established in Nigeria by Sir Hugh

* Achimota School is on a gentle hill, about one mile from the village of Achimota. The name comes from two Ga words meaning: one does not, or one should not, mention names. That is, don't mention anybody by name here. This was because the village of Achimota was an end 'station' of the 'underground railway' to which former slaves and runaways from northern Ghana escaped to freedom. Once they reached this village they were safe, because everyone kept everyone else's secret.

† The Lagos Town Council had already, in 1920, seen the first African elected representatives of a legislative body, but this was in local govern-ment. The 1922 Clifford Constitution was the first to introduce the principle into central government in the then African colonies.

Clifford in 1922. Moreover, in conjunction with the new harbour, Guggisberg had also expanded the railway services and constructed new roads in the Colony itself as well as into Ashanti. Thus he had increased manyfold the volume of trade in imports and exports, opened up the country immeasurably to both internal and external contact, and made the Gold Coast a subject of discussion abroad in respect of these pioneering development projects.

Frederick Gordon Guggisberg was a combination of administrator, technician, and humanist – for many ex-colonials the only kind of man that makes the contemplation of colonialism, with any degree of charity, possible. Sir Gordon was born in 1869 in Toronto, Canada, and educated at Portsmouth and the Royal Military Academy, Woolwich. He served in the First World War with the Royal Engineers and rose to the rank of Brigadier-General. He had done special survey work both in the then Gold Coast and in Nigeria before the War. After the War he was appointed Governor of the Gold Coast in 1919. In 1925 he was given an extension of two years at his own request and, at dreadful material cost to himself, in order to enable him to complete his dearest project, Achimota. These projects demonstrated Sir Gordon's many-sided personality, catholic ideas, and practical approach to the problem of colonial development, which was then a question depending as much on the daring and determination of individuals as on their humane insight. Sir Gordon was, in short, an idealist as well as a man of action – almost the complete antithesis of the contemporary colonial type. He attacked the problem of development on the Gold Coast by a comprehensive programme which saw in 1922 the opening of Africa's finest and largest hospital for Africans at that time; in 1925 the opening of Achimota School (at the time an idealistic experiment in comprehensive education from kindergarten to intermediate degree standard, and today still notable as a co-educational secondary school); in the same year (1925) the swearing-in of the second group of elected African members of a central legislature in colonial Africa; and in 1926 the opening of Takoradi Harbour, which had cost £6,000,000 – a heavy investment even by present-day standards.

Not less important was Guggisberg's road-building

programme, and the development of local government under the same impetus of his comprehensiveness. If these two additional efforts get only second-class treatment in the history of this period, it is not because they were less important in their context, but only because they lacked the drama of Korle-Bu, Achimota, and Takoradi. Most of all they lacked the appeal of the 1925 'Guggisberg Constitution', and of Guggisberg's 'gift' to Achimota of the charismatic personality of Dr Aggrey, whom nobody could forget, living or dead: 'the legendary Aggrey of Achimota', as yet another recent commentator has described him. It was Achimota School and Guggisberg that had brought Aggrey back home, and in the years of his active presence or living memory most other institutions were apt to be slighted. Most, not all, for Guggisberg himself was held in great esteem by the people, as well as A. G. Fraser, the Scot he brought from Ceylon to mould Achimota to the Governor's dream; as well as the school itself, and the hospital.

The services they offered were eagerly accepted. Korle-Bu Hospital, in spite of widespread distrust of and disbelief in western medicines, was crowded, and everyone soon knew the tragic story of the great Japanese doctor, Noguchi, who had sacrificed his life there in 1927 to the urgent necessity of discovering the dread secrets of yellow fever: he had let himself be bitten by infected mosquitoes in the effort to discover the nature and course of the disease. Achimota School, too, could not build classrooms and houses of residence for the boarders fast enough for the number of anxious parents who wanted to register their children there. In four or five short years Governor Guggisberg had established institutions and produced further plans for a rate of political, economic, and social progress the magnitude of which was probably unmatched in those days. It was a record achieved under a system whose claims that it had provided real benefits for its victims have been challenged, when examined in relation to modern progress and economic viability. Especially would this be true elsewhere than in a relatively favoured country like Ghana.

The Guggisberg régime introduced a period of local colonial development, then, on many fronts. The 1920s was the decade of the great world boom in cocoa, with the Gold Coast producing more of this commodity than any other country, and teaming with Nigeria to supply more than half the total world tonnage. It was principally this trade that had spurred Guggisberg on to build Takoradi. To the economic paths thus laid open was added the stimulus of a line of political development in the elective break-through provided by the Guggisberg Constitution of 1925. Educationally, too, 'the enlightenment' had been promised, even if it had not yet actually come, at Achimota. The school was already producing pupils who slowly but surely were getting to feel at home in their own culture – a reversal of the normal policy of denigration of native cultures.

The 1920s also covered the last phase of the life-and-times of J. E. Casely Hayford, who died in 1930. Beginning his public career during the last decade of the nineteenth century, this early West African Pan-Africanist eventually developed into the outstanding West African political figure in the first thirty years of the twentieth century. It was Casely Hayford who initiated the Pan-West African (English-speaking) movement of 1919–20 known as the National Congress of British West Africa, and it was the Congress that in 1920 had demanded elective representa-tion for their several countries. Their demands had been turned down at Westminster, but two years later elected representative government had come to West Africa, even if in strictly limited form. Not only did Casely Hayford live to see this indirect fruit of his aborted Congress, but throughout the Twenties he waged a legislative, jural, and journalistic* campaign on all questions affecting the general progress of his countrymen, as well as of black people everywhere.

His media were, first, the Legislative Council itself, to which he was elected† as soon as election became a right in 1925; and secondly the press, in which he had been persistently active since 1874. Casely Hayford's own *Gold Coast Leader* went out of business only with his death in 1930, but the standards of patriotism it had upheld were continued by its contemporaries

* His first appearance in journalism was on the *Gold Coast Times* (1874–85).

† He had in fact served in the Council before as a Nominated Member, one of the class around which the fires of the later nationalism raged relentlessly until its disappearance in the post-War conflagration.

and successors. Casely Hayford's efforts as a nationalist and the forces he represented during most of his life, but especially during these last ten years, inspired that continuity. The next year after his death another lawyer, J. B. Danquah, a brilliant young Akan with degrees in philosophy from London, entered the field of journalism too. His paper, the *Times of West Africa*, was only the second daily in the press history of Ghana and the first since 1897. Thus Dr Danquah was a kind of second-generation pioneer. He lived long enough to become one of West Africa's most distinguished scholars, as well as one of the oldest and best-known figures in Ghana's modern nationalist history, often succeeding, often failing, but always bravely persisting.*

The *Times* joined several other papers, former contemporaries of the then defunct *Leader*, to take up the challenge of constitutional reform. Among these were the *Gold Coast Independent*, *Vox Populi*, and the *Gold Coast Spectator*, and between them and the *Times* they created the atmosphere into which Nnamdi Azikiwe stepped in 1934. At the particular moment of his appearance that atmosphere was charged and in great disequilibrium.

There had been much agitation and unrest earlier that year over three Bills passed by the Legislative Council, a body which, until 1946, had the power to make laws in every case regardless of any opposition by the African members. The three bills passed in this instance, over vociferous, angry popular opposition, were on water rates, income tax, and 'seditious disaffection'. The 'Sedition Ordinance', as it came quickly to be called – the real title was the Criminal Code (Amendment) Ordinance No. 21 of 1934 – gave particular offence and raised great alarm among the people. Led by the Press and the politicians, in and out of the Legislative Council, they demanded the withdrawal of the three 'obnoxious bills', but especially of the one re-defining the crime of sedition and re-designing the range of punishment for it. The Governor then in office, Sir Shenton Thomas, a completely unsympathetic character, refused to shift from his position, and thus drove the country to the extremity of organizing an expensive protest deputation to the Colonial Office in London.

* Dr Danquah died on 4 February 1965 at Nsawam prison, while a political prisoner.

The deputation was an utter failure. Led by that extraordinary personality, Nana Ofori Atta the First, Paramount Chief of the area known as Akim Abuakwa, and with his half-brother, the same Dr J. B. Danquah, as secretary, it met with a series of disasters. Sir Philip Cunliffe-Lister, the Secretary of State for the Colonies in Neville Chamberlain's Cabinet, turned down their request for the repeal of the offending ordinances. To make matters worse, the deputation lost one of their members, Mr James Mercer, through a motor accident in London. In addition, they had to endure the mortification of a duplicate appeal to the British Government and people by a 'rival' delegation from the Gold Coast, even though this was in effect a private one. It had been sent by the Aborigines' Rights Protection Society, the body formed in 1897 to combat government threats to the country's communally-held lands. But the A.R.P.S. had long ceased to be representative of the country's public interest, and its delegation to London only piled confusion upon national distress.

It was in these unhappy circumstances that Nnamdi Azikiwe returned to the Gold Coast in 1934, to start his life work.

Chapter 14

A Brief Re-union

The man who was responsible for Azikiwe's career in the Gold
Coast was Alfred J. Ocansey, a successful businessman from the
small coastal town of Ada. Mr Ocansey, like many 'provincials'
or 'small-town boys' with talent, had moved into the capital
town (Accra) and had there established a many-sided business
enterprise. One after the other he had gone into the different
and difficult fields of cocoa, transport, timber, merchandising,
the cinema, and the Press. It was both to expand his newspaper
business and to break new ground for himself that he decided
upon the bold venture of hiring Azikiwe.

By this time Ocansey was known to be quite a rich man, but
there were also widespread stories about his parsimoniousness.
He had provided work for hundreds of men and women, information and popular knowledge for thousands, and entertainment
at his 'Palladium' cinema* for tens of thousands since 1925.
Nevertheless, his workers in all branches of his business empire
grumbled and complained incessantly about their low wages and
other unfavourable conditions of work. Machines and types in his
press workshops were used until they could hardly continue to
function, before they were replaced. Often, these machines, and
much other equipment, were originally of inferior make or
quality. Still, A. J. Ocansey's was an evocative name in those days.
It ranked with those of Frans Dove, Akilakpa Sawyerr, Charles
Quist, A. W. Kojo Thompson, Woolhouse Bannerman, Kobina
Sekyi, Dr C. E. Reidorf, Dr F. V. Nanka-Bruce, all of them
professionals and leading personalities.

The news that Ocansey was bringing 'Professor Azikiwe' – as
they called him – to Accra to edit a new daily for the City Press
Limited was thus greeted with a good deal of excited curiosity.
How much was the old man going to pay this young one.

* It was at the Palladium that the 'talkies' were first introduced into
Ghana.

especially with the reputation that had already preceded the latter? 'It is said he's to be given £40 a month, plus commission,' said one. 'More,' answered another. 'I have heard £50 per month, *plus* commission.' 'Well, whatever it is to be exactly, it will be higher than any African is getting in the country as a salary. At any rate in a private African company.' It must be remembered too, at this point, that until this time no one even included journalists in the class of respectable salaried workers, in spite of the outstanding role of the Press on so many occasions. '. ... Journalism,' wrote Obafemi Awolowo, 'was an unprofitable, frustrating and soul-depressing career at that time [1934] in Nigeria', a judgement then applicable to the whole of West Africa with equal aptness.

In the end none but a few in Ocansey's offices and among Zik's own chosen confidants ever found out the details of his total emoluments. All suspected, though, that it was at any rate far in excess of the average salary of Africans of similar status. More than that, it was completely out of the class of the ordinary editor. They then concluded that the correlation between the man and these 'extraordinary' terms of employment must be close indeed, that Azikiwe must really be something phenomenal. Later on, in fact, Azikiwe himself disclosed in a court hearing that by then he was in fact a shareholder in the City Press Ltd.*

Zik finally arrived, inauspiciously at first, in Accra, completed formalities with his first and last African (or any other kind of) employer, and was shortly ready to leave for a brief re-union with his family and home in Nigeria. Before he left, however, there were a few matters which claimed his instant attention. First, he met an old acquaintance, Bankole Awooner-Renner, a man to the far left of centre in colonial politics, with whom he had had some contact in America. Then there was I. T. A. Wallace Johnson, of Sierra Leone, with whom fate was to link Zik dramatically later on, as narrated in Chapter 16. Finally, some Ibo residents of Accra arranged a reception for him at which they presented the usual illuminated address. In this they told Zik: 'What increases our happiness more is your early attachment

---

* But the truth of the matter of his initial salary was that he received for some time only a £10 basic monthly payment, plus a percentage in commission on sales.

to journalistic occupation because we believe that it is the best field for the exposition of your knowledge and promulgation of your patriotic feelings for the sufferings of the African in general. We doubt not that your activities will open a new page in West African Journalism. . . .'

At last Zik reached Lagos, and immediately had to face a test of attitudes. The Ibo community of Lagos split into two camps, with the Onitsha group claiming that Zik was their own son particularly and that they ought therefore to have the exclusive 'right and honour' to give the reception. All the others, the non-Onitsha Ibos, insisted that the overriding fact was that the young man was an Ibo, and this entitled all Ibos to involvement in the organization of the proposed function. When the conflict could not be settled mutually between the two camps, they actually sent a joint deputation to seek the guidance of the guest himself. Naturally, he gave them the obvious answer. This resulted in a combined reception rightly enough, but it also earned for Azikiwe the disapproval of the conservative, clannish elements among the Onitsha Ibos of Lagos.

A curious feature of the programme at the reception was also an ironic commentary on the preceding intra-group manoeuvrings of the Ibos. On the speakers' platform that day there was not a single Ibo dignitary to be seen, in an affair they had organized themselves. The creation of an élite class among the Ibos just had not yet reached the same level of development as among the Yorubas, and there could of course be no competition with their sophistication in their own metropolis. So there had been no Ibos of educational or professional status in Lagos to put in company with his Worship the Magistrate who chaired the meeting: J. Jibowu, Esq., who later became a judge and, ironically, an antagonist of Zik (see Chapter 23); the Honourable T. A. Doherty, Member of the Legislative Council; Barristers A. Kayode, J. C. Zizer (a Sierra Leonean settler), and Dr Kwao Sagoe, of Gold Coast origin, who with Mr Kayode had been two of Zik's teachers at the Wesleyan Boys' High School.

The address of welcome and congratulations on this occasion surpassed that which Zik had received in Accra, in comprehensiveness and elaborateness. It traced Zik's entire career in America, praising him in grandiloquent terms for his achievements in scholarship, in sports, in what they called 'the social life of America' in journalism, authorship, and much else. The address ended by urging Zik to aim for the greater education of his country and countrymen of Africa. This, they said, was their 'sore need'.

Zik's reply, which created wild enthusiasm, was typical of his early speeches in Africa. It was entitled 'The Revolt of African Youth', and was a challenge to both the 'juvenescent old people' and 'the senescent young ones' (characteristic Zikist terminology employed by one admirer) to assert their belief in a New Africa. This would make both groups young at heart, the only kind of youth the New Africa required for the necessary reform of its political, economic, spiritual, and social life. Here Zik enunciated for his audience, in person, the 'five Zikist Postulates':

The realization of New Africa can only be possible by the African cultivating *spiritual balance*, which leads to the practicalization of *social regeneration*, to realizing *economic determination*, becoming *mentally emancipated*, and ushering in a *political resurgence*.*

Zik gave three lectures in Lagos before going east to his own home. The other two were concerned with African and Islamic contributions to Western civilization. In the choice of his third subject Zik there and then displayed a phase of that flair for political and social propaganda, that ability to capture confidence and votes, which later came to be admired by some and hated by others. Zik was always the universalist, whatever the motives that may be imputed to him for this philosophy. He has been bitterly attacked at various stages of his public career with 'tribalist' tendencies and dealings, of the most deep-seated, most fundamental kinds. But his writings and speeches, for one thing, and, for another, the stated ideals and appeal of his National Convention of Nigerian Citizens (formerly National Council of Nigeria and the Cameroons) posit, on the contrary, a universalist, unitarian-secular outlook on the problem of political communities at large. . . .

* 'Social Regeneration' was often rendered as 'Social Resurgence', and 'Political Resurgence' as 'National Risorgimento' – after the great Italian patriot Count Cavour, who, with Count Cesare Balbo, founded the nationalist paper *Il Risorgimento* in 1847.

From Lagos Zik proceeded to Onitsha to meet his father and mother, and his sister. The journey took the best part of two days and one night, by lorry. It was rough and tiring – as always for long-distance travellers using primitive means of transportation, and with no services on the way. But Zik had the strength and stamina to stand it well. He was in good condition and high spirits when the river-boat *Shanahan* finally set him down on the Onitsha Marine Ferry landing stage. His parents and sister, and the assembled relatives, had almost to compete with the crowds for the honour of shaking hands with the returning hero and remaining at his side. Everyone's pride was raised to its loftiest. His father's sacrifice, his mother's cares and worries over him, were now fully compensated. One of the most pleased was J. M. Stuart Young, an Englishman long resident in Onitsha. He was a Doctor of Philosophy who, as 'Odeziaku', had written articles and poems in the Nigerian papers for years, and had taught and inspired many youngsters there, including Benjamin Azikiwe. Here, at last, was one notable fruit of his labours.

Chapter 15

The *African Morning Post*

When J. B. Danquah left the Gold Coast with the 1934 Ofori Atta deputation for London he took some of the journalistic excitement of the day away with him. The *Times of West Africa* continued publication until 1935, but without Danquah it was not the same. Then, by a stroke of fate, Azikiwe appeared to take his place. The press was at that moment principally composed of the *Gold Coast Independent*, the *Spectator*, the *Vox Populi*, and the *Daily Echo*, and these papers were in full operation when Zik arrived. He immediately proceeded to add his quota to what became one of the most notable periods in the journalistic history of Ghana.

We have already analysed the political and something of the economic situation in the country at that time, at least as far as development was concerned. Socially, there was a truce among all 'classes', chiefs, professionals, general intelligentsia, journalists, and the rest, due mainly to the recent united front against government legislation. Before the 1934 disturbances there had been considerable disquiet among these classes, a psychological conflict to which Zik was soon to give definition, shape, and articulation.

Traditional African society, as many know, is very nearly classless. There is distinction and economic privilege, there are dynastic royalties, feudalistic residues, deep tribal rivalries and animosities, but hardly any social separateness. To put it shortly, there is some distinction but little social distance in African society. The chief, the professional, the clerk, and the fisherman are physically very close. They could not in the past, and cannot for some time yet in the future, be otherwise. The clan-family system, or kinship complex, involving much obligation and responsibility for members of an extended family at all levels, social and economic, will not let them erect a rigid class-structure yet, and the exceptions to this rule are not many. But naturally there is nevertheless psychological stress and strain among groups, which every now and then responds to current external forces and breaks out in overt, if not violent, conflict.

Throughout the 1920s there was such a situation in Ghana: Casely Hayford and his class of educated, modern élite had been angered and frustrated by the part played by some Gold Coast chiefs in the failure – in immediate, concrete terms – of the National Congress of British West Africa in 1920. With Casely Hayford leading his faction and Nana Ofori Atta his, the quarrel thus engendered lasted until Casely Hayford's death in 1930, after which there was an hiatus. The dispute which broke out between the Governor, Sir Shenton Thomas, and the Gold Coast people in 1934 over the sedition ordinance was the occasion for the truce between the chiefs and the educated, older élite. Many among the young, and the intelligentsia generally, were on the side of the élite.

Truce or no truce, however, Azikiwe had decided that the traditional leaders of Africa had outlived their usefulness to their communities in their present state of mind, and must be reformed or removed. They, their old minds, and the calcified conditions of yesterday which surrounded them, constituted the *Old Africa*. And '. . . the Old Africa must be destroyed because it is at death-grips with the New Africa. . . .' The *New Africa*, on the other hand, meant 'the Africa of tomorrow. . . . It is the Renascence of Africans and the reformation of African society'.

Pieced together from several of his expositions and spelled out in full, this was the 'philosophy of the New Africa' which Zik taught the youth of West Africa – for it was to them that he addressed himself principally – through the columns of the *African Morning Post* and later the *West African Pilot*.

The fate of the indigenous black man in Africa itself, Zik said, was the human factor in the struggle of European nations for territorial expansion in Africa. However, as far as these European ambitions were concerned, the human factor was of little consequence. Raw materials for Europe and man-power for its imperial and militaristic purposes were to them far more important than a full life for the African in Africa, such as the European himself enjoyed in his own native land. But the Africans were not destined to accept for ever the old idea of imperialism, as if it were some Mosaic law; on the contrary, the twentieth-century African is bound to become renascent, and to command attention as a 'concrescent factor in the peace of the world'.

Turning to the Africans themselves Zik analysed to them in detail the image of themselves which *he* had conceived *for* them, the image of their revolutionary role in the total remodelling of African life and the fitting of it into the general pattern of world life. There was the Old Africa of yesterday and the New Africa of tomorrow. Between them was the Renascent African, who existed in 'a transitional stage between the Old and the New. . . .' In the Old Africa, society had remained stagnant, in spite of 'the immortal contributions made by the ancestors of the African', in antiquity 'when Ethiopia was at the height of its majesty', and in medieval times 'when Songhay was in its splendour'. The Slave Trade and certain evils of imperialism had helped to per-petrate the static conditions complained about, and both evils and static conditions offered a challenge: 'that the New Africa must come to pass'.

The New Africa must of course have a philosophy, and the philosophy must be predicated upon the five principles Azikiwe's early enthusiasts called the 'Five Zikist Postulates'. Postulate One, *Spiritual Balance*, required that renascent Africans cultivate a sense of respect for the views of other people. In the old Africa, differences of opinion were allowed to widen gaps between various sections of the community.* Under Postulate Two, *Social Regeneration*, African society must be changed to conform to 'what is ethical, just, and equitable'. It must be made demo-cratic. It must consist of *Africans* and *human beings*, not just 'Fanti or Ga, Temne or Mende, Yoruba or Ibo, Bantu or Tuareg, Bubi or Hausa, Jolloff or Kru'. Thirdly, '*Economic Determinism* must be the basis of African economic thought'. The new African cannot hope to create a new order without a sound economic foundation. But here there must be no monopoly of wealth by the few, and the profit motive must not be allowed to capture the *life-itself* of the African. *Mental Emancipation,*

---

* This statement was tenable only in the general context of early Zikist proselytism. Other students of traditional African political and social organization may have a quite different view of the matter, as stated in this bald way by Zik.

fourthly, should teach the youth of Africa to have faith in themselves as the mental and physical equals of any other races of mankind. Under its influence they can and must rid themselves of their inferiority complex.

When all this shall have been done by or shall have happened to renascent Africans, their *National Risorgimento*, that is, their revolutionized political status, 'cannot be in doubt'. Expanded, contracted, varied, specified in the detail, generalized in whole and illustrated profusely, this was the main teaching of Azikiwe in the *Morning Post*.

... There is something one forgets when one tends to glorify Youth or Old Age.

It is the state of mind of the two.

Youth is immortal.

The thought processes are immortal.

No matter how old an individual may be, no matter if he is young or old, if he thinks in accordance with the times he is immortal. ...

One may or may not believe in the immortality of the soul. But it is too evident that it is immaterial whether Socrates lived until he had grey hair or wrinkled brow, etc. One thing is known; what he taught had [sic] made him immortal. *Gnothi seuaton* – Know thyself. Is there not immortality in these two words?

Youth and Old Age are not synonymous with the terms old and new. Some elders seem to be youthful perennially. This explains the justification of the use of the terms 'Young Old Man', and 'Old Young Man'.

Upon the young, as well as the *young in mind*, depended the success or failure of the programme of emancipation, said Zik. And let us not forget that that struggle has to be on all fronts. On the economic front renascent Africans must make tomorrow secure for their posterity, thereby bringing Africa into line with the economic interdependence of the whole world. To this end African business must change its nature; the African businessman must learn the lessons of efficient business operation. 'Probably,' Zik wrote, 'the main reason for the difference between African and European business administration is the principle of *cooperation*. The two words, linked together, mean *working together*.' Zik continued by laying bare his own beliefs and attitudes towards business and economic power, principles bearing directly on his later personal financial history:

The European, by pooling his financial resources together obtains a great capital with which to transact his business. . . .

With this capital, he gives employment to thousands. He organizes branches of his business. . . . He makes important contacts. . . . He has good banking references, and thus his business prospects are indicative of success, if not in the immediate, then in the remote, future.

The African, on the other hand, prefers to work alone . . . spending the greater part of his life in accumulating capital, the African proceeds to control his business single-handedly. For a one-man's business, it will work out temporarily, but [the] time will come when that one man will face problems which require many heads to solve. . . .

Zik tried to analyse for his readers, not always successfully, the different theories and practices of economics. The various definitions and explanations he gave sometimes missed the essential point altogether, or lost it by over-simplification, or stated it inadequately. Examples come readily to hand:

2. *The Struggle between Capital and Labour.* In the attempt to answer the challenge of economic determinism, two groups arise: the land-owners or bourgeoisie, who are the capitalists, and the proletarians, who are the workers. Having no capital, the latter become a permanent wage-earning class, of whom the erstwhile serfs and slaves are the prototypes.

4. *The Dictatorship of the Proletariat.* Workers must have the right of collective bargaining. They must be allowed to use strikes and boy-cotts as media to secure higher wages, shorter hours of work, social legislation, and more leisure. But history shows that Governments have, at times, aided only the capitalists, and would not protect the workers to achieve economic emancipation.

But, however Zik put his case, the important thing was that he was addressing people who needed to be told about these matters, in most cases for the first time. Secondly, he was aiming at a cumulative and long-term effect, not a specialist or *ad hoc* response. His gifts did not lie in simplicity of language or presen-tation, and there certainly was no elegance in much of the Zik prose. What he had was a flair for drama and for evoking the maximum of enthusiasm, which he always hoped to make perma-nent by making it encompassing. Hence his habit of the *compre-hensive attack*. To give hope for the future he examined the present minutely; to do that effectively, in *his* sense of effectiveness, he explored the past, right in front of his audience; and not just the past but antiquity. Often it was all very superficial, especially as Zik had no time to give a finish, daily, to his material. But the rivetting of attention was the motive, and this aim was achieved to the exact requirements. Was it political interest he wanted? Then we must see how *all* of the British West African colonies are doing: how well, that is, or ill. But we must have a reference-point, a check-back – ah! *Ethiopia*:

Ethiopia is the last vestige of black autocracy. It represents the type of government which the forefathers of Africans established on this continent.

I am not superstitious, but the continued existence of Ethiopia after its contemporaries and their descendants had vanished from political history, is, and should be, an object of admiration.

These historical facts purport to show that the black man, as demonstrated in the political history of the Ethiopians, has political capacity. ...

From here the article, of the famous 'Inside Stuff' series, goes on to examine and to comment freely, at many points devastatingly, upon men and politics in the West African colonies, where the 'Africans are still living in a period of suspended animation, politically speaking'. 'They have a form of government which is neither conducive to democratic government nor does it hold out for them any distinct promise for political manhood.' Zik continues:

In this circumstance, I have to consider why Africans are still the footstool of little Belgium, inconsequential Portugal, fourth-rate Spain, resurgent Italy and so on down the line.

Is it because they are lacking in political capacity? It cannot be. If the Negro race produced a State which has existed from aeons past, it cannot be logical to conclude that that race lacks political capacity.

Is it because they are lacking in political acumen? Probably so. Most of those who are the self-professed leaders of the various sections of West Africa are, in reality and with all due deference to them, worthy of one piece of job, that is, to commit *felo de se*.

In all sincerity and candour, the main reason why the shibboleth of the inferiority of the African for social and political capacity lingers, is due to the *imbecility* of most of African leaders. That word is not so musical to the ear, but it is the truth.

Here we must pause and consider some of the most significant features of the above passage, one of many in which Zik threw down the gauntlet through the columns of the *African Morning Post*. The first point to note is that Zik was one of the earliest journalists in the ex-British colonies to hold up the European Powers in Africa to the light of ridicule, to 'make them small': 'little Belgium', 'inconsequential Portugal', 'fourth-rate Spain'. Up to then there had been stronger language used by the West African Press against the colonial Powers, but this had created anger and resentment against them, not laughter, not contempt. Now, fourth-rate Spain and inconsequential Portugal cut laughable little figures. And fun reduced fear considerably.

Next, there is the indictment of the colonial 'form of Government which is neither conducive to democratic government' nor holds out for the African 'any distinct promise for political manhood'. It is almost needless to say that the indictment of colonialism was the central aim and purpose of 'Zikism'.

But perhaps the most important feature of the above passage is the attack on the African leadership of the time. This was, in other words, the battle against 'Old Africa', unavoidable in the strategy of war for the freedom of the continent, and of its people of socially regenerated, spiritually balanced, and economically emancipated youth. The two things: attack on the Establishment and encouragement to the young, brought Zik and the *Morning Post* into sharp, often violent, conflict with several members and institutions of the Old Guard. Said the late Nana Ofori Atta,* 'We have heard so much of a "New Africa" coming to birth. The protagonists of the New Africa are spreading doctrines which can only tend to cause trouble in this country. ... But if the youth of the Country', continued the Nana,

are to be taught and educated to disrespect and to show open contempt to their Chiefs and Elders and leading public figures with whose views or with whose persons those 'teachers' are not in agreement, or for whom they have an animosity, then there is a real danger.

The *Gold Coast Independent*, a paper established before the turn of the century, on 20 July 1935 challenged the *Morning Post*'s

* Nana Ofori Atta, Omanhene of Akim Abuakwa, chief African opposer of the West African National Congress in 1920–21, and leader of the 1934 deputation to the Colonial Office. (See Chapter 13.)

theory of youth and declared that politics was not 'the right business and aim of youth'. It made its case (in part) in these words:

It [politics] is intricate, perplexing and difficult, and for which is suited only those who have experience, the true value of things socially and economically important, and are acquainted with human life and conditions. This is essentially the business and concern of only those who have assumed the *toga virilis*.

To all of these Zik answered with spirit, repeating with telling effect where he aimed his social propaganda, that 'new ideas imply new minds, and these in turn imply a new order'. The corollary to this was of course a foregone conclusion: 'old ideas imply old minds', and these in turn, etc. 'That is why,' Zik added slyly, 'Tennyson wrote that the old order must change, yielding place to new, lest anachronistic customs might corrupt the world.'

Not the least confirmative feature of Zik's general attitude in the Gold Coast was the fact that he did not merely show interest in the local politics of the day but identified himself actively with the side he favoured. Thus he was an Executive Committee member of the *Mambii* (*Ga* for People's) Party, from the second year of his sojourn in the country until his departure for Nigeria in 1937. This was the period of intensified Press wars as well as political conflict, the result mostly of Zik's sustained attack upon the old order. It was unquestionably under the stimulation of the *Morning Post* and the *sensational* personality of its Editor-in-Chief that the combative drives of the people were aroused into action over colonial policies and domestic issues. When both elements met at election time, Zik, his paper, the party and policy he favoured, and that party's candidate or candidates became the objects around which passions rose and fell like massive waves.

So charged was the atmosphere on these occasions that fiercely-contested 'election petitions' became for the first time a feature of political life in Accra. There was one such petition towards the end of 1935 at the High Court, which Zik's paper reported *verbatim* in his 'Inside Stuff' column for several days. A portion of the evidence he gave in court himself on 22 November illustrates some of the major points made about Zik's political aims and methods. Mr Frans Dove, who in 1937 was to free him from the conviction of having published seditious matter, appeared on this occasion for the other side, against the Mambii Party. The Petitioner was Dr F. V. Nanka-Bruce, the Respondent Mr A. W. Kojo Thompson, a lawyer and the victorious candidate in the 1935 election for a seat in the Legislative Council. Here follows the portion of the evidence:

MR DOVE: In Exhibit 10 (*African Morning Post*, 9 August) at page 4, is an editorial headed 'Wanted: A New Leader'. (Counsel read last paragraph and passed it to witness.) That was written by yourself or one of your staff?

MR AZIKIWE: Yes.

MR DOVE: There is another one on page 5 headed 'Youth and Politics' by Kofi. (Counsel passed it to witness who read it in a clear voice.) At whom was that directed?

MR AZIKIWE: So far as I can observe, I do not think there is any reference to Petitioner or the Respondent.

MR DOVE: There is an editorial headed 'Stop Dr Nanka-Bruce' in your issue of 1 August. (Counsel read last paragraph and passed it to witness.) To whom does that refer?

MR AZIKIWE: It refers to the Petitioner.

MR DOVE: Was it before he was made O.B.E.?

MR AZIKIWE: I think so.

MR DOVE: Is there any connection between that editorial and the article headed 'Youth and Politics'?

MR AZIKIWE: I do not think there is any connection between the two.

MR DOVE: I refer you to page 4 of your issue of 14 August. (Counsel read last paragraph and passed paper to witness.) Will you tell us what this means? Who may resist the temptations of imperialism?

MR AZIKIWE: It means that Mr Thompson may or may not resist the temptations of British rule.

MR DOVE: What temptations of British rule do you refer to?

MR AZIKIWE: I am afraid I cannot say. The wording is self-explanatory. We leave readers to form their own conclusions. If there is any misunderstanding we try to explain.

MR DOVE: The new leader suggested, according to the editorial, is the Respondent?

MR AZIKIWE: Yes.

MR DOVE: And the old leader?

MR AZIKIWE: That is not suggested.

MR DOVE: Are there any old leaders who failed to resist such temptations?

MR AZIKIWE: Old leaders have failed to resist such temptations.

MR DOVE: Give me the names of such leaders.

MR AZIKIWE: Throughout the British colonies there have been old leaders who have failed.

MR DOVE: I am referring to Accra.

MR AZIKIWE: I can think of one – the Petitioner.

MR DOVE: In what has he failed?

MR AZIKIWE: By accepting an honour of British imperialism.

MR DOVE: You mean the O.B.E.?

MR AZIKIWE: Yes. ...

It should be mentioned here that it was Zik who started the habit of calling into question the practice of African leaders accepting British honours. He insisted in his writings, as he stated in court, that Africans who accepted these awards let themselves and their people down badly, for such baubles only served to confirm the African's inferior colonial status. He soon got the young men talking sneeringly about *O*bedient *B*oys of the *E*mpire' and '*M*ute *B*oys of the *E*mpire'.

Chapter 16

Marriage and Court Trial

The year 1936 was a memorable one for Azikiwe. Two events of the utmost importance in his life made this so: his marriage in Accra to Miss Flora Ogoegbunam from his home in Onitsha, and his court trial for publishing seditious matter in the *Morning Post*. His marriage has lasted him the rest of his life up till now; his conviction for sedition lasted only a few months. Both had a profound effect on him, at the time they happened and afterwards.

Flora Ogoegbunam was but a pretty school-girl when Zik returned home on his brief, pre-employment visit in November, 1934. However, she was soon to become of marriageable age, for she was sixteen at the time and in very many countries at all periods of human history that age in a female is very near to the time of her eligibility; indeed in many countries even today sixteen is already past the age of marriage. Certainly in most of Africa there could be no question about it. Moreover, Mrs Azikiwe is a woman of tall build and large bone, and even as a schoolgirl of fifteen or sixteen must have looked quite mature.

Vincent Ikeotuonye, in his *Zik and New Africa*, gives an account of the 'courtship' which contains this passage: 'Many Onitsha girls of marriageable age made their appearance, and from them all was chosen the light-coloured, beautiful Flora Ogoegbunam.' This seems to Mrs Azikiwe today to suggest that she had been deliberately put on parade by her parents for the appraisal of this young man whom everybody obviously considered the most eligible bachelor in the world, whereas her own memory of the occasion offers a totally different kind of situation. She remembers one incident in which, rushing off to school for the afternoon session, she was called back to be introduced formally to a young man sitting in the front room. After which she did run off, and never thought of the matter again.*

* Personally the present author considers that there is here only a slight

But that was only as far as she was concerned. As far as the *system* was concerned the arrangements for the eventual union of the two individuals and the two families had in fact begun then. Indeed it had begun even before that brief confrontation. Today in educated, westernized African communities the essential initial moves towards marriage are made by the two individuals most concerned, and there is no difference between them and the social custom of England or America in this respect. But in the rest of Africa, as indeed in many other countries even now, marriage is very much a parents' affair, and parental bride-choosing will apparently last an indefinite period into future human history. Especially so, of course, since the refinements are so subtle and so progressive.

Even so, the two parental sides in this particular case do not appear to have been completely agreed immediately about the overwhelming advantages of the proposition. The senior Azikiwes feared both Flora's beauty and her brains, the beauty presumably because it was a snare for their son and a temptation to other males, and the brains – or at least her education – because it would enable and may well induce her to read her husband's letters and examine his pass-book! All difficulties and any lingering doubts were finally disposed of, however, and the young maiden was dispatched all the way from Onitsha to Accra to be united with her future husband.

Before Azikiwe's marriage it had been impossible to say whether he was for or against this institution, in one form or another. For one thing, the people of Accra had been rather impressed with his singleness of purpose and hard work, which seemed to rule out socializing from his life. True, he played tennis at the Rodger Club and had provided fascinated glimpses of himself as an athlete to the Accra sporting public. But on the whole his seriousness and his prestige as scholar, lecturer, and popular writer predominated as the rooted image he left on his audience.

For another thing, Zik was at this time rather shy, uncomfortable,

---

problem of intention and of meaning. I believe Ikeotuonye simply meant that, in the process, Azikiwe saw, or was shown, many young girls, of whom Flora eventually proved the most desirable.

and awkward in mixed company. Though an immensely charming personality and full of private fun, he was, as in many similar cases at all times, ill at ease in this society in which he was still both a 'stranger' and also something rather special. He was admired and cheered by thousands, but most people stood in understandable awe of him when in close, personal social contact. They flocked around him smiling broadly and shaking hands after his lectures, but that is different from intimate small-talk on equal terms, different from the concord of hearts attuned to the interest of personal matters. In the absence of blood ties and common community origins, time and mutual liberality of spirit are the only guarantees of social *rapport*. Zik did not have any of the first and Accra society could not offer much of the second in those almost mutually exclusive circumstances.

There was one other cause for the uncertainty about Zik's personal position in this matter, and that a delicate one. Dr Aggrey, his beloved and abiding hero, had had a wonderful married life, blessed with children, and is described with grace in Edwin Smith's biography. But Aggrey died at a comparatively young age – fifty-two – after his very promising start in the Gold Coast from 1924 to 1927. One of his most poignant experiences during this fateful period was the return of Mrs Aggrey 'home' to America from 'home' in the Gold Coast, as the result of a series of disastrous experiences, on this, her first visit to his country and people. The time of year was all wrong for weather conditions; her first contact with Aggrey's people in Fantiland (from Accra) left her near to physical collapse; they (the Aggreys) were badly housed at first (though only temporarily) and had incompetent and roguish house servants. Other things went wrong. Not only did life become unbearable under these conditions; Mrs Aggrey's health, already made delicate by her fourth pregnancy, began to be affected. Much to their sorrow, therefore, they decided she had to go back to America. Later, it became evident she couldn't return to Africa, at least not soon. . . . Somehow, Azikiwe did not like this story, and indicated as much in his column, 'Inside Stuff', in the *Morning Post*.*

* It would be appropriate to recall here the story of Azikiwe's childhood misery as a result of his father's adoption of polygamy (Chapter 5).

So that, all in all, it came as a surprise to the Gold Coast community and Accra society when, first, the arrival of Miss Ogoegbunam was announced on 30 March and the rumours began to make the usual rounds; and when, next, the marriage ceremony took place soon afterwards at the Methodist Church in James Town, Accra. The date was 4 April 1936, but before man and wife had had a chance to begin learning the difficult art of married life, the blow fell: Zik was facing his first serious trouble with the law.

The *Morning Post* had published on Friday, 15 May 1936, an article captioned: 'Has the African a God?', written, as it was duly proved, by I. T. A. Wallace-Johnson, a Sierra Leonean labour leader and politician then resident in Ghana. The article was severely critical of European rule in the colonial empire and used some very strong language: 'The European has a God, Deceit, whose law is "Ye strong, you must weaken the weak. Ye 'civilized' Europeans, you must 'civilize' the 'barbarous' Africans with machine-guns."' These and similar words were considered by the Police and the Judicial Department to be seditious, under the definitions of that same ordinance which only two years earlier had caused so much political trouble in the country.

Both writer and editor were arrested and charged, the case immediately becoming a *cause célèbre* and creating a state of widespread, anxious excitement in the country, as well as in Nigeria, Sierra Leone, and beyond West Africa. Wallace-Johnson was eventually convicted, and his appeal to the Privy Council later on was dismissed on the grounds, so to speak, of definition: the Gold Coast law had defined sedition as 'bringing the Government into hatred and contempt', which the offending article was held to have been proved to have done. Azikiwe, in his turn, was convicted at first for having published this so-defined seditious matter in his paper. But his appeal to the West African Court of Appeal was allowed, in March 1937. Out of a total of eight grounds of appeal, the very first to be raised at this hearing was enough to reverse the judgement of the lower court. This was on the ground that it had never been established, either at the hearing in the Magistrate's Court or at the trial in the Supreme Court, that Nnamdi Azikiwe – so-named in the action: '*Rex v.*

Nnamdi Azikiwe' – was in fact editor of the *Morning Post* on the material date, and that he had checked on and/or authorized the insertion of the article in the issue of the paper for 15 May 1936.

Those were the bare facts. The proceedings themselves, occupying but a few minutes, provided for those inside the court that day enough drama and excitement for a few years. An unofficial reconstruction and summary of the hearing would perhaps be of interest here.

On the Bench of the West African Court of Appeal that day sat Sir Donald Kingdon, Chief Justice of Nigeria, President; Sir C. Petrides, Chief Justice of the Gold Coast, and Sir J. E. Webber, Chief Justice of Sierra Leone, members. For the Crown the chief Prosecutor was H. W. B. Blackhall, Esq., K.C., newly arrived at his post of Attorney-General of the Gold Coast: elegant, learned, suave, and with a pronounced bench-side manner. For the defence stood Frans W. Dove, Esq., Leader of the Gold Coast Bar and winner of a thousand notable cases: distinguished, experienced, deceptively mild-mannered at will. With Mr Dove were the Messrs A. Molade Akiwumi and K. A. Bossman, themselves elevated to the bench years later. The bar was tight with lawyers; the court was crowded, expectant, anxious.

When the President called the case, and it came to Frans Dove's turn to speak, he said he wanted to raise, as a preliminary but basic point, the matter of the identity and status of the appellant. The question was, why had Nnamdi Azikiwe, the appellant, been prosecuted in the first place, by a court which had nothing against him? Who *was* Nnamdi Azikiwe and what connexion was there between him and the original cause of this case? That was the question he wanted the Crown to answer, as a basis for this appeal. Mr Blackhall feigned surprise and distress at this opening thrust, but replied that of course Nnamdi Azikiwe was 'Zik', and every schoolboy in the country knew who Zik was: the editor of the *African Morning Post*, whose appeal case this was. Mr Dove replied that, with great respect, the popular identification of Zik with Nnamdi Azikiwe and of Nnamdi Azikiwe with the editor of the *African Morning Post* meant nothing to the law. Nnamdi Azikiwe, he insisted, was not properly answerable to the charge that had been brought against him, since he had not, at law, been properly identified as editor of the *Morning Post*.

Mr Blackhall replied with spirit that he was surprised at his learned friend attempting to mislead this honourable court; he would gladly provide their Lordships with the legal proof of identity which his learned friend was attempting to discredit and set at nought. He called for the record of the original 'arrest' of Azikiwe by Police Superintendent D. G. Carruthers on a date in late May 1936, and read, amidst mounting tension in the packed but silent court, words to this effect:

POLICE OFFICER: Are you Nnamdi Azikiwe?
AZIKIWE: Yes.
POLICE OFFICER: Are you the editor of the *African Morning Post*?
AZIKIWE: Yes, I am.
POLICE OFFICER: I have a criminal writ for you.

'That was the record, my Lords,' he went on; why had his learned friend for the appellant come here to try to mislead the court? ...

On Mr Dove's next move – that is, on his ability to meet this challenge successfully – now hung precariously the outcome of the appeal and the fate of his client. Judges, lawyers, the prosecution, the defence, the spectators, Mr Dove, and Mr Azikiwe – everyone knew that this was the point of crisis. ...

The defence had left nothing to chance in preparing this case, even from before the action in the Supreme Court, where Zik had been convicted. Mr Dove and his junior colleagues had gone to the extent of seeking advice from solicitors in London, who had confirmed the main legal question and suggested the line of defence. Mr Dove was fairly confident about his trump card. ... Yet there were many unpredictable possibilities in a court case, and even Frans Dove at this point could hardly expect to win this one now in a matter of a few words more.

He got up again, and played his trump. The record to which the learned Attorney-General had referred the court, he said, did show that Nnamdi Azikiwe, by his own admission to Mr Carruthers on the occasion of his 'arrest', was indeed editor of the *African Morning Post* on 23 May 1936, or whatever that date was. But had the prosecution established in law, anywhere and at any time during the previous hearings, that Nnamdi Azikiwe was the editor of the paper *on the material date of* 15 *May* 1936, and that he had either (a) authorized, (b) edited, or (c) inserted the seditious matter himself, on which proof alone he could be prosecuted? . . .

Even breathing seemed to have stopped in the court while the three judges held an ominous tête-à-tête, during which they referred to one or two legal tomes on their desk. Then – Well, Mr Attorney?

Mr Blackhall's flair had by this time noticeably left him, and his next movements were not as spontaneous as before. But he was able to struggle to his feet at last, to admit to the court that the position was as his learned friend had just stated: Nnamdi Azikiwe had not been legally identified as editor of the *African Morning Post* on the material date of Friday, 15 May 1936.

And that, Mr Attorney, replied Sir Donald Kingdon, is fatal to your case.

When convicted in the lower court a few months earlier, Azikiwe had made a short speech outside the Supreme Court in Accra to a group of friends and supporters, some of whom were in tears. He had said, in part:

The fight for liberty has just begun in Africa. Only those who are prepared to face odds with a will that knows no defeat – having Right as their armour and the Sword of Truth as their weapon – must follow the thorny road which was trodden by Socrates, Jesus of Nazareth, Paul of Tarsus, Saint Peter, Thomas More, and other immortals of history. . . .

As far as I am concerned, I am prepared for the inevitable, if through this oblation Africa will speed on its way towards redemption and self-determination.

Now, on his release in March 1937, a great shout went up in the court and was taken up by the multitude waiting outside. They carried him shoulder-high, triumphant, and uncomfortable, all the way back through the streets to his office.

Derrick A. Sington, a former B.B.C. Talks Chief, has in a small book recently made a comparative study of the vagaries of law legislation, in the context of freedom of thought and expression. The book, *Freedom of Communication*, finds appropriate examples of the handling of this question in the courts, in the Wallace-Johnson-Azikiwe case as contrasted with a similar case in Singapore eighteen years later. But first Sington shows how both the intention behind law legislation and the interpretation of the law, when passed, can differ from metropolitan to colonial area, for instance, and from colony to colony or court to court. These matters cannot fail to retain great historical interest.

In 1770 an English printer, John Miller, was acquitted by the jury (against the expressed wishes of the judge, Lord Mansfield) of the charge of sedition. He had printed a letter by Junius criticizing George III in the words: 'You have never been acquainted with the language of truth until you heard it in the complaints of your subjects.' Jury trial, Sington points out, had alone succeeded in saving a subject from punishment for printing and publishing a vigorous criticism of the King, but which was no more than vigorous criticism. Then, in 1909, Mr Justice Coleridge gave a definition of sedition which the Privy Council in 1937, reconsidering Wallace-Johnson's case, still admitted as being valid, namely, that a seditious publication must be 'calculated to incite others to public disorders, to wit rebellions, assassinations, outrages or any physical force or violence'. But, said the learned Law Lords, this definition was not applicable to the Gold Coast, where the law plainly said that sedition is any expression that brings the government into hatred and contempt. The conclusion is inescapable that Wallace-Johnson's merely verbal violence against European rulers in the colonies would not, if done in England itself, have earned him a conviction for sedition.

Indeed the Singapore case of 1954 mentioned above did not earn the accused a conviction either, though Singapore, like Ghana in 1936, was a colony. The Singapore student magazine, *Fajar*, had made a bitter attack against British colonial rule, and had included in its article phrases like 'Western barbarities'. The students and their magazine were taken to court for sedition, but the outcome of the case was quite different. The judge dismissed it after defence counsel, among other submissions, had pleaded that the prosecution of such an action was 'an attack on the ordinary public rights of controversy'.

A curious footnote to the history of the sedition-trial episode is that years later Zik remembered, in his 'Odyssey', with considerable bitterness and even with some anger, aspects of Wallace-Johnson's relations with him in Accra, especially in connexion with the way he, Zik, had got involved in the case.

Almost immediately after the appeal triumph, Zik and his young bride left Accra for Lagos and home. Flora Azikiwe had gone through months of torture; only the amazing strength which an unexpected crisis often gives, even to the very young, together with the carefulness with which her husband had planned their future in case the worst should happen to him, sustained her through this unusual experience of a young bride so far away from home. After the case certain foreign financial interests involved Azikiwe in discussions on the prospect of setting him up in business again, this time on a partnership basis. But there were legal and moral considerations which finally made Zik, urged by his wife, decide to go home instead.

A few days before he left Accra, a car in which he and a number of his reporters were riding was involved in an accident which could have ended the whole Azikiwe saga only just past its starting point: it nearly dispatched him home to his ancestors. Fortunately Zik survived and, instead, simply returned home to his parents.

One final word to this chapter, the most appropriate place to dispose of an interesting point about Zik and the law. The fact may not be of great significance one way or the other, but it is a fact that in all the turbulence of his active nationalist career, Zik never suffered political imprisonment, or even a true arrest. The Ghana sedition trial and initial conviction was the closest he ever came to it.

Chapter 17

The Return Home

'When Gandhi returned to India he had the prestige of a leader', says Romain Rolland in his book *Mahatma Gandhi*.* In a different way, when Azikiwe returned to Nigeria in 1937, he too already had the prestige of a leader. Gandhi had had professional training in England but had returned to start work not in India but in South Africa, that is, discounting an exploratory and abortive year he spent at home before migrating to South Africa. Azikiwe had come back from America and had started work in the Gold Coast, not in his native Nigeria. ... But we must not press the similarities here, lest the parallelogram should get knocked out of shape. Gandhi's career and Azikiwe's, though in principle leading to the same results – the political freedom of their countries from colonialism – were in their principal features widely dissimilar. The two men themselves were dissimilar: in background, character, and approach. Also, Azikiwe was not quite the only focal point in Nigerian nationalism that Gandhi was in India: Zik did not carry the burden of independence practically single-shouldered, the way Gandhi had.

Yet, when all is said and done, there *were* similarities. At any rate we must emphasize that when Azikiwe returned to Nigeria in 1937 he already had, like Gandhi in India in 1915, the reputation and standing of a leader. Remember that the *African Morning Post* had established him in the popular imagination since 1935 in the Gold Coast, Nigeria, Sierra Leone, and other parts of English-speaking West Africa. Remember that the sedition trial of 1936 and the appeal acquittal of March 1937 had enhanced that attraction enormously. Remember that behind these two factors there lay also Azikiwe's brief visit home in 1934, when he had been lionized in both the east and the west. Besides,

* Translated from the original French by Catherine D. Groth and published in London by The Swarthmore Press in 1924. The above quotation is on page 19.

October 1934 to July 1937 was less than three years, and yet those two fairly close points in time had in addition been bridged by recurrent episodes and incidents calculated to freshen the memory of enthusiasts, where memory was not even yet due to begin to fade.

By 1937 Nigeria was getting back on its feet economically, like many other countries, from the disasters of the 1929–33 depression. She too had enjoyed some of the benefits of the boom of the 1920s, but had been hard hit in the slump. In 1914, before the Great War began, the value of her trade had amounted to only £4 million (that is, for both exports and imports). By 1920 – at the highest point of the graph – it had risen to over £40 million. After a sharp drop in 1921 to just over £20 million, trade had risen in 1925 to £34 million, and had remained between thirty and £35 million from then until 1928. Then in 1929 the slump began, and by 1931 Nigeria's value-of-trade reading was lowest since 1915: £15½ million. The year Azikiwe returned home, recovery from the Great Depression had been such as to have raised Nigeria's trade level back to £37 million or more. Unfortunately, the Second World War burst upon the world only two years later, to put a brutal halt to the recovery from the first, and dash men's hopes.

Politically, the country had been passing through what Michael Crowder has described as 'superficially some of the dullest in Nigerian history'. Little had occurred of a spectacular nature since the Clifford Constitution of 1922. The Pan-British West African National Congress Movement had petered out by 1925 – indeed in Nigeria it had never been any great force at all, in spite of Herbert Macaulay. The reforms of Governor Sir Donald Cameron between 1931 and 1935 had been reforms chiefly in local government and judicial matters; they had been fundamental, important, but unexciting. 'Nothing shows more clearly the political spirit of the age,' says Vincent Ikeotuonye in *Zik of New Africa*, 'than the report of an address, or debate between the Governor, Sir Bernard Bourdillon, and a delegation of the Nigerian Youth Movement led by Mr Ernest Ikoli: "the Governor was the wise master who freely offered to his colonial agitators the doctrine and the drill-book of nationalist agitation. ..."' Ikeotuonye continues:

In the end the group dispersed, voluble with gratitude and pleased that their names were recorded in the Government Guest Book. In the same year the President of the Nigerian Youth Movement was granted a Government scholarship to do a specialized course in Medicine in the United Kingdom. Within the next two years the Secretary of the Party was given a most profitable appointment in the Civil Service.

Brilliant, devastating sarcasm; but Ikeotuonye's judgement on the whole Nigerian political situation of the Thirties – which this is – must be rejected as deliberately selective and unnecessarily harsh. Especially as he adds: 'Into this soulless Nigeria, Zik stepped fortified with the philosophy of the New Africa. . . .' – a sequence which prompts the question whether the condemnation of the first party was not merely so that the second, the hero, could be the more easily commended?

The truth of the matter is that though there was dullness on the surface, naïveté on the periphery, and sycophancy in high and low places, there was also a very great deal of vital political development taking place under the surface. Ikeotuonye's hero himself – who is after all the hero of this book also – admits the fact that he met much better than a soulless Nigeria awaiting him in 1937. In his speech in 1957 on 'The Development of Political Parties in Nigeria', Zik showed at Rhodes House, Oxford, that between 1922 and 1937 there had been no fewer than seven or eight political or quasi-political parties or movements organized in the country. In their different ways most of these had been very active and had enjoyed remarkable support in some instances. That they did not measure up to modern notions and standards of mobilization, organization, activity, and extent of appeal, does not diminish the reality of their existence during those years, nor of their very great service in giving some basic political training to their adherents. It is, on the whole, more reasonable to accept Michael Crowder's comment on these years he described himself as 'some of the dullest'. He continues:

Yet they mark the emergence of a new class of Africans who began to think of themselves as Nigerians rather than Ibo, Hausa, and Yoruba. And it was to be this group, initially confined almost exclusively to Lagos, that wrested control of affairs from the British Government and attained independence for Nigeria in 1960. So, though there are no dramatic upheavals to record during the period between the world wars, though there are few administrative changes to describe, there was the slow but all-important development of national consciousness amongst peoples of widely varying religions and cultural backgrounds.

Or, if a more cautious but nevertheless confirmatory tone were desired, then perhaps it is better still to turn to James Coleman. Summing up the opinions of various personal observers, among them Sir William Geary, W. R. Crocker (author of *On Governing Colonies*), and Lord Hailey, Coleman concludes that 'on the basis of evidence drawn from a study of interwar political activity in Nigeria, these appraisals* have a certain validity. The interwar period was largely one of nationalist gestation, when new influences were being felt, new associations were being formed, and a new generation was coming of age.'† Dr (now Professor) Kalu Ezera also found that 'Forces making for political progress were at work in Nigeria before the Second World War. . . .'

So it is not accurate to describe the Nigeria Azikiwe stepped into in 1937 as a complete political void, or despicable, or dead. But there was *a* void which he met and which, as it were, had been created precisely for him to fill. It was 'a journalistic vacuum', in the very sound description of Chief Awolowo (page 84 of *Awo*, his autobiography):

* *Sir William Geary:* 'No unrest in Nigeria – no political assassination – no non-cooperation, no bombs. The Prince of Wales had a universal welcome of enthusiastic loyalty.' (1927)

W. R. Crocker: '(Nigeria) has fewer problems than any other governing unit of the same population in the world. There is no problem of racial antagonism; there are no economic problems, ... and there are no political problems, internal or external, of any kind ... political problems like nationalism, as in India, are all non-existent.' (1936)

Lord Hailey: '[In British West Africa] one encounters movements of a more definite political nature ... [and] a class which more nearly resembles the Indian political type than can be seen elsewhere in Africa. But prominent as this class is in local politics it has not proceeded beyond the ideals of early Victorian radicalism; ... it seems to make little appeal to the un-educated or rural element.' (1937)

It is evident that foresight did not help these three commentators much; hindsight, on the other hand, has certainly helped Coleman, Crowder, Ezera (*Constitutional Development in Nigeria*), and others, to show how much more there was to the inter-war years than met the eye.

† James S. Coleman, *Nigeria: Background to Nationalism*, 1958, Berkeley and Los Angeles; University of California (Chapter 9).

... things were happening which aroused the just resentment and indignation of young Nigerians. As there was no effective vehicle for the vigorous ventilation of suppressed grievances, a journalistic vacuum was thus created which Dr Azikiwe very cleverly exploited and usefully filled when he returned to the country in 1937 to establish the *West African Pilot*. ...

Awolowo was of course writing from personal experience, and adds that '... when Azikiwe arrived, he found waiting not only a large number of young Yorubas who were dissatisfied with the conservatism and moderation of their traditional Lagosian leadership, but also all the educated elements of one of the largest tribes of Nigeria which until then had had no spokesman. Azikiwe at once became a symbol of Ibo (indeed, of non-Yoruba) achievement and emancipation, and he was able to mobilize the political support of Ibos. ...'

The Azikiwe image in his own country before his appearance had been built up out of several elements. The first was advance notification of his impending arrival from America, which by various means had been received in all the ex-British colonies in West Africa. With this news were attached not only accurate as well as wild reports of his extensive academic studies but also the news that he had written a book – a miraculous feat for an African in those days! – a book called *Liberia in World Politics*. It had been published in the same year of his return from his American career, and now 'there was a general belief that he was the most outstanding Nigerian scholar in the academic history of the country.'* Then had come Zik's brief visit home, on his way to the Gold Coast. On this occasion he was given a tumultuous reception in his native East (Onitsha and elsewhere), and in Lagos at first a cautious then an equally enthusiastic welcome, according to Awolowo's eye-witness account.

The enthusiasm was caused not only by the reputation of the man, but also by his lectures and speeches. In Africa, even today and in the most unlikely quarters, it is possible to create a

* Awolowo, op. cit., pp. 86 and 87. Indeed, in the address of welcome offered to Zik by the Ibo Union in Lagos in November 1934 he was credited with 'detailed studies in Psychology, Sociology, Political Economy, Economics, Education, Philosophy, Rural Sociology, and the Principles and History of Law. ...' (One thing at least is certain: Zik could not have told them he had studied both political economy and economics!)

veritable sensation by a display of learning in which long words abound, especially if they have a foreign, unusual flavour. Since nobody can accuse Zik of being shy of long, technical, unusual, and foreign-sounding words, his effect on the wholly unsophisticated audiences of West Africa in the 1930s and early 1940s was such as has already been described. Zik's speeches are less cluttered these days, but in the opening years of his African career they were more so. Anthony Enahoro wrote in 1949, in a pamphlet entitled *Nnamdi Azikiwe: Saint or Sinner?*: 'First of all, the man himself appealed to the masses. They flocked to his lectures to enjoy his oratory. They did not, perchance, understand his long words nor many of the "scintillating, titillating and vibrating" editorials of the *West African Pilot* of those days, but they respected this man who had such a copious vocabulary. . . .' The following extract from one of Zik's Lagos speeches during this visit provides an illustration:

. . . Heirs and heiresses of the New Africa must now consecrate themselves for scholarly research into all the aspects of world society in general and African society in particular.

Herodotus said that Africans ruled Egypt but that does not necessarily mean that it is true. That Professor Bonehead taught that the African race have not shown any capacity for civilization, and therefore could not have ruled Egypt, except in the mythology of the Greeks, does not mean that this view need be accepted. The true scholar studies Herodotean literature and the writings of his contemporaries, analytically examines the archaeological remains of the pertinent period in history, judiciously observes and critically studies the reports of archaeological expeditions together with the data, hypotheses, theses, and *obiter dicta* connected with other evidences adduced, validates them in the accepted style of scientific research, and then formulates his conclusions. If he is competent, and if his conclusions are accepted by the confraternity of scholars, then his opinions are just as valid and acceptable as those of his colleagues.

The third factor in the development of the Zik image in Nigeria was made up of (a) his reputation as 'Editor-in-Chief' of the *African Morning Post*, Editor-in-Chief being in itself a great dazzler mostly from the American exoticism, (b) his stand against conservatism in all African affairs and his publicized clashes with notable members of this class, (c) his appearances in the witness-box at election-petition cases in Accra, always the occasion for an extra public stir, and (d) most of all, his 'arrest', trial, and subsequent acquittal in the sedition case episode, 1936 and 1937.

As if these were not enough to overwhelm the young people in Lagos with anticipation and the old with apprehension, Zik arranged to have his second major publication – the book *Renascent Africa* – coincide with his departure from the Gold Coast and his arrival in Nigeria. ... Azikiwe had a life-programme ahead of him; he had to have success to carry it out, and knew it. In spite of his unassuming exterior and 'charming and disarming' manners – as Awolowo later put it – Zik had an iron will and the ruthless intention of using it for success. For, to him, his success would mean also the success of a programme of advance in Africa. Both by his own adroitness and by the blessings of chance everything he did and everything that happened to him between 1934 and 1937 was but part of the preparation for the return to Nigeria.

Chapter 18

The *Pilot*

We have seen in the last chapter something of the nature of the political and economic situation upon which Azikiwe entered on his return home from the Gold Coast as it then was. It would be useful for us also to mention some of the prevailing social conditions of the time.

It was stated in Chapter 17 that Nigeria was just getting back on her feet economically by 1937, when the volume of trade had risen back into the high £30 millions. But this was not to suggest that Nigeria was therefore economically prosperous and stable, nor, even less, that the social conditions inseparable from economic factors were anything like satisfactory. The standard of living of the few was still high enough, but the majority had not yet felt any benefits from the rise in national income. Besides, there was now developing a new danger in the area of employment and unemployment, namely that the schools were now turning out more numbers than before of youngsters who could not be absorbed into government work and for whom there were no other prospects of employment. In other words, the expansion of the Civil Service, which had begun under the policies of Sir Donald Cameron (1931–5) had slowed down considerably, especially as a result of the Great Depression.

But again there is no suggestion here that education itself, therefore, had a brilliant picture to present of its own internal development. British colonial policy and operations in Africa had nowhere been able to achieve more than a pitiable five to seven per cent literacy in English, or any other language, up to and including the Second World War. The exceptions, one or two urban areas like Freetown (Sierra Leone) ,were few enough to be ignored as a serious contradiction of a general fact. Certainly by 1937 neither Nigeria nor any of her sister-colonies had an impressive educational record to show. Between 1900 and 1937 the gain in Nigeria was from $5\frac{1}{2}$ to 11 per cent; or, to put it another

way, 11 per cent only of the people (of the south) had been
educated since the capture of Lagos from the slavers in 1851.
Moreover, much of the credit in any case belonged to the Christian
missionaries.

Unemployment of course creates dangerous tensions of related
nature among different classes of people. Among the young
school-leavers of Nigeria there was, according to Awolowo, a
condition of 'suppressed grievances'; Enahoro, for his part,
thought 'Nigeria was on the eve of a mild revolution'. The ordinary people did not count a great deal with the more privileged
ones: literate and illiterate alike seemed to belong together in the
one faceless mass. Nor had they any means, as Awolowo reports,
of protesting against their disadvantages. The Press of the day was
interested only in news concerning the members of 'high society',
namely lawyers, doctors, and the like. Zik thus came as the
answer to the prayers of the people on the other side of the
dividing line between the privileged and the under-privileged.
They, the under-privileged, were the great majority. They always
are, except that in 'old' welfare states like New Zealand or the
Scandinavian countries the term can be modified to read *less*-
privileged. ...

Zik had saved quite a considerable sum of money from his
Gold Coast employment to use in establishing himself in Nigeria.
'Considerable' is of course a relative term, and in this case
describes, according to Zik himself, no more but also no less than
a sum of '£1,000-plus'. This amount was raised to some £5,000
by contributions from his family, and it was on this initial
capital that the 'Zik's Press Ltd' was founded. His first business
and printing premises were in one of the most congested corners
of commercial Lagos, Market Street. Later, he moved into
slightly more suitable and spacious quarters in Broad Street, part
of the property of the family of the man who eventually became
and still is Chief Justice of the Federation (now Republic) of
Nigeria, Sir Adetokunbo Ademola.

The association broke up in bad blood. Barrister Ademola, as
he then was, complained that the operation of Zik's printing
presses and other machines was a source of nuisance to him on
account of the constant noise and vibration. Secondly, and worse
still, the vibration was in turn a source of danger to his building,

because he felt – and had expert confirmation – that the foundations as well as walls were being undermined. Zik replied that he
had put all his money and hopes into the present establishment,
and had no prospects whatsoever of acquiring suitable alternative
accommodation at short notice. He thought Mr Ademola's fears
about the building were out of proportion, but undertook to do
his best to abate the nuisance of the noise by a readjustment in
hours of operation. Mr Ademola did not think this was satisfactory; Zik thought Ademola's attitude was unsympathetic and
unreasonable. Eventually the case went to court. Zik lost. He was
ordered to move from the lawyer's premises – to his immense
distress.

Today both men have long 'buried the hatchet', and both
avow there was nothing violent in their feelings towards each
other, at the time or subsequently. But in fact the case had results
and repercussions of negative significance for the Zik image.
Some of the earliest accusations of vindictiveness and ruthlessness
levelled against him arose out of this action. Zik was said to
have subsequently attacked Mr Caxton-Martin on municipal
affairs for the sole reason of the latter's success on behalf of
Ademola in the eviction case. Moreover, on the occasion of the
appointment of Ademola and Mr J. S. Cole to the magistracy,
the *Pilot* had shown, according to Zik's critics, approval of Cole,
who was European – which laid Azikiwe open to the accusation
of being a philistine.

But the second direct repercussion from the court incident was
far more important. It had a pointed significance, in fact, for
this question of racial feelings and relations in the Azikiwe story.

Zik had his share of personal clashes with individuals of the
white race, and his whole life's work has been, as we know, concerned with 'rescuing' black people, generally, from white. But,
like many other African leaders throughout the continent, indeed
like most Africans today, Zik has no personal racial hatred in
him. This is why one must be profoundly sorry that no less a
person than Sir Eric Ashby could, after all these years, have
misread Azikiwe so much as to have accused him – in 1962! – of
racialism. When Zik had said at University College, Ibadan – as
it then was – 'we have produced learned men in all walks of life.
There is now no need to be running helter-skelter abroad begging

for experts to come and guide us', he was not thinking merely of foreign academics in the West African universities, but of the necessity of African graduates hurrying up to assume responsibility in guiding their own countries in the new problems they face daily. Sir Eric's charge that Zik was promoting racialism in university employment policy in Africa thus missed a point somewhat. Otherwise the magnificent address Sir Eric gave at the University of the Witwatersrand in Johannesburg in 1962, entitled 'Universities under Siege', was suffused with progressiveness and truth, as it laid bare the evils of academic *apartheid*.

In his case with Barrister Ademola Zik happened to have received unexpected generosity from two white persons, which, if anything, confirmed his natural attitude that race-hatred in principle and on a personal basis is a terrible, unnecessary evil. His benefactors were, first, none other than Sir Bernard Bourdillon himself, Governor of Nigeria (1935–43), and a Swede called Rasmussen. Sir Bernard's sympathetic interest in Zik's desperate position resulted in the acquirement of a large piece of Government-controlled land, and the Swedish financier and contractor (Rasmussen) built on it, on credit, the premises which came to house the press and which still does so today.

The *West African Pilot*, when finally launched on 22 November 1937, rapidly became in Nigeria what the *African Morning Post* had become in the Gold Coast soon after first publication. Again we can do no better than to take evidence from sound, discriminating eye-witnesses of this history. Obafemi Awolowo, one of Nigeria's foremost architects of independence, was never, except at the very beginning,* a hero-worshipper of Zik; this fact gives the greater weight, therefore, to his words. The *Pilot*, he has written, 'whatever its literary defects, was a fire-eating and aggressive nationalist paper of the highest order, ranking in this regard with the *Nigerian Daily Telegraph* under Ikoli, and the *Lagos Daily News*, but much better produced'. Awolowo goes on to give a complete but concise picture of the paper, its impact and significance:

It was naturally very popular, the very thing the youth of the country

* 'Because of my admiration for the man, I was given an assignment to cover the three lectures which Dr Azikiwe delivered on his arrival in Lagos towards the end of 1934. ...' (*AWO*, p. 86.)

had been waiting for. Newspapermen in the employ of the *West African Pilot* were better paid* and they assumed a new status in society. Civil servants, teachers and mercantile employees resigned good and pensionable posts to lend a hand in the new journalistic awakening. Some of these enthusiasts were eventually disappointed and disillusioned on other grounds, but the fact of a journalistic revival and revolution was widely recognized and acknowledged.

To this should be added one of the few other personal-experience accounts committed to print, Anthony Enahoro's:

... When, in addition to the romance which had been built round the man by the publication of his odyssey, the *West African Pilot* blossomed into every corner of the country as the champion of the common man – the teacher, the trader, the clerk – it went right to the top.

Nigerian journalism, wrote Enahoro, had only played-up doctors, lawyers, and senior civil servants of the status of Dr Henry Carr, the most senior African in the service for years, and Dr C. C. Adeniyi-Jones, one of the distinguished settlers from Sierra Leone. 'Those among the poorer people who were so privileged as to read the newspapers', he continued, 'looked upon them as the property and the mouthpiece of the gods of their time. But here was a novel type of newspaper, catering to the taste of people even in the remotest corners of Nigeria and, above all, edited by that colourful personality with those degrees! The people fell for him. The *Pilot* was made.'

But it was not quite as easy as all that, nor were the initial financial problems of the *Pilot* merely those that have already been briefly mentioned. Zik's £5,000 capital, though substantial and able to give him and his family the controlling share of the business, had not, of course, been large enough to provide both initial operating costs *and* security. For security he had to have two sureties, and a Dr Okoroafor Smart and a Dr Caulchrick agreed to back him. This was on the intervention of two other men: Dr J. C. Vaughan and Mr Herbert Macaulay. Dr Vaughan and Mr Macaulay were in fact the two most prominent figures in

* One of these better-paid men was Adolphus Kofi Blankson, a half-Nigerian, half-Ghanaian who had followed Zik to the *Pilot* from the *Morning Post*. Blankson, the most faithful and longest-serving of Zik's former employees, next got the important position of head of Nigeria's international telecommunications service.

Zik's life during his early struggles in Lagos. But Dr Smart and Dr Caulchrick (according to a chronicle confirmed in general by Zik himself) withdrew their support without notice or warning in 1938. This was after the defeat of the candidates of the Nigerian National Democratic Party, whose staunch members both guarantors were.

The *Pilot* was now threatened with failure by this crisis, and Azikiwe was in a serious situation. He was saved by the generosity of Dr (now Sir) Kofo Abayomi and Dr Akinola Maja, who were also leading Lagos Yorubas. Until this point, therefore, it is quite clear that the greatest support of the financial sector of Zik's enterprise was the Yoruba élite of Lagos. From this arose the extreme bitterness, in part, of the complaints against Zik by a large section of this class, who in later years charged him both with the insult of political enmity and the injury of ingratitude.

There was one other source of difficulty for Zik in the first years of the *Pilot*, namely competition with the *Nigerian Daily Times*:

The *Nigerian Daily Times* was very swiftly reorganized, in order to meet the challenge of the *West African Pilot*. A substantial amount of foreign capital was injected into it, and the dead wood in the editorial section cut out to yield place to younger and more imaginative elements. R. B. Paul, Esq., head of the 'West African Newspapers' came to Nigeria himself and, for a while, personally directed the initial operations. An expatriate editor, Mr H. C. E. M. Bates, was appointed. He and Dr Azikiwe soon fell foul of each other, and there was a fierce press war. . . .

Fred V. Anyiam in a partisan account goes much further than this analysis by Awolowo, and claims that during this period there was a concerted effort to hamper Azikiwe's plans, 'and it was directed that no stone should be left unturned to ruin his plans'. Towards the end of 1938 Mr Bates and the *Daily Times* on the one side and Zik and his *Pilot* on the other were suing and counter-suing one another at court, with damage claims running into many thousands of pounds. There was no holding back the *Pilot*, however, and the balance slowly tipped in its favour. 'My sympathy and that of all Nigerian nationalists was with Dr Azikiwe,' said Awolowo.

A few short excerpts from early issues of the *Pilot* will illustrate its handling of (a) economic questions, (b) the basic political theme, and (c) the emotional appeal to Zik's countrymen on the subject of Africa and her sufferings. The first example is from Zik's own column, 'Inside Stuff' (29 December 1937), and was part of the answer to a questioner:

> The argument that Africans have no chamber of commerce will not hold water. There is nothing to stop the Africans forming their own Chamber of Commerce, if they find it difficult to gain admission into the European Chamber of Commerce. ...

Nothing much in that passage, but it is to be noted that when the Africans 'have no chamber of commerce' that institution has no respectability either; when they are being presented with the inspiring prospect of 'forming *their own* Chamber of Commerce', however, the institution – though still unestablished – goes into Capital Letters at once, suggesting the equality being aimed at. Then there was the well-aimed but anonymous hit at one of the *Pilot*'s early economic enemies, delivered by Zik in an auxiliary column called 'It Seems to Me':

> My Prague Correspondent tells me that a child ... recently born at — had three arms and eighteen fingers. This monstrosity is still alive.
> But I know a monstrosity with as many arms and as many fingers which is interested in strangling everything within reach so as to enable it to declare dividends regularly. ...

The next example deals in part with a subject that was to recur a thousand times in the paper, until in 1946/7 the 'Richards Constitution' made complete nonsense of it in more ways than the obvious one:

> The West African Colonies have a political common foe properly decorated with red tape – [the] Official Majority.
> So long as we think in terms of Nigeria, Gold Coast, Sierra Leone, Gambia and not as one United West Africa we must be content with a Colonial Dictatorship instead of a Government of the people by the people and for the people – namely Democracy. (Editorial, 21 July 1938.)

Our final example is made up of the last six evocative lines of a sonnet, by one J. Harvey L. Baxter (a name that could have belonged to anybody: a Sierra Leonean, a West Indian, or a sympathizer from an English-speaking country):

O natal Mother, how your heart bewails!
Bereft of vineyards, and of freedom too;
Kissed and betrayed, rifled, rent of sails
By godless thugs that care not what they do.
Brood nor despair, this hell is not your doom,
God is not dead, nor guarded in a tomb.

A frequent early contributor of poetry was Dennis Osadebay, one of Nigeria's senior politicians, a former President of the Senate, and now Premier of the new (fourth) region, the Mid-West.

Chapter 19

The First Ten Years Begin

We have seen Azikiwe return home to Nigeria and have followed his career during the forming and the initial years of the *West African Pilot*. In this chapter it would be useful to survey the first decade of the Zik story in Nigeria, that is, from 1937 to 1946. As a help we may start by mentioning the major events of this period, noting explicitly or implicitly, where necessary, Zik's connexion with each.

Before anything else, there was the founding of the *Pilot*, No. 1, Vol. I of which came out on 22 November 1937. Next, Zik joined the already well-established Nigerian Youth Movement (formerly *Lagos* Youth Movement). The following year, 1938, the N.Y.M. entered the political lists for the first time and defeated the hitherto lone political party, the Nigerian National Democratic Party. In 1941 Azikiwe resigned from the Youth Movement and later joined the National Democratic, which was a creation of Herbert Macaulay. The break with the N.Y.M. was 'a devastating blow from which it never really recovered', in James Coleman's words. Next, there was the West African Press Delegation to the U.K., led by Zik, in 1943. The National Council of Nigeria and the Cameroons was formed the year after the Delegation, on the suggestion of Zik. The N.C.N.C. became and remained, until his withdrawal from politics in 1960, Zik's main platform, apart from his newspapers. Of these papers, Zik founded or took over a total of six: they were strategically located throughout the whole country, north and south. The same year he founded the African Continental Bank, which was to provide high drama, and some tragedy, twelve years later. In 1945 the General Strike, led by the African Civil Servants Technical Workers' Union, resulted in two of Zik's papers being banned by the Government. Finally, this ten-year record closed when the first President of the National Council of Nigeria and the Cameroons, Herbert Macaulay, died in 1946, and was succeeded by Zik. Zik thus became leader of Nigeria's first country-wide political party, *de jure,* as he had been, *de facto,* all along.

To this catalogue must be added, separately, the famous incident of 'The Assassination Story' of 1945/6, which it will be possible to bring up-to-date in this book, by the addition of a piece of evidence not hitherto released in public.

It is necessary for us at this point to attempt to evaluate and put into perspective the Zikist contribution to political and social change in West Africa, during the first few years of his development. For it was during this time that he excelled all others. The Old Guard in the four British colonies had played for some time the role of patriotic élite; during the preceding forty or fifty years various combinations of them had mounted numerous campaigns for political, social, and economic reform in favour of their people, though many had also been but imperial sycophants or conservative time-servers. In later years Herbert Macaulay and Casely Hayford had stood out among politicians on the West Coast as nationalist leaders. Aggrey, in the early Twenties, had also made his great impression among millions of his countrymen of both east and west. But it was Zik – complete contrast to Aggrey* as he was – that brought new political life to West Africa in 1934. His contemporaries, even those opposed to him in many things, had no doubts about his effect on the current scene. We have already quoted Obafemi Awolowo several times in Chapters 17 and 18, not necessarily, and certainly not always, in praise of Zik. In a further quotation, Awolowo showed both that he ('Awo') was critical, and that Azikiwe was effective:

The Nigerian Youth Movement was already popular with the masses before Dr Azikiwe's return. But he brought with him a propaganda technique which was new in politics and journalism in Nigeria, and which further boosted the popularity of the Nigerian Youth Movement and disarrayed its opponents. Little wonder, therefore, that in opposition to the veteran N.N.D.P. (Nigerian National Democratic Party) the N.Y.M. won in 1938, and in a resounding manner, all the three

* 'Whereas J. E. K. Aggrey ... had emphasized the need for both black and white piano keys to achieve musical harmony, a European friend of Azikiwe's noted that "most of Zik's music is played on the black keys and it is sweet, exciting, and stirring in African ears; ... the white keys when used are often employed to stress a contrast or a disharmony".' (Coleman)

Lagos seats in the Legislative Council, and all but one of the elective seats in the Lagos Town Council.

Nnamdi Azikiwe brought into West Africa, first, a new 'call for greatness'. Zik initially directed a universalist 'Negro' – 'black man' – appeal to an equally universalist audience: 'Africa', 'Africans'. On a second level, he spoke to 'Gold Coasters', 'Nigerians', 'Gambians', 'Sierra Leoneans', 'Liberians', not to Fantis, or Yorubas, or 'Creoles', or 'Americo-Liberians'. Later he was to be accused of tribalism, but in the crucial opening stages of his campaign he addressed himself to 'nations', not to 'tribes'. Unlike Aggrey, Zik's approach was aggressive and combative. It created a corresponding atmosphere, first in the Gold Coast and then in Nigeria, with long-range effects in Sierra Leone and the Gambia.

Secondly, Zik's appeal touched elements which had previously been largely ignored by other leaders or else underrated: schoolteachers, clerks, workers at all levels, and, most of all, young people. Even more important than the variety of group-interests was their geographical distribution. For the first time in their experience, these groups were brought into the stream of national consciousness through a popular press, whether they lived in the few urban centres or in what the urbanites always called 'the bush'.

In line with this approach, Zik's contribution to Nigerian political development of a nationalist, country-wide political organization was significant. The National Council of Nigeria and the Cameroons, organized in 1944 partly on the groundwork done by Zik, was the first party in the country with such a wide-based appeal, even including the former Cameroons in its embrace. The N.C.N.C. was not so much a party in the normal sense as 'a confederation of trade unions, smaller parties, tribal unions and literary groups', as Crowder observes in *The Story of Nigeria*. It was, in short, an experiment in fusion, and gained its initial massive membership for that reason. The importance of the N.C.N.C. in the development of the nationalist drive justifies a full and correct account of its genesis. No one has ever given a better account than Zik himself, and for the sake of the record we reproduce it here. Zik said:

Unlike other political parties, the N.C.N.C. did not begin spontaneously as a political party. Early in 1942, a dozen thinkers formed themselves into what they ultimately called the Nigeria Reconstruction Group. They met every Sunday morning at 72 King George Avenue, at Yaba, which was my residence. They discussed political, social, and economic problems which affected contemporary Nigeria and sought answers to them. Most of the members of this group were connected with the Yaba Higher College and its associated institutions. Their sole aim was to apply scientific methods in the solution of practical problems.

In course of their researches and discussions, they began to feel that a national front organization was necessary to act as a mouthpiece for expressing the aspirations of Nigerians in various walks of life. The aims of such a national front were stated to be the immediate improvement of social conditions and eventually the bringing about of far-reaching social progress which should include the exclusion of foreign exploitation and the establishment of self-government in Nigeria. Such aims could not be attained by only one section of the community working independently but must be faced by a front constituted of men and women who wished to see the setting up of an independent Nigeria. It was believed that only by agreement on practical measures of common action, whilst making allowance for differences of conviction, could Nigeria attain this desirable goal.

Representatives of the Nigeria Reconstruction Group then exchanged views with officials of the Nigerian Youth Movement, which was then under the leadership of Mr Ernest Ikoli. They did the same with representatives of the Nigerian National Democratic Party, under the leadership of Herbert Macaulay. The Nigerian Youth Circle was also contacted and ideas were exchanged with its leaders in the persons of Messrs H. O. Davies and J. Udochi. Having contacted other organizations, like the Nigeria Union of Teachers, the Union of Young Democrats, certain trade unions and tribal organizations, the N.R.G. requested all of them to form a federation which would be an All-Nigerian National Congress.

In the meantime, a youth rally was organized to take place at the Ojukoro Farm of E. J. Alex-Taylor in November 1943. Hundreds of youths stormed this suburban estate and a most impressive aggregation of nationalists demonstrated the possibilities of a Nigerian nationalist front. The thought was unanimous that the Nigerian Youth Movement should spearhead this front and so the N.R.G. joined in suggesting that the Movement should summon a representative meeting of various organizations with a view to crystallizing the national front which was the dream of most nationalists. After six months of vacillation and inaction, the Nigeria Union of Students decided to assume responsibility for summoning such a meeting, which took place on 26 August 1944, in the Glover Memorial Hall, Lagos, under the chairmanship of Duse Mohamed Ali.

Subsequently, it was decided to adopt N.C.N.C. as the name of the new national front and Herbert Macaulay was elected its first President, with your humble servant as General Secretary.

It is pertinent, at this stage, to give you the names of the thinkers who, without any political ambitions and without any thought of personal gain, sowed the seed which has now germinated to become the N.C.N.C. They are as follows: T. O. na Oruwariye, M. O. Balonwu, B. O. S. Adophy, T. E. E. Brown, S. I. Bosah, M. E. R. Okorodudu, E. E. Esua, E. C. Erokwu, Henry Collins, C. Enitan Brown, A. I. Osakwe, O. K. Ogan, and Nnamdi Azikiwe.

In January 1945 the N.C.N.C. held its Constitutional Conference. The aims it set down included (1) the extension of democratic principles and the advancement of the interests of the people of Nigeria and of the Cameroons under British mandate; (2) the imparting of political education to the people of Nigeria, in order to prepare them for the achievement of self-government; and (3) the provision of a medium of expression for members of the N.C.N.C., through which they would endeavour to secure for Nigeria and the Cameroons 'political freedom, economic security, social equality, and religious toleration. . . .'

Another inspiration Azikiwe gave his country and countrymen was that of commercially successful business. Zik was of course determined on this from the beginning. We have seen previously that he considered an economic foundation to be necessary for all social progress. Secondly, successful African business was a means of employment for his own countrymen as well as a source of inspiration. His six newspapers were thus doubly potent. They were a sound economic means, and, through them, Zik's 'combative and provocative journalism' gave him his 'principal source of fame and power' and was 'the most crucial single precipitant of the Nigerian awakening'. (We shall say something about this last statement presently.)

Here, in connexion with the question of his economic philosophy and activities, must be told the story of the circumstances immediately responsible for Azikiwe's decision to go into banking, a decision of fateful future consequences. By the time of his return from the 1943 Press Delegation, Zik's financial affairs were in a dangerously unhealthy condition. He had to have capital from somewhere, and in his desperation he turned to the manager of the branch of the British-owned bank with which he had done business all along.

Zik's own account of what happened is as dramatic and stirring as only he could make it. He had of course gone in virtually as a beggar, cap in hand, and for a long time at the interview the relationship between him and the manager was just that: beggar and alms-giver – if, that is, the manager would be a giver. But he would not, and instead was subjecting Zik to a humiliating lecture on business ethics, African business methods or the lack of them, and so on and on, until Zik suddenly called a halt by an abrupt and violent movement. . . . It was the manager's turn then to listen, half-frightened, to a volcanic lecture on other facts and future possibilities. . . . It was out of this experience, buttressed by memories of 1937 and 1938, that Zik emerged sworn to establish an African bank of his own as soon as humanly possible, where Africans could receive financial assistance without humiliating lectures, and where the established banking monopoly of the British firms would be broken. The African Continental Bank was established in 1946/7. Ten years later the Foster-Sutton Commission was appointed for what became in effect a second trial of Zik, in connexion with certain funds of the bank. This famous incident is narrated in Chapter 23.

It was, to continue, no small feature of the Azikiwe complex that under his influence and by his moral or financial support many young Nigerians and Gold Coasters found their way to America, for the same kind of education Aggrey and Azikiwe himself had both brought back. President Kwame Nkrumah of Ghana mentions this influence – of both Aggrey and Zik – on him, in his autobiography, *Ghana*.

Among those who went from Nigeria were three Ibos who published the only Nigerian nationalist literature during the 1940s and before they left America for the return home. They were: Mbonu Ojike, who wrote *My Africa* and *I Have Two Countries*; K. Ozuomba Mbadiwe (*British and Axis Aims in Africa*), and A. A. Nwafor Orizu (*Without Bitterness*). Their books were the first of their kind since *Renascent Africa* in 1937.

The 'Zikist Movement', which was launched in 1946 in Lagos and rapidly developed into the militant wing of the N.C.N.C., was widely held to have been founded on the 'Zikist Philosophy' propounded in Orizu's book. The only other effort of intellectualization of nationalism on this scale and during these years was Awolowo's *Path to Nigerian Freedom*, published in 1947.

A Yoruba Moslem who went to the United States under direct assistance from Azikiwe, A. K. Disu, concentrated on the journalistic interests inspired in him by Zik. After considerable service as an information officer, Disu became Private Secretary to the Governor-General. Many others of Zik's followers and protégés have risen to high positions in many walks of life. Among these originals may be mentioned Dr Ikejiani, a medical doctor who became Chairman of the Nigerian Railways Corporation; Dr J. B. C. Okala, an educational psychologist at the University of Nigeria, Nsukka; I. U. Akpabio, a senior Minister in the East Region Government of Dr Okpara; and Nwankwo Chukwuemeka, industrial engineer. A Sierra Leonean whom Zik 'rescued' from Hampton Institute (simply because he was in the wrong place for his field of interests), and re-directed to Lincoln University – David Ekundayo Boye-Johnson – in time became head of the Medical Services in his country.

So far, so good. But we must now modify Coleman's opinion that Azikiwe's 'combative and provocative journalism was ... the most crucial single precipitant of the Nigerian awakening'. It would be much safer to say the Nigerian *re*-awakening. We said at the beginning of Chapter 17 that Zik's position in the fight for Nigerian independence was not quite comparable to Gandhi's in India, in the sense that Zik was not as peculiarly alone as Gandhi was, not as unique. There was the still-towering figure of Herbert Macaulay when Zik arrived, to whom he deferred without hesitation. There was the existing Nigerian Youth Movement and its leaders, whose claims to past-performance and present activity could not be disputed. Furthermore, the status of the Lagos Yoruba élite and the talents of Ernest Ikoli, Oba Akisanya, H. O. Davies, and Awolowo himself were not automatically obliterated immediately upon the appearance of Azikiwe. As a matter of fact Zik and 'H.O.D.' formed an attractive team for a considerable time, as Awolowo has testified.

It is for these same reasons that we must also quarrel with another summation of the Zik phenomenon similar to Coleman's. This is one made by Babatunde Williams, of the University of Ife, in his able analysis of Nigerian nationalism.* 'Indeed, it would be impossible to understand Nigerian nationalism,' wrote Dr Williams, 'without being acquainted with this vigorous personality who dominated it for so long and acted as its sole motive force.'

Why 'sole motive force', when Dr Williams's own exhaustive analysis of antecedental as well as current conditions clearly showed otherwise? It is much fairer to Zik to opine that his was the most powerful motive force operating on the nationalist scene during the critical period under review. And to add, as Dr Williams says earlier on in his summary, that 'undoubtedly the most important development for Nigerian nationalism in the Thirties was the arrival of Dr Azikiwe' is no more than the whole truth. But the other word – like Coleman's – is slightly unfair both to our hero and to his contemporaries. If there is no basis for comparison there can be no true evaluation of worth either; and an equation in which one side is equal to zero renders the other side equally valueless.

This was certainly not the case on the Nigerian scene of the Thirties. Zik's great advantage over his rivals was his charismatic personality. What he brought to the scene was a *new approach* which at first reinforced the appeal of the old régime and re-vitalized interest, then later assumed leadership by a broadening, nay, a metamorphosis, of the popular base of that interest. It was Zik's quickening of the political pulse, as witnessed by Awolowo himself, Anthony Enahoro, and others, that brought the youth to their feet in larger numbers than before. It was his encouragement of them, and his backing, when they came to him and said that they were ready but lacked leadership, that resulted in the moves through which the N.C.N.C. was founded. And it was his subsequent leadership of the N.C.N.C. that was in many ways responsible for much of the speeding-up process for independence. Finally, and perhaps as good as any other contribution, Zik more than any other single individual helped his countrymen

* *Nationalism and Federalism in Nigeria*, unpublished dissertation for the Ph.D. degree of the University of Illinois, 1959.

to begin to do away with conservatism and anachronistic humbug of all kinds. And here Babatunde Williams's assessment is flawless:

Zik arrived in Nigeria when the nationalist movement needed further extension and an effective leadership. He came at the right psychological moment when the old Yoruba leadership had not grasped that times had changed and that old cures would not suffice for old wounds. In this sense, Herbert Macaulay and Dr C. C. Adeniyi-Jones, although patriotic to the last and adamant in their opposition to British rule, were of the conventional mould, believing in 'self-government within the Commonwealth' and singing 'God save the King'.

Just the same, it is true to say that much good foundation had been laid before Zik's arrival, and that he bested his contemporaries, compeers, and rivals only by his hard work, superior political and social propaganda techniques, and his vote-winning personality.

The record of the Nigerian Youth Movement is proof of the existence of strong foundations. Organized in 1934 to 'canalize this resentment' – to use Awolowo's expression – against the proposals for establishing a 'higher' college which few of the Lagosians believed in, the Lagos Youth Movement became in 1936 the Nigerian Youth Movement. Those concerned in the founding in 1934 included Dr J. C. Vaughan (who was later one of Azikiwe's backers), Ernest Ikoli, and Oba Samuel Akisanya. Later, it attracted to itself many of the younger, dynamic elements, including H. O. Davies, Awolowo, and, soon after his arrival, Azikiwe himself. Ignoring all partisan opinion about the N.Y.M., it would be enough to quote parts of its aims and objectives to show what it stood for:*

THE PRINCIPAL AIM The principal aim of the Nigerian Youth Movement is the development of a united nation out of the conglomeration of peoples who inhabit Nigeria. ... We will combat vigorously all such tendencies as would jeopardize the unifying process.

THE POLITICAL CHARTER The goal of our political activities is a complete autonomy within the British Empire. We are striving towards a position of equal partnership with other member States of the British Commonwealth of Nations. ...

* Awolowo, *Autobiography*, pp. 121–2.

The Movement aims at the abolition of property or income qualification for the exercise of the franchise and the substitution of universal suffrage. ...

THE ECONOMIC CHARTER We pledge ourselves to demand for our people economic opportunities equal to those enjoyed by foreigners. ...

CULTURAL AND SOCIAL CHARTER We believe that mass education ought to be the true pivot of the educational policy of our Government. We will therefore urge on the Government to make elementary education progressively free and compulsory. ...

Awolowo's evidence is thin as to the 'Nigerian-ness' of the appeal and the activities of the N.Y.M., but there can be no doubt that the Movement had in hand a programme intended to apply to the whole country, and that it was advanced in its demands. When Zik broke with the N.Y.M. in 1941, followed by all his Ibo countrymen, other Easterners, and many Ijebu-Yorubas, he undoubtedly smashed a potential national front. Moreover, though he could not have intended it to, the incident did further aggravate tribalism in national politics, especially since Zik soon afterwards identified himself with the existing Ibo State Union. The split created an hiatus in national politics and resulted in considerable confusion. But it also developed into a sort of victory for Zik, because out of the ruins of the N.Y.M. arose relentlessly his image as the dominant nationalist force in the country.

One link of fate after another – cruel to the other leaders, kind to Azikiwe – forged the chain of factors which took him to the top. In 1943, two years after the break with the Youth Movement and while the Second World War was still on, the British Council invited a group of eight West African journalists to visit Britain-at-War. Zik was chosen leader of the delegation, and used this opportunity to present a West African Press Delegation memorandum of demands on the British Government for constitutional, economic, and social reform in the four British territories. 'The Atlantic Charter and British West Africa' memorandum demanded, among other things, immediate annulment of the Crown Colony system, immediate Africanization of all services, the award of 400 scholarships to young West Africans annually, and ten years of representative government followed by five of fully responsible government. In this way the four countries were to be independent by the year 1958.

In spite of the widespread attack on colonialism during the war, not least from the United States, the British Government paid scant attention to the Press Delegation. Indeed Sir (then Mr) Winston Churchill in those days was irritably repudiating all pressure on him to 'liquidate the Empire', regardless of the mounting criticism at home and abroad. Zik returned to Nigeria terribly disappointed and bitter. But there was no national vehicle through which the frustrations of the war-years could be massively conveyed immediately, thanks partly to his own disagreement with the Yoruba leadership in 1941 and the violent Press wars which followed that break, and worsened relations among the ethnic groups.

During the three years 1941–4 the Yoruba leadership 'withdrew' to Ibadan, where Obafemi Awolowo was attempting an earnest internal reconstruction among his own group. 'After the 1941 election crisis in the Nigerian Youth Movement,' he has written in his autobiography (page 163), 'I re-opened the issue [of the necessity for a federal form of government, on the basis of linguistic and ethnic divisions]. I was now emboldened to argue my case before a larger number of friends and colleagues in the Ibadan Branch of the Nigerian Youth Movement. . . .' These efforts and these arguments were kept up, off and on, until Awolowo left for England in 1944 to study law. They were the beginnings of two important factors in Awolowo's career as a nationalist: (1) his founding in London of the Yoruba cultural organization – the *Egbe Omo Oduduwa* – on which the Yoruba political party, the Action Group, was later built, and (2) the development of his own political ideas for Nigeria which he has himself described as the 'evolution of a Federalist'.

But in 1943/4 'Awo' was also preoccupied with his ambition to study law in England. Brilliant, mercurial, unpredictable H. O. Davies, too, had left his key position and functions in the Movement to take a Government job, Oba Akisanya had returned to his home to become a chief, and the older generation in Lagos had almost retired or were mere figure-heads. It was thus that Azikiwe found himself temporarily alone in the field.

In 1942, before the Press visit to England, he produced a monograph on *Land Tenure in Northern Nigeria*. In this he analysed, *inter alia*, the 'Hausa Customary Law of Land Tenure', and discussed the law of treaties, and treaties between Northern Nigerian rulers and the British, concluding at one point (Chapter VI, page 20) that 'from all accounts, it is now clear that most, if not all, of the treaties negotiated between the Royal Niger Company and the Kings of Northern Nigeria, contained lacunae which make their validity questionable'.

The memorandum to the Secretary of State for the Colonies by the 1943 Press Delegation was of course mostly Zik's work, and in November and December after his return from London he published two of his most-often cited smaller works: the *Political Blueprint of Nigeria* (on which the Press memo was based) and the *Economic Reconstruction of Nigeria*. Both appeared, as did *Land Tenure*, under the imprint of the African Book Company, one of the many branches of the Zik Group of enterprises.

Chapter 20

A Postscript to History

Both the *Blueprint* and the *Economic Reconstruction* booklet were in fact two separate collections of serials on those subjects, written in that year and first published in the *West African Pilot*. They exhibited the two main streams of Zik's nationalism: one, the belief in the African – in this case the Nigerian – resources of men and material, and (2) the total repudiation of the hold of the colonial system on these resources. The December publication, he said, was 'an attempt to prepare a blueprint for our political future'. Zik continued:

Previous Constitutions of Nigeria (1866, 1886, 1900, 1906, 1914, 1933) have merely perpetrated our political serfdom. At best, they are crumbs of benevolent despotism. We appear complacent about this national humiliation because of our proneness to wag our tongues like parrots instead of mobilizing our intellectual and physical energy for an all-out assault against the rampart of colonialism with its destructive effects on our national character.

In the *Economic Reconstruction of Nigeria* Zik wrote:

I believe that political autonomy must proceed *pari passu* with economic autonomy, in the social evolution of any people, because both are *sine qua non* of each other. With all the political power in the world, no state whose economic structure is not sound can attain maximum happiness in the commonality of nations, as many nations have proved in recent years. But that should not prejudice the claim and exercise of political power, because same enables the development of any country to be accelerated without unnecessary brakes, caused by political machinations.

Zik's political plan advocated a two-stage development to last fifteen years, at the end of which Nigeria would be ready to take over her own government. He recommended a Commonwealth of Nigeria made up of eight 'Protectorates' and headed by a

Governor-General and his Lieutenant, and by Governors and Lieutenant-Governors in the unit divisions. A Cabinet should complete the Executive power of the Commonwealth, with Executive Councils at the Protectorate level. The Legislative power proposed would consist of a Commonwealth Parliament, Protectorate Legislative Councils, and Municipal and Rural Councils. The Judicial power was to bear a correlative structure: Commonwealth Supreme Court, Protectorate, Municipal, and Rural Courts. A '*corpus juris Nigeriensis*' would be the basis of the legal system, and the corporate instruments would comprise (1) a written Constitution (constitutional law), (2) Acts of the Nigerian Commonwealth Parliament (statutory law), (3) Acts of the Nigerian Judiciary (case law), and (4) the laws and customs of the 'aborigines of Nigeria', or common law. . . .

In the years of Our Lord One Thousand Nine Hundred and Forty-Plus, it would have been a philosophic and political miracle for anyone to have devised more theories and structures of government or economics which were original and new; the cleverest or most learned men since Adam Smith and Marx can now manage no more than ingenious arrangements of the established parts and, in addition, perhaps smoother-running political mechanisms. Certainly Zik's blueprint proposed nothing fundamentally new; on the contrary, it repeated proposals which in one form or another, to a greater or lesser degree, had been put forward by the old Pan-Africanists, the post-First World War Pan-West Africanists, and the later nationalists of the pre-Zik era. But in the year 1943 it was also true that, although it had been done before in other ways, one required tremendous moral courage to push, not mere theories of government, but demands for self-government in a British West African colony; even more, to do it in the terms employed by Azikiwe. Other leaders were getting ready to; Zik was actually doing it.

In 1944 he got a boost in morale, with the founding of the N.C.N.C. By now he had established his chain of newspapers, and with them as propaganda media for the Party, Zik was a formidable power in the country. In January of 1945 the N.C.N.C. drew up its party constitution of aims and objectives. In March of the same year the famous Richards constitutional proposals were put forward by Sir Arthur for the first time, and from that moment a new phase of nationalism-versus-colonialism had been reached. Richards and Azikiwe, 'the leading imperial representative and the foremost nationalist', became the symbols each of their respective sides and 'the principal antagonists in the struggle'.

The Richards Constitution was attacked from all sides, partly and selectively for its different shortcomings but universally for the authoritarian way of its introduction. 'Largely for the arbitrary manner in which it was introduced, and not necessarily for its defects, the Richards Constitution embittered and alientated the nationalist elements of the country . . .,' wrote Kalu Ezera in his *Constitutional Development in Nigeria* (page 81). Among the contemporary individual critics of note were Awolowo: '[The Richards Constitution] retains some of the objectionable features of the old, contains unsavoury characteristics of its own and falls short of expectations'; Chief H. O. Davies: 'Sir Arthur Richards' scheme of constitutional reform for Nigeria is ingenious but unpalatable'. It was even criticized, significantly enough, by Sir Arthur's immediate predecessor, Sir Bernard Bourdillon. But Sir Bernard's quarrel was only with the manner of the introduction of the measures, not with their content, much of which he declared to be of good intention and fair merit.

The most vehement of the critics was, of course, Nnamdi Azikiwe, leading the N.C.N.C. attack and with his Press in full cry. First they sent a memorandum to the Governor, denouncing and condemning the proposals as 'autocratic in origin' and 'also as designed to create a false impression of providing for an unofficial majority when, in fact, the "unofficials" were either chiefs who were officials appointed by the Government, or their nominees'. The memorandum then proposed alternatives: to divide the country on semi-federal lines; to have the central legislature control the Colony area, but to be responsible for the Provinces only in matters of defence, currency, and foreign affairs; and other proposals.

While the constitutional agitation was still on, a labour crisis also suddenly developed, over the twin-complaint of high costs and low wages. By then labour unions had grown in number from twelve in 1940 to eighty-five (1944), and in membership from

4,300-odd to some 30,000 or more. These unionists complained bitterly not only about their economic hardships but also about the relative disparity in treatment as between European and African staff, under Government authority. Zik threw himself into the fight on the side of the workers, the situation deteriorated rapidly, and finally it ended in a general strike. A link between the constitutional troubles and the General Strike was established at once by the authorities with respect to Azikiwe's activities; thus for the first time in his career and in the history of the nationalist struggle, Zik and the Government came into open legal clash. The Government closed down both the *Pilot* and Zik's second Lagos paper, the *Comet*.

Immediately upon the heels of this incident came another which was to reverberate around the world and create a sensation of alarm, incredulity, out-and-out disbelief, ridicule, anger, and a passion of protectiveness among Zik's devotees. This was the 'Assassination Story'. In Zik's own words (published in the east soon after the incident it narrates):

1. On 21 June 1945 the technical workers of the civil service of Nigeria went on strike at the instance of the African Civil Servants Technical Workers Union. They demanded an increase in the cost of living allowance due to [a] rise in the cost of living, and [the] Government refused to accede to their demands.
2. On 13 July 1945, at about 5.45 p.m. or thereabouts, Mr C. U. M. Gardner, Managing Editor of the *West African Pilot*, handed to me a wireless message which, he said, Mr Paul West, one of the three Wireless Operators of the *West African Pilot*, a licensed station in accordance with the laws of Nigeria, told him he had intercepted on Metre 51.5 at 5.15 p.m. or thereabouts on that day.
3. I took delivery of the wireless message and read same. I was shocked and terrified, as would any other human being, to observe that my assassination was contemplated. ...

It will have been noticed that there is no connexion whatsoever between paragraphs (1) and (2) in the above account, which is the opening of Zik's own *The Assassination Story — True or False?* That was because he was at the time operating well within the given context of time and place. This led him to assume the precognition, in his readers, of the matters under narration; but it was an unfortunate slip in judgement. He himself had created a world-audience, but had not, in this account of the matter, supplied them with all the facts, the connecting links. True, he had written a much better pamphlet: *The Suppression of the Press in British West Africa*, giving a well-narrated story of the events leading up to the banning of his two newspapers during the General Strike. In this he had described how on Saturday, 14 July, at 00.01 a.m., he had 'left Lagos as a "fugitive" from assassination', though not before he had 'contacted the Colonial Office and many other organizations in the United Kingdom and the United States'. But all of this was missing from its proper place in *The Assassination Story*, a circumstance which added to the puzzle and confusion.

It is not necessary to go into the full details here. Suffice it to say, Zik immediately left Lagos in secret and went into hiding at home in Onitsha. But before doing so, he took steps to ensure thorough public information on the alleged plot. He drafted letters, telegrams, and cablegrams to the Secretary of State for the Colonies at the time (Oliver Lyttelton); to the then Chief Secretary to the Government of Nigeria, and to organizations and individuals in Britain and the United States. When the story broke in Lagos, the relations between Zik and his estranged Yoruba contemporaries took a violent turn for the worse; the Press wars between the Zik group on one side and the *Daily Service*, the organ of the N.Y.M., were intensified to a point where the situation became very ugly. Since the nature of the alleged wireless message had suggested that the plot had official backing of some sort, with both Lagos and London possibly implicated, Government circles also greeted the story partly in outrage and partly with contempt. Zik himself reported 'a garbled communiqué published in the *Daily Service* and the *Nigerian Eastern Mail* [by] the Public Relations Officer alleging that I had not submitted any evidence either to the Police or to the Government regarding the alleged attempt to assassinate me. ...'

'Half the world' refused to believe this story; the other half, Zik's followers and adherents, gave it full credence. So much so in the latter case that, with Zik undoubtedly under some of the heaviest fire of his career, the young men rallied round him and, early in 1946, formed the 'Zikist Vanguard' movement, primarily to protect him from his enemies. By April 1946 Zik had recovered his poise. With Richards still the main enemy, he was off on a spectacular tour of the whole country, with his old chief, Herbert Macaulay, heading the N.C.N.C. delegation of enlightenment. For the first time, thousands of Nigerians were confronted personally with national issues, just as Zik had previously involved them in national discussion through his press. Not only that: their active coöperation against British colonialism, in the present form of Sir Arthur Richards and his Constitution, was sought and won by the missioners. But the latter suffered one tragic loss. Old 'H.M.' was stricken down in the north during the tour and died soon afterwards, at eighty-two. The mission had to return to Lagos for the funeral. When it resumed again, Zik was the head of the organization as well as undisputed leader. But he was in fact still to encounter some of his biggest tests and triumphs yet.

Was that, then, the end of the 'Assassination Story' of 1945/6? Not at all. 'The "Assassination Story",' writes Ikeotuonye, 'will remain one of the greatest controversies in the biography of contemporary Nigerians.' He continues:

The greatest argument against it is historical: there is no case of any nationalist assassinated by the British. This apart, the stupidity of the method makes it unlikely. Who would send such a message broadcast into the air? And finally, the conduct and integrity of the wireless operator is not unexceptionable. ...

Perhaps so. Perhaps the wireless operator suffered a 'stroke' or some species of dementia: of hallucinations, or 'visions', or such-like. Perhaps excessive hero-worship turned his head, and led him to mislead Zik and throw the whole country into double uproar – for nothing. But perhaps not. Perhaps the wireless operator was himself the first victim of a colossal international hoax. *Could* it have been a hoax, originating, perhaps from the source of the broadcast itself? Or was it, maybe, a deliberate 'bomb scare'? For isn't it still true that facts are sometimes stranger than fiction? ... However it may have been, these speculations and questions were dramatically restored to life on or about 2 June 1961 – some sixteen years later – when the letter reproduced below was received at State House. *It bore the full* *name and signature of the writer, and an almost pin-pointed Lagos address.** It was dated '1:6:61', and read as follows:

Mrs Flora Azikiwe,
State House,
Lagos

Dear Mrs Azikiwe,

Please forgive me for addressing you in this manner. It is a *private* letter hence I decided to address it so. Looking at the above name you cannot imagine who I am. But remembering the year 1945, when the political cloud of your illustrious husband was thick with a fore-boding of an assassination, and how the ingenuity of a wireless operator saved his life, you will perhaps suspect that the writer of this letter is the man who saved his life. I was then known as M. P. WEST, but later changed the name to the above when the authorities were looking for me – the wireless operator.

Sensing there was trouble after my employer had fled, I quickly took a ship to Freetown Sierra Leone where I hid for six months and finally left for England. . . . I am sure that during this sixteen years, Dr Azikiwe might have been wondering if I am dead or alive; if alive why not come to see him. So this is the reason for writing you, to beg you to make it possible for me to see him if even it is for ten minutes during his leisure any evening; it will afford me the opportunity to shake his hands and congratulate him. I need not add that today I think I am the proudest man alive in Nigeria; – the man who saved the life of our Governor-General. Our political opponents and those who hate him have disbelieved the Assassination story; but what have we lost, we who have endeared ourselves to him, we who love and idolize him. If other political leaders in other parts of the world who were assassinated, [had] received a pre-information of their impending doom and fled as Dr Nnamdi Azikiwe, their own assassination stories would have been false; but for the simple fact that they were not pre-informed and were shot through the heart, their own assassination stories were believed. So whether it was true or false, one fact still remains – DR NNAMDI AZIKIWE is alive, and has led Nigeria to Independence; and that is why I am so proud. Believe me Mrs Azikiwe that I am very proud. I am the man who saved his life. Therefore do me the favour by making it possible for me to see him PRIVATELY even for ten minutes. I am sure

* These, and the writer's service posting after wartime training (the details of which were stated in the letter) are the only matters left out of his text, otherwise here reproduced in full. The reasons for these exclusions are explicit in the letter.

he will love to see me and give me all the encouragement in life. I dare not address a letter to him in his high office as it may be opened by his secretaries, hence I have addressed it to you. You too will have the opportunity of seeing the man who figured so prominently in the Assassination story, and thus saved your husband's life.

LONG LIVE ZIK,

LONG LIVE NIGERIA.

Yours very respectfully,

(With all due respect may I implore you to keep this letter secret.)

Eventually, the ex-wireless operator did visit Zik to confirm the contents of his letter to Mrs Azikiwe.

'The Assassination Story – True or False?' That is the question. And one answer, in the form of the postscript to history thus presented here, will undoubtedly be examined with the open-minded attention it demands.

Part Five

CONQUEST

This is a glorious day. It is an occasion for personal rejoicing because it reminds me that now is the beginning of the end of our political servitude. The announcement that Her Majesty's Government will recognize 1 October 1960, as the date of our national independence is a message of hope. It is also the fulfilment of my life's mission and the realization of the dream of Nigerian patriots.

From fifty-fourth birthday statement, at sea,
16 November 1958

As for me, my stiffest earthly assignment is ended and my major life's work is done. My country is now free, and I have been honoured to be its first indigenous Head of State. What more could one desire in life?

From First Inaugural 16 November 1960

It is only on a very rare occasion that a nation confers on its son the unique privilege of incorporating his name in a written constitution as its first citizen.

From Second Inaugural, 1 October 1963

Chapter 21

Azikiwe, Awolowo, and H. O. Davies

15 November 1960

My dear Zik,

Tomorrow, you will be installed as the Governor-General of the Federation of Nigeria. Since 1941 until some three months ago, you and I have been keen political opponents. It must be emphasized, however, that both of us have differed only on public issues, *never* on personal grounds. Though in your capacity as a politician I had fought you with all my might, yet as a person I have never wished you ill.

*

On behalf of all the leaders and members of the Action Group of Nigeria and of my wife and myself, I congratulate you and Mrs Azikiwe from the bottom of my heart. I do sincerely wish you peace, health, and all the best in your new office. I also fervently pray that it may please Almighty God to so rule and direct your heart that your tenure of office may be a success, a real blessing to our people, and a shining example to those that will follow after you.

Those are the first and last paragraphs of a letter which closed 'with my warmest regards and affectionate good wishes', and was signed by 'Yours Very Sincerely, Obafemi Awolowo'.

In between the opening and closing lines Awolowo had spoken to Azikiwe about his initial objection to the move to make Zik Governor-General – 'purely on political grounds' – and about his subsequent reconciliation to the proposal. This change, said 'Awo', was due to the fact that he had 'kept a careful watch on your utterances since then', and was now satisfied that Zik was 'striving conscientiously to cultivate an attitude of mind' which would enable him to play properly the completely non-partisan role the office would demand. Awolowo then gave his recent opponent and long-time political rival his personal evaluation of that role and its importance for their country and people. He also offered advice on constitutional procedure and conduct, pledging himself and his party not to 'try to peer behind the curtain' in an attempt to ascertain what private advice Zik, as constitutional Head of State, was or was not giving to his Ministers. 'Even your public speeches,' added Awolowo, 'will be regarded as representing the policy and views of the Federal Government, and will be criticized as such, unless they are expressly denounced or disowned by the Prime Minister. . . .'

Thus (for the purposes of this book) closed formally a personal relationship between two remarkable men. It had lasted, as Awolowo said in his letter, from 1941 until 1960 – some twenty years – and had run through the entire spectrum of political passion. It had witnessed warm years of unity of purpose; long periods of bitter mutual denunciation and ethnic warfare; the embrace of 1953 when the N.C.N.C. and Action Group leaders were once more united in political aims, calling for self-government for Nigeria in 1956. It had seen more fights (for instance, over the question: 'Lagos with the West Region, or Lagos as separate, Federal territory?'), more breaks, more compromises, more hostility . . . then back again to the beginning.

The studies and histories of the period are already being written. Every account of the twenty years specified by Awolowo will continue to contain at least a partial record of his contributions to Nigerian nationalism and the struggle for independence. For his role was a stellar one, perhaps second only to that of Zik himself. There had been others, of course (like H. O. Davies), whose parts were not minor either, and who cannot be ignored in the histories. There were, naturally, considerable differences between the personalities and temperaments of these leaders. We are including a brief appraisal of H. O. Davies here, because of 'H.O.D.''s own importance in the story of Nigerian independence, and also for the sharp contrast in political and personal character which he presented with the other two, while playing his part in the common cause along with them, for much of the time. But Zik and 'Awo' were undoubtedly the key men of the period. They were outstanding not merely for their political acts and activities but for the theoretical foundations upon which these were based. To consider Awolowo first and in his own words:

I began the study of law on 1 October 1944, and sat for my Bar Finals as from 3 October 1946. In the two years, I worked much

harder than I ever did before. In addition to working for the two exam-
inations already mentioned, I wrote several articles for the *Daily
Service* and *West Africa* and some for the *West African Review*. For a
while, I did a Fortnightly Bulletin of interest to West African students,
for the British Council. I also wrote *Path to Nigerian Freedom*, a book
published by Faber and Faber and exceedingly favourably received
by both the press and the public.

Awolowo could have added without immodesty that in fact he
created quite a stir with *Path to Nigerian Freedom*. For in those
days people like him were rare. Today books by Africans are
appearing as regularly as their new states, but right up to the
Second World War there was virtually nothing to mention. The
work of J. Africanus Horton, of Sierra Leonean origin (*West
African Countries and Peoples*, 1868); Samuel Ajayi Crowther
(*The Journals*) and Samuel Johnson (*History of the Yorubas*,
1921); the Ghanaians John Mensah Sarbah (*Fanti Customary
Law*, 1896), Casely Hayford (*Gold Coast Native Institutions*, 1903,
and *Ethiopia Unbound*, 1911), and Danquah (*The Akan Doctrine
of God, Akan Laws and Customs*, and *Cases in Akan Law*); and
Edward W. Blyden (*Christianity, Islam and the Negro Race*, 1887,
and *West Africa Before Europe*, 1905), and a few others, were
known to Western scholars and students of the African scene, but
to few others. The African had no status and was widely and
'authoritatively' reported to have no history either. The most he
could expect was the goodness of some missionaries, and the
paternalism of abolitionists, philanthropists, humanists, altruists,
anthropologists, sociologists, and humbuggists. All of these
people wrote about Africans, both for the Africans and for
themselves; but the African could not write about himself
because (a) there was nothing serious to be said that *he* could say,
and (b) the rest of the world just was not ready to hear him say it
anyway.

So Azikiwe's *Liberia in World Politics* and *Renascent Africa*
(1934 and 1937) were an almost unbelievable feat. After them
there was hardly anything more until Zik's young countrymen
turned out their productions in America in the mid-Forties. *Path
to Nigerian Freedom* thus arrived as one of a very few. But more
than that, it was unique in those years for its long-sustained
stand on Nigeria's future constitution and the reasons which just

had to make it a federal one. Alone among Nigerian nationalists, Awolowo had consistently maintained – '. . . for more than eighteen years' before 1951, he tells us (in his 1960 autobiography) – this particularistic notion of political organization for Nigeria, from start to finish. He says he was 'a convinced federalist' long before he wrote it up in *Path to Nigerian Freedom*; indeed it had all started as far back as the early 1930s. By then a still earlier admiration for Gandhi, Nehru, and Subha Bose had developed into an appreciation of their idea of redrawing India's provincial boundaries along linguistic lines, thus assuring each ethnic group a cultural identity even within the framework of political government.

From this point Awolowo developed rapidly into the theorist who insisted in *Path to Nigerian Freedom* that 'Nigeria is a mere geographical expression', that 'all these incompatibilities among the various peoples in the country militate against unification', and that 'a federal Constitution is the only thing suitable for Nigeria'. (The last proposition – repeated in *Awo* almost word for word some fifteen years later – redeems the second, in which the phrase *militate against unification* might otherwise have had alarming implications.) This makes Awolowo a 'cultural pluralist', an unrepentant realist standing upon a set of given facts and rejecting any alternatives that do not agree with the logic of the facts that he sees.

As against all this, Azikiwe's basic idealism stands out the more clearly. Both men were revolutionaries in the nationalist sense, yes; but on the question of the elements involved and of methodology they were profoundly different. Azikiwe's principles were always universalist by nature, as against Awolowo's ever-present particularism. For Awolowo it was ethnic nationalism; for Azikiwe at one time or another a unitary state would have been as acceptable as the reality of federalism came to be – as long as self-government in its complete form was the end-result sought, and as long as unity was preserved. What could be more revealing than the difference between these two statements:

AWOLOWO: As long as every Nigerian in Nigeria is made to feel he is a Nigerian first and a Yoruba or Ibo or Hausa next, each will be justified to poke his nose into the domestic issues of the others. The one thing of common interest to all Nigerians as such and in which the voice of one must be as acceptable as that of any other, is the Constitution of the Central or Federal Government of Nigeria. The constitution of each national group is the sole concern of members of that group. (*Path to Nigerian Freedom*, p. 53)

AZIKIWE: We should emphasize our belief that the idea of *one Nigeria* could become a reality, provided each co-ordinate unit of the Federation was allowed ample scope for local autonomy within a framework whose task would be to weld our diverse peoples into one organic whole by guaranteeing fundamental rights and by establishing common nationality. (*Zik*, C.U.P., 1962, p. 185)

And again:

In this connexion, I should like to place emphasis on the belief of the N.C.N.C. in one Nigeria, especially as it effects me as a candidate for election. We of the N.C.N.C. believe that no region is socially compact enough to reserve to itself the sole right to autonomous existence politically, unless such a region is headed towards Pakistanism. (op. cit., p. 178)

The difference in the two temperaments is also heavily underscored by their attitudes towards economic matters. We have already shown how from the first Azikiwe was always fascinated by economic forms and practices, and how even on the personal level he weighed one system against another, wondering which one would enable him to do most for himself and other people in accordance with his fundamental notions, and also which was better, in itself, for the community. In 1938 he was reminiscing about his first awareness of the 'rapacious tendencies of Capitalism', almost in the same breath as he was contemplating more capitalistic means of acquiring wealth – though having altruistic and philanthropic ends in view:

I thought that after my education ... I would start a business of my own with a view to accumulating wealth until I was in position to have sufficient money to bring my ideas of a new social order into realization.

According to my philosophy of life then, as soon as I had barely sufficient money, I would begin to offer scholarships; later I would start helping those who needed the necessities of life. And ultimately, I would build a University for the education of those who breathe the free air in Africa.

I still believe in the above philosophy and I have begun the spade-work towards its realization. But I am still far from accumulating wealth. . . .

In 1948 Zik declared in Kaduna: 'Competition is the soul of business', and as he drew nearer to the goal of economic security with personal altruism, Zik spoke more and more of the right to private property and entrepreneurial activity, less and less of the need for socialism or nationalization: the well-recorded Ibo individualism and trading propensities would not be suppressed. To Awolowo, on the other hand, the question of a personal choice of economic systems had never even suggested itself. Before proceeding to England in 1944 he had already tried his hand at business, falling naturally into the economic patterns he had met and raising no questions about them except those raised by the whole colonial régime; in *Path to Nigerian Freedom* there had been no economic discussions as such. Awolowo's economics, in short, has been defined only in connexion with the state (public finance and economic planning), especially during his régime as Premier of the West Region. Here, as he tells us in his autobiography, he would not be drawn into the prevailing ten-dency towards socialism, refusing 'to be wedded to any particular ism' and declaring that 'in the circumstances of Nigeria, it would be reckless and [would] lead to economic chaos to adopt a rigid socialist policy, or [on the other hand] drink the cup of undiluted capitalism'. Zik was always incurably eclectic in the examination and choice of economic means or methods; until 1960 Awolowo had not even thought of a choice of systems. A Nigerian welfare-state was his nearest to socio-economic commitment, as fully restated in 1958.

What happened to Awolowo after 1960 is not a matter for this book – except to regret that his talents were for the time being removed from the scene of his long public career. It is pertinent to observe in passing, however, that in 1961 he visited Ghana and embraced Dr Nkrumah and his policies. But the Nkrumah policies include socialism, on which Awo's 1960 views have just been stated; and also Pan-African political unity, which Awo had heatedly attacked in recent times, prior to his 'conversion'. On the other hand, though in 1944 Azikiwe in the *Pilot* called for state socialism, 'because only Socialism can galvanize principles

into action for a cause worth living for ...'; and though in
London in 1949 he said 'we are determined that Nigeria should
now evolve into a fully democratic and Socialist Commonwealth
in order to enable our various nationalities and communities to
own and control the essential means of production and distribution ...', he was by 1955, as Premier of the East Region, facing
his immense task of 'economic rehabilitation' with an entirely
different policy. He was recommending purely *laissez-faire*
principles for his sub-state, except for limited periods of government participation in the form of loans and managerial assistance.

Politically, an intriguing similarity between the two men
stopped short with terminology, where Zik also came to use
'federation', 'regions', 'tribes and nations of Nigeria', 'a real
federal system', and the other terms in this class which had long
been the idea-tools of Awolowo; and where in 1950 Zik again
advocated a 'division of the country along the main ethnic and/or
linguistic groups. ...' But the terms he used here, and at all other
times, were simply a convenience, a medium through which the
'national will' would be ascertained; a democratic process in
which 'a feeling of oneness among the people of Nigeria' would
be cultivated.* For Awolowo, on the other hand, 'every ethnic
group, and there may be as many as a hundred of them, should
in the long run be constituted into a separate state'.

And what about H. O. Davies? The riddle of 'H.O.D.' is
implied in the question why he did not come out 'an ace' with
Zik and Awo; why he has never really been one of the top few in
the power-structure of Nigeria during the last days of the revolution. And the short answer, as he graciously admits himself, is
that he lacks that last bit of drive, of ruthlessness, of the will to
political success, which sets the pure politician apart from the
pure idealist. In short, H. O. Davies is an idealist who was temporarily caught in the game of politics, for which he had the
head but not the stomach. With a powerful, ready-made party
machine Davies could perhaps have been a Stafford Cripps,

* In 1955 Zik delivered a lecture in London to the Nigeria Union entitled 'The Evolution of Federal Government in Nigeria', in which he said
he had supported federalism for Nigeria since 1943, and cited the N.C.N.C.
'model constitution' presented to Mr Creech-Jones in 1947. But this was
really a document for *regional local government* and not the kind of *separate
state* units Awolowo, for his part, meant by federation.

or even a Hugh Gaitskell; a Thomas Jefferson he never could have been, because that takes toughness and resilience beyond the supply under Davies's skin. It implies no derogation to say so, or to add that in a case like this, lack of toughness means the incapability of accepting and using some of the more lethal weapons of politics, if necessary with intent to 'kill' an opponent. The corollary – and a judgement we are obliged to accept in good grace – is of course that one may be afraid of being 'killed' by an opponent too.

This tenderness of feeling often results in sudden and distressing withdrawals from the fray. It is often costly to the individual politician and may lose his party some otherwise clear advantages. In effect this is what happened in 1941 when Davies suddenly left the Nigerian Youth Movement secretaryship and the management of the *Daily Service* to join the Government as an Assistant Marketing Officer. Even today, so to speak, Awolowo winces when he remembers the incident. In his autobiography he gives Davies his full stature and enumerates his merits in terms as glowing as any ever employed by one compeer to describe another; at the same time he recounts the great let-down in this vein:

We of the Ibadan Branch were shocked. When the news that he was going to accept a government appointment first reached us, I dismissed it as fabrication by the enemies of the Movement. It was too much for me to believe that the Davies I knew could be lured into the civil service at that juncture in our nationalist struggles and in the life of our great Movement. He was a remarkable man with many distinguished accomplishments: a brilliant scholar and writer; a fearless and resourceful nationalist; the sole author and genius of the 'Youth Charter'; a dazzling theoretician who propounded one new idea after another with such rapidity that he was later written off by most of his colleagues as an unstable visionary. I went to see him in Lagos, and I was acutely distressed when he confirmed the news.

Elsewhere Awolowo described Davies as 'one of the famous, volcanic nationalist quartet: Mr Ikoli, Oba Samuel Akisanya, H. O. Davies, and Dr Azikiwe', of the turn of the decade of the Thirties. Other chronicles, covering the same period of some twenty years as the Zik-Awolowo political relationship, have also given 'H.O.D.' his deserved place in contemporary Nigerian history. It is unlikely that he would claim more space in it than he has already got. His true role is that of an intellectual and theoretician, and recently he has gone a fair way to prove it. Through a U.S. State Department grant to the Centre for International Affairs at Harvard, Mr Davies published in 1961 his first major work, *Nigeria: The Prospects for Democracy.*

It is a study of the Nigerian nationalist movement and its outcome, with a comparative analysis of analogous situations in other new states like Pakistan, Burma, and Sudan. It also examines Nigeria's economy, pluralism, tribalism, the causes of breakdown in parliamentary democracy, and the role of several political institutions like the military and the civil service. In a detailed and distinguished Foreword, the Prime Minister of Nigeria, Sir Abubakar Tafawa Balewa, puts the capstone to the description of the H. O. Davies phenomenon when he says:

Many non-Nigerian readers of Chief Davies's book will little realize that Chief Davies himself was one of the *dramatis personae* on the Nigerian political stage during the fifteen years or so preceding independence. . . . It is to the credit of Chief Davies that his book is completely devoid of any justification for the part he played or blame for the part played by his political opponents, . . . the charitableness with which he presents unpleasant conclusions is bound to commend his point of view to many a reader.

It is certain that H. O. Davies – still ambitious for a role that has so far thus eluded him – is one of the few Nigerians with political leanings and a political past who can write about his contemporaries in the way he has done and which is so aptly described by Sir Abubakar.

Chapter 22

The Second Ten Years

Once Zik had recovered from the immense strain occasioned by the 'assassination-story' episode, he was ready to move forward again on the momentum of 1943 and after. We must not lose sight of that important year. Its catalogue of events was complex and crucial, not in a final sense but for the prodigious future into which it flowed. A brief recapitulation here of the major events preceding the second ten-year period would perhaps be in place. It could set the scene.

The 1943 West African Press Delegation led by Zik had brought many things to pass, apart from the jolt it had administered to Azikiwe himself. One of the most important had been the arousing of most of the West African student body abroad to a new sense of political urgency. In particular, the West African Students' Union (W.A.S.U.) in London, that spawning ground of nationalists, had joined forces with the Delegation, thus re-asserting W.A.S.U.'s importance. This re-eruption of youth had carried over into 1944, when it both followed Zik and led him into organizing the N.C.N.C.

We are not free, in this connexion, to recount at length but only to refer briefly, again, to the part played by the West African Students' Union at headquarters, three of whose leading members at the time (Messrs Ladipo Solanke, H. O. Davies, and Dr Akinola Maja) had cabled Azikiwe in 1944 in support of the demand for self-government immediately; also to the importance of the contribution of the African Students' Association of the United States and Canada, whose foremost Nigerian members were from 1942 to 1947 making the only major efforts in writing on African self-rule, except for Awolowo, as mentioned before. (They were also trying at the same time to educate Americans to an understanding of Africa, which they did by extensive lecturing and cultural demonstrations. In 1943 they too supported the Press Delegation memorandum.)

In short, 1943 had sharpened Zik's nationalist resolve and re-aligned the youth to his leadership. Directly from these circumstances had come the principal event of the following year, 1944, providing Zik with his second major tactical weapon – the N.C.N.C. – his first having been the newspaper chain. And with the formation of the new party Zik's personal appeal had taken another sweep upward.

The next year, 1945, saw a continuation of this trend. On that and on other grounds, as we shall see forthwith, 1945 also became another historical important year for Nigerian nationalism. It was notable, first, for the N.C.N.C. Constitutional Conference in January; secondly, for the initial publication of the Richards constitutional proposals in March; and thirdly, for the General Strike of June to August, which unexpectedly revealed the existence of new sources of strength and new configurations of power for the nationalists, in particular, for Nnamdi Azikiwe.

Out of the strike episode came that of the 'Assassination Story', a fierce conflagration which at first seemed to have cremated Zik but later turned out merely to have ensured his emergence, phoenix-like, out of other people's ashes and with the new image of a martyr. Furthermore, there was the genesis of the 'Zikist Vanguard' by the N.C.N.C. youth wing, embattled for their hero but also impatient with the suspicion of a developing enervation in the limbs of the older generation. Lastly, at the end of the year, a renewed punitive war against the Zik's Press was executed by the Government of Sir Arthur Richards, in the form of the banning of Zik's reporters from the Legislative Council chamber for alleged misrepresentation of the Governor.

One other occurrence of 1945 must be mentioned briefly here and then held over for later discussion where it has its proper place in the 'second ten-year period'. This was the formation of the Yoruba cultural society, the *Egbe Omo Oduduwa*, by a group of Yoruba students in London, led by Awolowo, who was then studying law in the British capital. Out of this organization, as an answer to the N.C.N.C., later came the Action Group political party.

The one direct carry-over from 1945 into 1946, the last year of the first ten, was the Zikist Movement. The leading founders were Kola Balogun (now an honorary Chief, lawyer, and former

Federal Minister of Information), M. C. K. Ajuluchuku, and Abiola Aloba. Balogun was a Yoruba, Ajuluchuku an Ibo, and Abiola Aloba a member of the Edo group of people in the West Region. The 'Zikists' took a pledge (as reported in the *Pilot* early in March): 'Nevermore shall we allow this evangelist to cry his voice hoarse when millions of youths of Nigeria can take up his whisper and echo it all over the world. . . .' We shall return to the Zikists in due course.

In 1946, Zik founded the African Continental Bank, the story of which is told in two parts in Chapters 18 and 23. During the year the N.C.N.C. toured the country to educate the population in all regions against the Richards Constitution. Mr Herbert Macaulay died during the first part of the tour, which was later resumed, with the party now firmly under Zik's complete command. The main aim of the tour was not only to educate the people to their present political disabilities and the greater threats of the future, but to get them to contribute to a fund to despatch a protest delegation to London. The 1946 N.C.N.C. tour was a significant venture, and formed the closing episode to Zik's first ten-year period in Nigerian nationalism.

The second opened with the completion of the tour, which eventually ended with the collection of £13,000 for the proposed N.C.N.C. Deputation to Britain. A delegation of the party duly left for London, and remained in Britain from June to October 1947.

This was an ill-starred venture in some ways. Led again by Zik, the carefully representative* delegation of seven made a poor job of keeping track of their expenditure, with the result that eventually this proved the greatest challenge they had to face when they returned home. Secondly, the Labour Party's Secretary of State for the Colonies (Mr Arthur Creech-Jones), though he received the deputation cordially enough, quite firmly rejected their demand for a revision of the Richards Constitution before it had been given a fair trial. Mr Creech-Jones urged the N.C.N.C. leaders to go back to Nigeria and give the new Constitution that chance. Again, not all friendly opinion was in favour of the

---

* Dr Azikiwe (Ibo), Prince Adeleke Adedoyin (Ijebu-Yoruba), Dr Abu Bakr Olorun-Nimbe (Ilorin-Yoruba), Mallam Bukar Dipcharima (Hausa), Chief Inyong Essien (Ibibio), Mrs F. Ransome-Kuti (Yoruba), and P. M. Kale (Cameroons).

deputation, even in London. This time the *W.A.S.U. Magazine*,* for instance (though the Union itself met with and helped the delegation in many ways), felt that the time for deputations and petitions to Westminster had passed. In an editorial comment the journal was of the opinion that West Africa was then in such a strong political and moral position that if the leaders would only do the right things at home they would not have to come to London to see Creech-Jones at all; Creech-Jones, rather, would have to go to West Africa to see them! (See Appendix B.)

Nevertheless, on their return to Nigeria in October the delegation was received by a tumultuous crowd, whose enthusiasm amounted almost to a frenzy. They saw in the whole venture another spectacular demonstration of their own feelings about the constitutional conditions of the day. The immediate achievement or otherwise did not matter at the moment. It was later that the troubles began, with the anti-Zik, anti-N.C.N.C. Press furious for an account of finances as well as of results. People like Awolowo were openly contemptuous of Zik and the whole business.

Before the delegation left for London there had been a series of events which had brought Zik and the N.C.N.C. to their highest point of popularity. One of these was the sweeping victory of the party's candidates for the three Lagos seats offered under the new Constitution. The N.C.N.C. had fought the elections mostly on principle but also because no one could afford any losses or disadvantages by default at such a time. Their victory had added greatly to the triumph of the money-raising tour for the deputation to London. When, on the return of the delegates, the people had received them like heroes, a reciprocal gesture of defiance against 'the imperialists' needed to be made. Zik and his newly-elected colleagues (Adedoyin and Olorun-Nimbe) promptly supplied this stimulant by promising to boycott the new Legislative Council.

(This was in fact Azikiwe's first legislative seat at that level – the first of a succession of public posts which ran from Legislative

---

* Then run by an editorial board of which the present writer was a member, and whose chairman was Mr F. Kankam-Boadu, until December 1964 Executive-Director of the Cocoa Producers' Alliance (headquarters in Lagos).

Council member, Minister, Premier of the East Region, President of the Senate, Governor-General, and finally President of the Republic.)

A few months before the departure of the London deputation another famous incident had occurred which had put a sudden though temporary end to the state of active bitterness between the parties. This was when a foreign-owned hotel in Lagos (the Bristol) refused to accommodate the second member of a two-man Colonial Office team, John Keith and Ivor Cummings, because Cummings was partly of African descent. For, almost up to the 1950s, Africans were subjected to this type of discrimination too, in their own countries; many foreigners – including some Indians, Lebanese, Greeks, and assorted others – acted in this way simply as a direct reflection of the political and social attitudes of the colonial masters themselves.

When news of the Cummings incident broke in Lagos the reaction was immediate. The feuding leaders of the Nigerian Youth Movement and the N.C.N.C. covered up their differences at once and organized a United Front Committee to fight for the elimination of racial discrimination in Nigeria, once and for all. A deputation of protest waited on the Governor, following mass meetings and demonstrations of a united will. It was composed of a cross-section of the leadership, old and new: Chief Oluwa, Sir Adeyemo Alakija, Dr Akinola Maja, Dr K. A. Abayomi, Dr Olorun-Nimbe, Nnamdi Azikiwe, Adeleke Adedoyin, W. H. Biney, S. O. Gbadamosi, Ernest Ikoli, H. O. Davies, and J. K. Randle. (Azikiwe, Olorun-Nimbe, and Adedoyin had then just won their victory in the Legislative Council elections, and H. O. Davies had just returned home from his law studies in London.) The conference with the Governor and his Chief Secretary, Attorney-General, and Administrative Secretary resulted in decisions to abate the evil of race discrimination in the country by both short and long-term measures. These results had been hailed by the populace.

Sir Arthur Richards, who had found no favour whatsoever in Nigeria and who had certainly not strained himself trying to please anybody there, was replaced in 1948 by Sir John Macpherson. The changes which came immediately with Sir John made 1948 a notable year in the history of Nigerian nationalism.

And this was in a positive as well as a negative way. Obviously armed with a mandate to strive for an assuagement of the ill-feelings created between government and people during the last régime, Sir John rapidly let it be felt that there would be many changes for the better.

Statements in which the new Governor established the new atmosphere concerned (a) the Richards Constitution and (b) Africanization – or 'Nigerianization', as it came to be particularized and known later. The Richards Constitution, suggested Sir John, could be considered for alteration before the nine years it was originally scheduled to run on its trial course were up: 'Reviewing our timetable', as the Governor put it. Then, completely opposite to the procedure Sir Arthur Richards had adopted, a select committee of the Legislative Council recommended an approach to constitutional change quite unprecedented in Nigeria, or any other African colony. They recommended that the entire population be consulted – from village level to Regional Conferences and from peasants to Emirs and legislators – as to the changes they would like to see made.

For the problem of Nigerianization, Sir John appointed a commission as early as May 1948. Included among its members was one of the most consistently vocal and vehement attackers of colonial appointments policy: Nnamdi Azikiwe, whose 1943 proposals on this matter had been a starting point. The other Nigerian members were: Mr (later Justice) Charles Onyeama, Mrs (later Lady) Onyikan Abayomi, Mallam Muhammadu Ribadu, and Chief Jacob Rosiji Turton. The first statement of the Commission's Report – which was completed in August – was that it was not only necessary to recruit and train Nigerians for higher posts as a way of increasing their share in the conduct of affairs, but that this was an essential condition for the 'development and progress of the country'. The Commission had seen in the situation a 'need for urgent action'. Their Report was the first major 'break-through' for Nigeria's Africanization programme. In the three years following the Report the number of Nigerian Senior Servants had risen from 182 to 628, or more than 200 per cent.

Equally important and dramatic was the great step forward taken in 1948 in the field of education. At the same session of the

Legislative Council which received the reports of the Select Committee on constitutional changes and the Nigerianization Commission, a new Education Ordinance was passed which was revolutionary in its scope and its provisions for the expansion of all levels of schooling. Most of all, 1948 was the year which saw the materialization of the 1945 Elliott Commission on higher education for West Africa: Nigeria, like Ghana, saw the opening of its first university institution, now the University of Ibadan and the senior member of a group of five.*

The fourth major change instituted under Sir John Macpherson in his first year of office was in local government. Here, the traditional system of Native Administration ('N.A.') and its Administrative Officers ('A.O.'s) was largely abandoned for one which accommodated elected membership and opened the door to educated persons for the first time. The process started in the East Region, where a campaign of consultation similar to that proposed for the major constitutional reform itself was carried out. On the subject of this conversion taking place first in the east, the comment of Dr T. O. Elias, Nigeria's Attorney-General and Minister of Justice, is illuminating. Dr Elias made the statement in India in 1956. He said:

> It is noteworthy that the chiefless societies which fared not so well under the Indirect Rule system proved to be the first to adopt the new British patterns of local government. Thus it was that the British system of County Councils, Urban and Rural District Councils, and even the Committee System were first established in the Eastern Region of Nigeria, and have since been copied elsewhere in British Africa. ...
> (*Government and Politics in Africa*, p. 29)

Fortunately for all, Nigeria was just then enjoying a great boom of post-war prosperity, which made it possible for the high cost of these undertakings to be met. Thus the Macpherson régime opened with a series of notable gains and the promise of substantial reforms on all fronts.

That was on the positive side. The negative side of these immediate gains made in the first year of the Macpherson régime was to the disadvantage of the nationalists. The progress already

* The others are: the University of Nigeria at Nsukka, Ahmadu Bello University at Zaria, the University of Ife, and the University of Lagos (which, like Ibadan, has a medical school).

recorded and the expectation of changes in the constitution induced a degree of euphoria in many people. The length of time required for the elaborate schemes of consultation brought everyone to a slow walk. And now that all the leaders were working out their own ideas of reform with an eye on their particular regions, parties, and people, they lost sight of the 'common enemy' and began to look warily at each other. For the reforms in view involved the problems of power in the future, of representation, regional boundaries, the distribution or allocation of revenue for development and services, of minorities, and of other vital questions. All this meant, in short, both regional and tribal rivalries all over again – the rocks upon which the ship of state had often foundered.

For the N.C.N.C. especially this condition of affairs was most unsatisfactory. The protraction of the method, as Coleman remarks, 'weakened' that party, 'whose *raison d'etre* had been agitation for constitutional revision'. Now that it was being done they could not, so to speak, complain, but the manner of the doing left them restless and touchy. They would far rather have had a national constituent assembly, where the fight could have been carried more by the nationalist and less by the traditional elements and the uninformed, which the Macpherson method otherwise made unavoidable. For in spite of the changed aspect and the 'new look' on politics, the main concern of the nationalists was that of the take-over of power, and they were afraid that in the complexities of the new procedures and in the involvement of the masses in these complexities may lie further set-backs, further delay.

At any rate, Zik's aroused youth felt the lull to be intolerable, and the 1948 decision of Azikiwe and his two new fellow-members of the Legislative Council to end their boycott and take the nationalist fight into the Council does not seem to have helped matters much. Here it is necessary to return to the story of the Zikist Vanguard. The movement, founded in 1945–6, as we have seen, spent most of its first three years just being the youth branch or wing of the N.C.N.C., holding up the image of Azikiwe by celebrating his birthday every November, arranging meetings and lectures, and like activities. But in 1948 all this changed suddenly. Although the vast majority of the masses had accepted Zik as *the* leader and champion of Nigeria, partly as a result of the 'assassination story', by the second half of 1948 his popular party, the N.C.N.C., was faltering, for reasons which will be explained presently.

At this point the Zikists decided to adopt a new strategy, to 'get tough'. The get-tough policy in fact got rough very quickly: there was 'A Call for Revolution', a call to 'drag ... down [the Governor] and take over', a violent speech on 'The Age of Positive Action', in which it was declared that Nigeria had 'passed the age of petition, ... of resolution, — [and] of diplomacy'. This, it said, was the 'age of action', 'plain and blunt'.

These declarations were followed by threats of violence and near-violence, not only against the ruling British but also against any Africans who did not see things the way the Zikists did. The ringleaders were finally rounded up by the Government, charged with sedition, and heavily punished with fines and prison sentences. This abated the situation for the time being, but the Zikists were not finished by any means. Before the end of 1948, they had founded the National (and nationalist) Church of Nigeria in Aba, with the late Mbonu Ojike one of its principal supporters and Azikiwe, in effect, its first saint. In 1949 they used the shooting of twenty-one coal-miners dead, and the wounding of many more, at Enugu, as a reason for more violence: at Enugu itself, Calabar, Port Harcourt, and Aba, all eastern towns. In February 1950 the Zikists reached a peak of frenzy, when one of them attempted to assassinate the Chief Secretary to the Government, Mr (later Sir) Hugh Foot (and now Lord Carodon). As a result, two months later the organization was banned, but it reappeared in Port Harcourt under a new name (the Freedom Movement) in the following May. A Lagos branch was also formed, but by the beginning of 1951 the Zikist Vanguard Movement had finally burnt itself out.

The Enugu incident was the result of labour troubles in the mines. The miners had staged a 'go-slow' demonstration in connexion with wage demands. The Government became fearful that some Zikists, or even the miners themselves, might seize the stock of mine explosives, which they therefore ordered to be removed to safety. The miners and their families, on the other hand, thought the mines could be closed down without further ado once the explosives were safely away. An excited and threatening crowd of them, with relatives and sympathizing townfolk, then marched on the mines with sticks and stones and even cutlasses; for their part it was their idea to prevent the removal of the explosives. The European officer in command gave an impulsive, frightened order to his Police to fire, and over seventy of the crowd were shot, twenty-one of them fatally.

This situation again resulted in a temporary closing of ranks by the nationalists, who once more formed an organization of unity, the National Emergency Council. The Council lasted only just under a year and then went the way of its predecessors. Yet by this time H. O. Davies and Obafemi Awolowo, who had both returned to Nigeria as lawyers in 1947, were there to add their strength and ability to nationalism. But the point was that in those days of preparation for constitutional change the call to every man was to the regional and ethnic ramparts.

Not least in Northern Nigeria was this call being heard. North and south had traditionally been two different and distinct countries, kept so by natural differences of religion and culture, as well as by the effects of British policy. But by 1949 modernistic young Hausas who had been south or had returned from England, and northern members of the Nigeria-oriented N.C.N.C., were forcing the old traditionalists there to look at their position for the first time from a wider angle of view. The Northern Peoples' Congress was founded in December 1949; its break-away, radical but smaller competitor, the Northern Elements' Progressive Union (N.E.P.U.), in 1950. Armed with this comparatively minuscule degree of experience or orientation, the north was ready by 1951 to challenge the south for political rights.

That year (1951) saw the replacement of the Richards Constitution by the Macpherson. The Richards Constitution had introduced regionalism into Nigeria, in a way which the previous Governor, Sir Bernard Bourdillon, said would tend to unify the country and which, to the contrary, Okoi Arikpo* (a former Federal minister) described later as the first step to a 'fragmentation' process 'based on the belief that a unitary and highly centralized constitution was unsuited to the size and diversity of Nigeria'. The Macpherson Constitution went one step further in

* Mr Arikpo was President of WASU during the late 1940s.

regionalization and introduced for the first time political units with distributed legislative and financial powers, representation in a central legislature as regional units, separate ministries, and other provisions of a federalistic kind.

But this, the newest, constitution proved unworkable too. In just one year of its operation all its worst features had been established, and regional, party, and tribal differences and rivalries were again to the fore. These had been building up all along since 1947 and the N.C.N.C. deputation to London, in spite of the periodic episodes of calm or of unified action during national emergencies. The year 1948, for instance, had seen a violent eruption with the local founding of the Yoruba *Egbe Omo Oduduwa*, and between then and 1951 there was constant provocation among the major parties and ethnic groups, as first one and then the other tried to capture the initiative or gain advantage for itself.

During this period Azikiwe used every strategy and tactic he could devise in the contest for supremacy. He deliberately chose to come as close as he and the N.C.N.C. ever did to Awolowo and his Yoruba following in advocating a federal structure, then repudiated that position when he said it seemed to him that others wanted to use federalism to break up the country and take what they could get out of it for themselves and those they represented; he objected to the three-way division of Nigeria as being the way of 'balkanization', and again advocated, rather, a division along major ethnic lines, which in fact meant as many as eight or ten different areas; ... and so on. It was during these years that the 'tribalist' arguments and accusations were most vehement, and Zik was charged again and again by his Yoruba critics with being the most pronounced tribalist of them all. This aspect got worse with the coming of Awolowo and the Action Group.

The Action Group, the political party that finally emerged from the *Egbe Omo*, was launched in March 1951. It was, naturally, composed mostly of Yorubas, and aimed at wresting power in the Western Region, which it did in the election of that year. Lagos, which Awolowo distrusted and which was Azikiwe's political and financial stronghold, was ignored by the Action Group at first. Subsequently, however, Zik was to be dislodged there and to return to the east, where he eventually became

Premier and where some of the most dramatic events yet of his eventful life were to take place.

Lagos had been incorporated into the Western Region under the 1951 Constitution. The Western House of Assembly was by these provisions the electoral college for Western members of the Central Legislature. Since Awolowo's Action Group defeated the N.C.N.C. in the election, their majority in the Western House deliberately froze out Azikiwe – a member for Lagos – from the centre; and that was how Zik turned to the east in 1953, and to a fateful career there. Some students of this history indeed consider not only that the return to the east was a turning point in Azikiwe's public life, but that he was thus forced out of his basic universalist philosophy of unity and coherence of the whole into the acceptance of a fragmentary, piecemeal polity.

Zik was the outstanding individual most affected personally by the shortcomings of the Macpherson Constitution, and his was thus the case that proved most dramatically some of the greatest absurdities of an instrument the people had themselves, this time, helped to fashion.

By its effect on Azikiwe in the west, the constitution had excluded from the centres of power (the Central House and the first Council of Ministers) the country's foremost politician and busiest planner. As somewhat of a compensation, the transfer gave Zik his first opportunity to display his powers to the full elsewhere: first as Minister of Local Government, and then as Premier, of the East Region. Nevertheless the case against the Macpherson Constitution remained a valid one, and not only in connexion with Zik: the said Council of Ministers at the Centre itself was weak, other leaders found themselves with ineffective powers or none at all, and frustration piled upon frustration.

During these years, and before Zik left Lagos and the Western Region to go to the east, it became really possible for his enemies and critics to accuse him of those traits of character which formed the other side of the coin in him. His impatience and *hauteur* with people and circumstances increased enormously. It became next to impossible to approach him, and even relatives and friends were turned away at the gates of his Yaba residence, or kept waiting indefinitely. His stand on the problem of the Zikists was vacillating

– some said opportunistic; indeed the most radical would date 'Zik's failure as a man', as they put it, from this episode. His handling of subordinates, especially ambitious young ones like Nduka Eze (of both the Zikists and the Nigerian Labour Congress), made many think of Azikiwe as a ruthless Napoleon who could brook neither competition nor failure; and Awolowo, of all Zik's political antagonists the most emphatic, devotes many, many pages in his autobiography to attacks on the other man's actions and motivations during the second ten-year period.

These conflicts came to a head within the N.C.N.C. itself, in the first major clash between Azikiwe and his party executive. When Zik was defeated in the Western House of Assembly for a seat at the centre, it was due partly to indiscipline in the party. There were three N.C.N.C. candidates for two House of Representative seats: Azikiwe and his two fellow-candidates, Adedoyin and Dr Olorun-Nimbe. In spite of moral and political pressure on them from all sides, each of Zik's junior party colleagues refused to step down for his chief in the candidature. The result was that Zik's enemies in the Western Assembly had him at their mercy and voted in Adedoyin and Olorun-Nimbe, leaving Zik out of the Central Government. It was clearly a tribally biased episode, demonstrating how a constitution could be frustrated and even aborted by extraneous and illegitimate factors.

Thus Azikiwe was left in the Western Regional House as the leader of a confused and demoralized opposition, [reports Kalu Ezera in *Constitutional Developments in Nigeria*]. Consequently, the leadership of the N.C.N.C. party, both at the centre and in the Eastern regional government, fell into the hands of a new set of men.

Four of these 'new men' became the Eastern Region representatives on the Council of Ministers at the centre: A. C. Nwapa, Eni Njoku, Okoi Arikpo, and the Cameroonian Dr Endeley. In the Eastern Region itself the party parliamentary leadership passed into the hands of the longtime philosopher-nationalist, Eyo Ita; he was then Deputy National President of the N.C.N.C. When Zik and his supporters tried to get what they considered to be an altogether anomalous position changed, there was resistance on the part of the N.C.N.C. central ministers, whose voice carried the day at a party conference held in Port Harcourt late in 1952. The four central ministers won the vote to give the Macpherson Constitution a trial.

Since the controversy in the party leadership got worse instead of better after this conference it was reassembled at Jos (in the north) in December. The central ministers refused to attend the Jos meeting and were expelled from the party. (Dr Endeley was not affected in this.) It soon became obvious that the ministers in the Eastern Assembly were in sympathy with their central colleagues, and when Zik and the loyalists of the National Executive tried to discipline them by an attempted 'reshuffle' of their posts there was a second rebellion in the hierarchy. The quarrel raged across the east, with serious reverberations in the other regions, throughout the first four months of 1953, and was not abated until the dissolution of the Assembly in early May.

Meanwhile, the dissident ministers of both the centre and the region had decided to form a new party, which they did in February. It was called the National Independence Party (N.I.P.) and was headed by Eyo Ita, with Jaja Wachuku and Dr Udo Udoma (a lawyer and now Chief Justice of Uganda, in East Africa) supporting the three expelled central ministers. The N.I.P. thus joined another small oppositional party, the United National Party, led by a dissident from the N.C.N.C. since 1951, Alvan Ikoku. At the new elections in December 1953 these two parties between them managed to win twelve seats, against the N.C.N.C.'s overwhelming majority of sixty-six to eighteen. By now Zik had left the west and come to his own home region. He went into the new Assembly and became Minister of Local Government as well as Leader of the House. With new provisions introduced into the Constitution in 1954 he became Premier of Eastern Nigeria.

The eastern crisis revealed many facets of the complex political and social phenomenon in the southern area of the country. The unworkability of the Macpherson Constitution was one: Ezera points out how even a dissolution of the Eastern Regional Assembly had been impossible during the crisis except by an Amendment decree to the Royal Instrument. Another was the indiscipline among the rank and file of the N.C.N.C., which came as an outstanding revelation. At British Labour Party conferences and conventions, as well as at the phenomenal American national party Nomination Conventions, there are often sectional revolts among the delegates, deadlocks, and upsets to planned programmes, through unexpected or even arbitrary behaviour. However, the pointed refusal to cooperate with the N.C.N.C. party leader, especially in an instance involving a parliamentary seat; and the wholesale refusal of ministers to agree with party policy, holding on to their seats in spite of 'dismissals' and 'expulsions' – these and the other types of non-cooperation displayed are hardly to be encountered in parliamentary experience among people who have accepted this form of political organization.

The intolerable position into which Nnamdi Azikiwe was put by this episode also served to demonstrate something else: Zik's strength in a crisis. He had been in a most exposed and dangerous position, where one false step – a show of weakness, for instance – could have toppled him from the leadership, perhaps permanently. In this, as in two other instances during the following five years, when the odds were stacked high against him, bold, aggressive action alone saved Zik from imminent disaster. The other two cases – another party crisis of leadership in 1958 and the Bank Inquiry – are narrated below. In the present case Zik made powerful statements of indictment and challenge against his rebellious juniors, exercised some of the arbitrary powers the loose N.C.N.C. organizational system conferred on him, and won the fight. A passage in a presidential address of Zik's, delivered in 1957 and cited by Post in *The Nigerian Federal Election of 1959*, is illustrative of the tough line adopted by Zik on these occasions:

...drastic control of the N.C.N.C., even in a totalitarian manner, has become necessary. The situation in our rank and file is to be likened to the Great Plague in London, which required a Great Fire to purify it.

The Macpherson Constitution had received its deathblow, however, in the House of Representatives on 1 April 1953, during the deadlock in the east. On that day Anthony Enahoro, a backbench Action Group member (now in prison on a conspiracy conviction), tabled a private member's motion for Nigerian Independence in 1956. The move precipitated an immediate crisis.

First of all, the Council of Ministers had been persuaded not to participate in the debate on the motion. But the four Action Group ministers said they would resign their seats rather than remain quiet on a matter like this. Then the Sardauna of Sokoto, speaking for the north proposed an amendment to the motion by changing 1956 to 'as soon as practicable'.

Awolowo thereupon delivered a bitter attack on the British, blaming them for making dupes out of the northerners. He was followed by an N.C.N.C. speaker, who also attacked British imperialism for what had just happened. After this both the Action Group and N.C.N.C. members walked out of the House, leaving only the N.P.C. and special members still in their places. Zik – who was watching the proceedings as a spectator – embraced Awolowo outside the House on the adjournment, and the two parties made common cause, temporarily, while practically all of Lagos booed and hissed and jeered at the northern members. The four Action Group ministers duly resigned their seats on the Council of Ministers, and business in that body was thus brought to a standstill.

Up in the north, meanwhile, the leaders of the N.P.C. were taking steps to make a recurrence of their terrible Lagos experience impossible. In May they passed in the Northern House of Assembly an 'Eight-Point Programme' whose effect would have been virtual secession of the north from the south. What hastened this break-away attempt was in the form of a sequel to the 1956 Self-Government motion and the ill-use of the northern delegates by the southerners of Lagos. The sequel to that was a tour of the north by an Action Group party led by S. L. Akintola, when bad feeling was at its height among the Hausas over the treatment to which their leaders had been subjected.

The tour touched off rioting at Kano – the famous walled city of the north – in which over thirty people died and scores were wounded. With that and the troubles in the east, the stand-still at the centre, and threats of secession from the north, the British Government decided it was time to review a constitution chiefly on whose account so much was going wrong. It was thus that the momentous Constitutional Conference of 1953 was scheduled for the middle of the year. In consultation with the Governor, the three regional party leaders (the Sardauna, Azikiwe, and Awolowo) agreed to the following terms of reference for the Conference:

1. The defects of the Macpherson Constitution.
2. Remedies for same.
3. Method of effecting such remedies.
4. The unanswered question of self-government in 1956.

The last item was included on the insistence of Awolowo and Azikiwe, who had not given up the idea in spite of the troubles and tragedies it had caused.

The Conference eventually agreed to: (1) the principle of a federal union for Nigeria, (2) residual powers being vested in the regions instead of the Central Government, (3) the drawing up of lists of subjects for which the regions or the centre shall have competence, provided that in case of conflict the federal law would be the superior law, (4) regional ministers being in full control over their portfolios and personnel, and regional Premiers over their cabinets, (5) the granting, in 1956, of internal self-government to any regions that would want it, (6) a review of these provisions not later than August 1956.

There were other important matters; on some of them the Conference was split. The delegates of the National Independence Party from the east, for intance, walked out on the deliberations, because they disagreed utterly with the degree of power to be allowed the regional governments; the N.C.N.C. and the Action Group, despite an alliance between them on a number of points, disagreed over the problem of the position of Lagos – the capital – in the federal-regional relationship; and so on. A year later, further changes were added to the scheme of 1953, and elections were held late in 1954 for the implementation of the provisions of the '1953/54 Constitution', which the Conference results amounted to.

In the Eastern Assembly Azikiwe became the Premier under the new arrangements. In 1955 his government and the Lieutenant-Governor of the Region, Sir Clement Pleass, came into a head-on collision over a civil service matter involving some expatriate posts. Zik, in the pursuit of new Nigerianization policies being put into operation in the country, especially in the southern regions, attempted to void a number of expatriate posts which he said were vacant or being only temporarily filled. The idea was that these posts should not be provided for in the new estimates for the coming fiscal year, so that they could be abolished then. Sir Clement saw the matter in an entirely different light, and, when repeatedly denied his request for the unprovided funds, used his reserve powers to certify supplementary estimates for the purpose. In Parliament in London, the Colonial Secretary, Mr Lennox-Boyd, supported the Lieutenant-Governor's action and in addition charged Azikiwe with breaking faith over a mutual agreement about overseas staff. To which Zik replied in kind, charging the Secretary of State, in turn, with 'adding insult to injury' by a false accusation. He angrily added that the Colonial Office was 'impervious to reason when it comes to matters affecting European civil servants'.

Meanwhile, in Lagos the old Governor-General, Sir John Macpherson, had gone away (in 1955) and Nigeria's last new colonial Governor, Sir James Robertson, had come in to take his place. Sir James proved to be the best type for the job. A warm Scotsman, practical, businesslike, and genial, he saw Nigeria through the last phase with as much success as any man could have had in the circumstances. Moreover, in the year following his assumption of office the country went through the all-engulfing welcome to Queen Elizabeth II, an event which made the world conscious of Nigeria and Nigeria conscious of itself as a unit of it.

After the excitement of the visit was over, everyone returned home to strengthen their region and prepare for the next stage. In the east Azikiwe called an important 'Summit Conference' for the purpose of organizing the East Region's manifesto for the expected London Constitutional Conference in 1956. This was in July, but before the 'Summit Conference' had met the first skirmishes had already taken place in connexion with allegations against Zik by a former Eastern Regional Government Chief Whip, E. O. Eyo. Mr Eyo made the charge that public funds of the region had been improperly channelled into the African Continental Bank, in which Dr Azikiwe still held personal financial interests. He was demanding a commission of inquiry into the matters forming the subject of his allegations.

In August, following the conclusion of the Eastern Summit

meeting, the Eyo-Azikiwe clash was resumed. And when a public inquiry became inevitable it became also inevitable that all national constitutional business should be postponed until the regional trouble had been disposed of and the position of the key figure in Nigerian independence politics clarified. The next chapter offers the facts of the case of the bank inquiry.

Chapter 23

The Second Trial

The 1956 case of the Tribunal of Inquiry into allegations reflecting on the 'official conduct' of the Premier of the Eastern Region of Nigeria, and of certain other ministers and public officers of the Region, was marked by several outstanding features. Principal among these were: (a) the politics and 'personalism' which surrounded the whole affair; (b) the vigorous offensive launched by Zik to shake the case of the opposition, as soon as the Tribunal was mooted; (c) the nature of the findings, and (d) the reactions of Zik's public – perhaps the most remarkable of the four – to the Report of the Tribunal. The purpose of this chapter is to summarize the facts along these lines, chiefly through the use of the documentary evidence.

The first thing to note is that the opening shots in this battle were fired by *politicians* at *persons*. Mr Effiong O. Eyo, who made the allegations against Zik, was a high party-man between whom and the party hierarchy trouble had arisen. He was widely held to have been the victim of a political vendetta in his loss of both face and place, though he had actually put in a resignation himself. In proof of all this, Eyo, in the words of the Tribunal Report, 'admitted antagonism between himself and Dr Azikiwe and his late colleagues in the N.C.N.C. ..., and ..., that he was prepared to believe anything bad about Dr Azikiwe, however flimsy the evidence'. In turn Zik charged Eyo with the crime of indulging in the 'pastime of character assassination', in the preliminary statement he made in the Regional Assembly under the title 'Character Assassination'.

This was in Nigeria. In London the then Secretary of State for the Colonies, Alan Lennox-Boyd, was not only questioned about a hurried amendment to the Nigerian Constitution made solely in order to give him the power to appoint the Foster-Sutton Tribunal; he also had to listen to the late Aneurin Bevan (*Hansard*, 25 July 1956, columns 420–424) charge him with racial bias.

Mr Bevan said the Secretary was actively interested in allegations made against the 'Prime Minister of Eastern Nigeria', 'who is black', whereas the Right Honourable Gentleman was 'so complacent' about charges brought in the same House against the Chief Justice of Seychelles the very next day. 'It is obvious from the cries of Hon. Members opposite,' cried Bevan himself, 'that so long as corruption is charged against the white man it is all right. Can we have an answer?'

The allegations made by Mr Eyo were, in sum, 'abuse of office and corruption in connexion with the deposit and investment of public monies of the Eastern Region in the African Continental Bank in which Dr Azikiwe had a substantial pecuniary interest'. The cash and securities involved in these transactions amounted to nearly two million pounds sterling.

In answer to and in challenge of these allegations, Zik issued or made four separate statements: the 'Character Assassination' speech in the Eastern House of Assembly on 26 June 1956; a 'Report on Banking and Finance in Eastern Nigeria', a statement on 'Banking Monopoly in Nigeria', and a statement on the 'Commission of Inquiry into [the] African Continental Bank'. In addition, Zik sued Eyo, claiming damages of £25,000 or more for libel. This was based on the correspondence which passed between Eyo and the Governor, Sir Clement Pleass, on the subject of Eyo's motion calling for the inquiry. (Since Sir Clement and Zik were never the best of friends (Chapter 22), this case, incidentally, sealed their enmity.)

In the 'Report on Banking and Finance in Eastern Nigeria' Zik set out the East Region Government's policy on this sector of its economic programme, in order to show how the African Continental Bank had come to be favoured in the depositing and investing of the Government funds under question. The four principles of the policy, he said, were:

1. To discourage a banking monopoly.

2. To liberalize credit facilities for Nigerian business entreprenuers.

3. To encourage indigenous banking.

4. To plan for the eventual establishment of a State Bank.

In respect of (1) and (2) he attacked heavily the expatriate bank which he singled out as most guilty of practices unfavourable to the country and its native businessmen. He then gave the facts and circumstances of the transactions forming the subject of the call for an inquiry, seeking to square them with the policy enunciated above and with his own role and conduct as the Premier who was also the founder of the Continental Bank.

In 'Banking Monopoly in Nigeria' Dr Azikiwe went into a minutely documented history of banking practice in Nigeria, and showed how African efforts in this field of business had always been ruthlessly aborted by foreign firms. He named many men in British public life who had immense holdings in banks and other large financial companies with interests in Africa, which shares they had not relinquished upon accepting office, though they had relinquished their many directorships, as required by official practice. 'Mr Speaker,' he declared at one point, 'this is the crux of the palaver between us and the Colonial Secretary who, as I have abundantly shown, is not alien either to share-holding operations or to directorates of industries keenly interested in the Nigerian market.' At another point he cried: 'This Government is not prepared to abdicate the powers vested in Nigerian Ministers of this Region by the Constitution, in respect of economic and financial matters, no matter how many Orders in Council the Colonial Secretary promulgates ... to have retrospective effect. This Government is determined to root out monopoly in banking from this Region. ...'

In the statement on the Commission of Inquiry itself Zik's principal targets were the Order in Council and the basis of choice of the personnel of the Tribunal. Of the first he said: 'Everybody knows that an Order in Council is an extra-legal device used to defeat the basic institutions of democratic government.' As for the Tribunal members, it was his 'humble submission [to Mr Speaker] that it would be most embarrassing to both Sir Stafford Foster-Sutton and Sir Maxime de Cormarmond to serve on this Commission of Inquiry, in view of the fact that they are members of the Federal Supreme Court of Appeal. I have in mind,' Zik continued, 'the various libel suits which I have filed against Mr Eyo. What if any of the parties to the dispute decided to appeal to the Federal Supreme Court? ...' Zik then made public a letter written to a third party in 1954 by Mr Justice Jibowu (since deceased), in which the judge had attacked Azikiwe and the N.C.N.C., at the same time praising Awolowo, the Action Group, and the Yoruba cause in general. This exposure was to support Zik's contention that politics had cast such a spell around the country that even 'persons who are expected, like Caesar's wife, to be above board' could go to great lengths 'to demonstrate their prejudice against Nigerian nationalists'.

The Tribunal opened the hearings on 3 September 1956. Its Report was presented on 7 January 1957. The principal findings were cited and quoted around the world next day, with Zik's enemies at home emphasizing the passages which said that his conduct in the matter had 'fallen short of the expectations of honest, reasonable people', and that he had been 'attracted by the financial power his interest in the Bank gave him'. The Report also blamed in similar terms some of the other Ministers and high party officials involved. In particular, they found it un-accountable that the then Minister of Finance, Mazi Mbonu Ojike (who died tragically before the end of the hearings) should have passed the final papers for the transfer of funds to the Continental Bank against departmental advice and without con-sultation with the whole Cabinet.

To Zik's friends, however, the position was not at all the way the Tribunal saw it, except where the Report granted that Zik's 'primary motive was to make available an indigenous bank with the object of liberalizing credit for the people of this country'. As far as this section of the population was concerned, that was the only relevant issue; and it was their quite unshakeable belief not only that Zik wanted to liberalize credit for his countrymen, but, equally important, that he had been out solely to break that banking monopoly he had complained so bitterly about, that hold the white man had over the Nigerian's economic life. All other issues, to them, were utterly irrelevant, even silly. So, during the inquiry they came in their thousands 'to show their solidarity with their hero', and greeted him repeatedly with that mystic, awe-inspiring crescendo: *Z-e-e-e-e-e-k !* And at the general election which followed the inquiry and which was in effect a test of his standing with the Eastern electorate, Azikiwe and the N.C.N.C. were returned to power with a large majority.

Chapter 24

The Last Phase

The drama and, in part, the tragedy of the Foster-Sutton tribunal was over: Zik was back in power by the decree of his people; the east was now able to accept its share of responsibility in the negotiations.... Nigeria, that is to say, was at last ready to do the last mile on her road to independence.

Immediately after the Report of the Commission was out, Azikiwe, on the advice of the N.C.N.C. National Executive, had turned over to the East Region Government all his rights and interests in the African Continental Bank. That done, the House of Assembly was dissolved by the decision of himself as Premier, and the date of 16 March set for new elections. It was the success of the N.C.N.C. at the polls that restored Zik's right to lead his region and his party at the new talks for finalizing the intricate arrangements and agreements for independence.

From this point on excitement succeeded excitement until the day of independence itself. The resumed conference was scheduled to take place in London beginning in May. Meanwhile, all leaders of all parties realized that they were now facing their final preparatory task, and that the most urgent need of the moment was a united front to present to the British Government on the question of a definite date. There were grounds for hoping that unity would not be too difficult of achievement. The hopes were based on an event going back to the year before: the unexpected and gratefully hailed announcement from the north in May 1956 that the Northern Peoples' Congress was now prepared to demand internal self-government in 1959 for the Region. It was the first time the Sardauna and the then Mallam Abubakar Tafawa Balewa had broken the deadlock of their previous stand on 'self-government as soon as practicable'.

This welcome move had struck immediate responses in the south. Awolowo stated that his party still thought 1956 a suitable year for independence but did not want to 'coerce the North' on the issue. Zik's response was more masterly. He proposed a compromise: let the two southern regions have self-government in that year (1956), and the whole country be granted its independence in 1959. He added that he had adopted this new date *because it suited the north better than the previous one proposed by the south.* In this way Zik obviously sought to weaken the northerners still further – to jump into the breach created at the northern stronghold by the 'besieged' themselves.

What followed less than a year later in the Federal House of Representatives proved that Zik had judged the position quite correctly and had made the best single strategic move in this chess game for unanimity. On 26 March Chief S. L. Akintola of the Action Group tabled in the House a motion to instruct the delegates to the forthcoming conference in London that they should press for self-government for the Federation in 1957 – a concession on the party's previous stand. Promptly upon this, Jaja Wachuku of the N.C.N.C. (Foreign Minister of the Federation since Independence) rose to offer an amendment: 1959 *in place of* 1957 – one step further, and the date suggested by Zik. Akintola accepted the amendment at once, because of the need for the 'utmost spirit of unanimity' in the prevailing circumstances.

The cheers had hardly died down before the House was given real cause for joy. For up rose Alhaji Abubakar Tafawa Balewa who, speaking for the Northern Peoples' Congress, put it in diplomacy's most impeccable phraseology: he could see 'no reason why we of the Congress should refuse to allow the House of Representatives the opportunity to instruct their political delegates to press for the fixing of a date for Nigerian Independence in 1959'. After the prolonged applause the motion was passed unanimously, and at last the representatives of the whole country were united on what to do with their old bone of contention. The next step forward was the drafting of a memorandum putting their unanimous demand before the British Government, which they agreed to submit at the beginning of the London Conference in May.

The Constitutional Conference of 1957 duly opened at the time and place scheduled. The British Government was represented by Alan Lennox-Boyd, Secretary of State for the Colonies

(Chairman), and his advisers and experts. Nigeria was represented by the Sardauna and Balewa, Zik, Awolowo, and the Leader of Government Business in Southern Cameroons; with them were a large cadre of ministers and advisers.

Apart from the spectacle such a gathering provides, with the movement and colour and busy activity all around, the 1957 Conference did not produce much drama. First, the unanimity of the leaders on the question of the independence date cancelled out any fights in that quarter among themselves. Next, this feeling of common aim had also encouraged the leaders to prepare themselves fairly thoroughly for the challenges of the round-table. True, their main demand – Independence in 1959 – was turned down eventually by the British Government, acting through Lennox-Boyd and his advisers. But there was too much at stake, the stages of negotiation were too far advanced, and the Nigerians were by then too anxious about independence, for anyone to have risked a collapse at this point.

So when the Secretary of State said he could not possibly accede to the request in 1959, because there were, in effect, too many unknown elements in the situation and too much preparation still undone, the delegates could only express their deep disappointment and reserve their 'right to pursue the issue further with a view to impressing upon Her Majesty's Government the necessity for granting independence to the Federation of Nigeria not later than 2 April 1960'.

Those were the words of Alhaji Ahmadu Bello, the Sardauna of Sokoto, who spoke for his fellow-Premiers, the Cameroons Leader of Government business, and the rest of the Nigerian delegation. With that the Conference returned to other matters, and their decisions on the main problems can be summarized briefly. First, it was agreed that the West and East Regions should be formally recognized as fully self-governing, effective from the coming August, and that the North Region should be autonomous in 1959. Secondly, the post of Federal Prime Minister was to be created forthwith. Thirdly, there would be a bicameral legislature at the federal centre, consisting of a Senate and a new House of Representatives. Fourthly, federal elections would have to be held before independence, following the dissolution of the present House.

The conference also decided to appoint commissions to deal with the technical problems of (a) minorities and the question of creating or not creating new states for them; (b) revenue allocation among the regions, and (c) the delimitation of new federal constituencies. A committee of the conference on electoral law, which had met earlier in London, was to complete its work, sitting in Lagos.

The Constitutional Conference of 1957 met again in Lagos in September 1958, to consider the results of the work of their commissions. The Minorities Commission's report created the greatest contest at this meeting. The Commission was against the creation of new states before independence, because they said you just can't draw lines through people; strong local feelings, they felt, were no argument against the encouragement of unity in the whole country. According to K. W. J. Post, in his 1963 book: *The Nigerian Federal Election of 1959*:

These views were not held by all the delegates to the 1959 conference. In particular the Action Group, which had sought allies among the parties representing the minority groups, strongly advocated the creation of new states. The states which the Action Group wanted to create were the 'Mid-West' State in the West, the 'Middle Belt' State in the North, and the 'Calabar-Ogoja-Rivers' State in the East.

But the other major parties agreed with the Willink Commission in this matter: that it would be difficult and undesirable to create new states before independence; a postponement of that was desirable, or else the postponement of independence until the new states had been carved out and made viable. Faced with the choice of outraging the whole country by postponing independence, or offending the minority peoples by withdrawing his demands, Awolowo chose the less of two evils. This was in fact the only choice possible in the circumstances, although in his autobiography Awolowo makes the Secretary of State bear the responsibility for creating the either-or situation in the first place. (*Awo*, pages 194–5. Zik, for different reasons, also had his reservations about the chairman's handling of the delegations.)

Soon after the final end of the 1957/8 Conference the decisions were put into operation. Alhaji Abubakar was appointed Prime Minister of the Federation, and he in turn formed a 'National Government' of twelve ministers comprising all three major parties. The three Regional Premiers – the Sardauna, Nnamdi Azikiwe, and Obafemi Awolowo – returned to their own assemblies to put through their regional programmes and get ready for independence when it should come; this everyone now hoped would be in 1960 at the latest.

Back in the east, Azikiwe was soon facing another intra-party revolt. K. O. Mbadiwe and Kola Balogun, long-time stalwarts of Zik, became disaffected – some said because of the complications of the Foster-Sutton bank inquiry episode and the initial failure of the Eastern Region's free-education scheme. Balogun was then the General-Secretary of the N.C.N.C. and Mbadiwe the second Vice-President. In the in-fighting that developed, the two rebels (who were Federal Ministers at the time) tried to unseat their party chief, but Zik was able, with support he won from the party, to have them expelled instead and replaced in their offices. (Balogun's General Secretaryship was taken by F. S. McEwen, who later become the influential N.C.N.C. President of the Lagos Municipal Council and, later still, also Managing Director of the African Continental Bank.)

Zik's victory in this case was complete and overwhelming. The rebel ministers, with some lesser parliamentarians, with (surprisingly) H. O. Davies, and others, eventually formed their own new party, the Democratic Party of Nigeria and the Cameroons. But they failed to make any impression on the electorate in the 1959 elections and collapsed. Eventually, both Mbadiwe and Balogun were re-admitted into the N.C.N.C.

In 1959 Zik bade farewell to the east and returned to Lagos; here he went into the new Upper Chamber (the Senate) as one of the twelve members from the Eastern Region; he became President of the Chamber. His farewell address was delivered on 17 December 1959, at Premier's Lodge, Enugu, the eastern capital, where Zik recalled his career and introduced his successor, Dr M. I. Okpara.

In his five years as Premier Zik had pushed the East Region into development as fast as it was physically possible to do so. He had brought in a large measure of educational advancement at the primary and secondary level, and had successfully carried through one of his oldest and dearest wishes, the establishment of the University of Nigeria at Nsukka. The establishment of the

Regional Central Library at Enugu by the Eastern Government in conjunction with U.N.E.S.C.O. was also a project largely due to Zik's enterprise and drive. He had personally made many visits to Europe, Britain, and the New World introducing his country and seeking economic advantages for the east. In this connexion it was notable that his government had raised the level of Treasury funds from £4 million to £18½ million during Zik's tenure.

My five years of legislative activities in this Region [he said] have been very instructive to me and I count them among the best years of my life.

Chapter 25

Governor-General or Prime Minister?

Azikiwe's critics accused him of being power-mad, of being intolerant of any political competition, of shunning any political movement unless he could dominate it, and of having a consuming passion to be Nigeria's first president. ...

This finding is stated on page 342 of James Coleman's *Nigeria*. To the extent that it connected Azikiwe and the first Presidency of Nigeria at all it was prophetic, either on the part of the able author himself or on that of 'Azikiwe's critics'; nor would it matter as to how either side came by the notion. Later observers were of the same opinion (that Zik wanted to go on to be first President) when speaking to the present biographer. But this was between 1962 and 1963, when Zik had already been Governor-General for more than two years. It was easier to speculate on this subject by then: after all, it could only have been one way or the other. In 1955, however, there was no either-or choice of prophecy, yet that was when Coleman, or Zik's critics, made their 'prediction'.

The fact that this accusation of a consuming ambition to be first President of a probable Republic of Nigeria, at some time in the future, has been 'proved' against Dr Azikiwe makes a return to our previous speculations inevitable. What were the reasons back of Zik's acceptance of the Governor-Generalship in 1960? Was that his only choice, and if so, why? Or could he have used certain obvious advantages to press Sir Abubakar and the N.P.C. into yielding the Prime Ministership to him? What 'obvious advantages' had Zik? Would it have been easier, braver, wiser for him to have gone in with the A.G. instead?

This matter is worth discussing here not only for its intrinsic interest but also because both Zik's friends and enemies insist on keeping the issue alive. Moreover, to professional political scientists this episode has presented an attractive subject for analysis, the attraction being inherent, *inter alia*, in the number and variety of alternative hypotheses which the case offers.

First: Either Zik had to accept the headship of state because that was the only practical course to take, in view of the prevailing political circumstances; or else, *secondly*, the alternative was possible but Zik secretly rejected it because he did want to be Governor-General, with the ultimate aim of capping his career by becoming the first President of a foreseeable Republic of Nigeria; or, *thirdly*, he was simply out-manoeuvered and outwitted by the northern strategists; or else, *fourthly*, there had been a secret, pre-agreed, pre-arranged pincer movement between the N.P.C. and the N.C.N.C., in which to catch and crush the 'common enemy', Awolowo and his Action Group. Let it be added in respect of the first hypothesis that this would imply an honest mutual appraisal and an acceptance, on both sides, of political reality; in short, that the arrangement that emerged from the negotiations, and the Federal Government that Nigeria got by January 1960, was a genuine, open compromise.

What can we make of these four possibilities, which by their very nature must be accepted as being mutually exclusive of one another? If any of them can be short-shrifted, let us do so at once, in order to get to the bone of the matter quickly.

The third argument, that Zik must have been outwitted and out-manoeuvered, is the easiest to get rid of, being untenable to the point of absurdity. It is inconceivable that the man whose career this book has followed and traced in the last ten chapters or more could have been as politically naïve as is here affirmed. It would be politically less uncomplimentary to say he had been opportunistic than that he had been naïve to such an extent. Postulate two must be rejected also, because it conflicts fatally with the first argument, which seems to be the most acceptable because it is the most consistent with the bulk of the evidence which emerged. For those who missed the occasion, let us present here a simple case of what seem to have been the most obvious details inherent in this first argument, dating it from pre-Independence to post-Federal Election.

After the leaders of the Northern Peoples' Congress had finally agreed in 1957 with both halves of the south on a suitable date for independence (1959, as they had then decided), the north had come into the national political game as fully and as competitively as any other section or party in the country. Indeed with the looming figure of the Sardauna in the ranks of negotiation this was not just competition but an assertion of rights. And 'rights' for the north at this time meant power through the suddenly available wonder of the *democratic majority*. From the moment during the 1949–50 constitutional revisions when the north had forced its way through to the acceptance by the others of its right to half the number of seats in the coming central House of Representatives, it had held the upper hand in all national political negotiations in which the mere counting of heads was ultimately to be determinative. And this, irrespective of an 'understanding' with the N.C.N.C. of which we shall hear more presently.

In the Federal Election of 1959, after all the peripheral bits had been drawn into the central mass, it developed that the N.P.C. had 148 seats, the N.C.N.C.-N.E.P.U. coalition eighty-nine, and the Action Group seventy-five. Here was the point, as far as the generality of people were concerned, at which the bargaining had to be joined, because this was when the locus of effective legislative as well as executive power had to be fixed. The N.P.C. had a large plurality, that is, a majority over each of the other two major parties but not over-all. It could never be sure of winning a single debate, much less carrying a single important measure through, in the new legislature, with its two southern rivals mustering 164 votes between them. On the other hand, the N.C.N.C. and the A.G. were even more powerless each by itself. There was therefore only one way out of an *impasse* which, on the face of it, was no one's fault but everyone's concern: the coalition of 'any two' of the three parties to form the Federal Government, with the third party left to become the Opposition. The question was: which two, and which one?

Members and sympathizers of the (Yoruba) Action Group party who were no more enamoured of northern domination of Nigeria than the northerners were of southern, saw ahead both actual northern domination *and* retrogression, or at least a probable condition of stagnancy for the country, if the N.P.C. got the upper hand. They were therefore the most anxious citizens in the country after the election, and they were the most shocked and alarmed at the settlement struck between the

N.C.N.C. and the N.P.C., led by Sir Abubakar but powered from behind by the Sardauna of Sokoto.

It is among these loyal Action Groupers, and their sympathizers both native and foreign, that the fourth hypothesis is held to be true. And the extreme statement of it was made, interestingly enough, by one of the outsiders, Stanley Diamond (in *Africa Today*, Vol. X, No. 9, November 1963). He said:

Awolowo had rejected the idea of a National Government, and following the elections in 1960, had gone to Azikiwe and the N.C.N.C., asking for a coalition Government, which would have been based on an almost identical vote, though a smaller number of seats than the present Coalition. Balewa, who was to become Premier, had made it clear that the North would not withdraw from the Federation, indeed he explicitly remarked that the North was prepared to form the Opposition, should the Southern parties coalesce at the centre. But the N.C.N.C. rejected the Action Group request. Dr Azikiwe's party chose the North, as it turned out, by *prior arrangement*, judging, perhaps, that they could command the South without Awolowo, and seizing the chance to rid themselves of Action Group rivalry. But in doing so, the N.C.N.C. forfeited their drive towards a sturdier central government, which had been part of Awolowo's platform, and they sacrificed their radicalism, for the sake, so goes the claim, of maintaining the Federation.

The West, the Action Group, and Awolowo were trapped in a pincer move from North and East.

Later, in his summary, Diamond asked: 'Did the N.P.C., which gained much, engineer this affair, with the acquiescence of the N.C.N.C., which gained less?' To which question he gave the answer himself, that the evidence for 'such an assumption' was quite good.

The problem here is not that Diamond's closely-argued, highly expert analysis is faulty, or that his conclusions – 'assumptions' – are wrong. The problem about 'Point Four', as stated in this article, is simply that on both the critical questions raised, only half-answers are given. The '*prior agreement*', according to Diamond, was the 'understanding' between Dr Azikiwe and the Sardauna, or between the N.C.N.C. and the N.P.C. *But many people had been hinting at or playing further politics with this idea for years;* it does not appear, that is, to have been all that secret or sudden – carried out only just before the election and provisional against its results alone. Secondly, there were widely disseminated accounts of the post-election negotiations. These give that other half of the answer left out by Diamond, to the second question his article raised concerning the negotiations and the eventual rejection of the Action Group approach by the N.C.N.C. In short, though many had speculated about an 'understanding', (a) this cannot be proved to have been entirely *ad hoc*, and (b) it is countered by accounts of factual happenings which diminish fatally the importance that could perhaps otherwise have been attachable to such an 'understanding'.

The earliest of these accounts were given by the local press and the principals themselves. The *Daily Times* of Lagos, for instance, reported on 22 December that Chief Awolowo had approached Dr Azikiwe with an offer to serve under him in a coalition, in exchange, so to speak, for an undertaking guaranteeing the creation of new states in all the regions. This account was amplified and given a second, crucial dimension by *West Africa* (London) on 2 January 1960:

Following the formation of Nigeria's new Federal Government, Chief Awolowo has issued a statement explaining the part the Action Group played in the inter-party negotiations immediately after the election results became clear. Chief Awolowo says he received innumerable messages asking him to join forces with Dr Azikiwe and the N.C.N.C. to form a government and, as a consequence, he offered to serve in a government under Dr Azikiwe – on condition that the N.C.N.C. agreed to create three new Regions. In reply Dr Azikiwe has publicly acknowledged the Action Group offer but said he refused it because he discovered that at the time Action Group spokesmen were making their offer to the N.C.N.C. other Action Group representatives were trying to negotiate a similar pact with the N.P.C. This allegation has been confirmed by Mallam Muhammadu King, N.P.C. principal organizing secretary, who claims that Chief Rosiji, on behalf of Chief Awolowo, suggested forming an A.G.–N.P.C. coalition government in Kaduna on 15 December.

The impossibility of proving a planned pincer movement by the top N.P.C.-N.C.N.C. leadership, merely to keep out Awolowo and the Action Group from Federal power, and without extensive consideration of other important consequences, is further demonstrated by Sklar (*Nigerian Political Parties*, page 508), who reported as follows:

Dr Azikiwe disclosed that within the N.C.N.C. 'two schools of thought emerged after prolonged discussion. One school conceded that a coalition between the N.C.N.C.–N.E.P.U. Alliance with the Action Group would no doubt produce an efficient Government, but it was stressed that majority opinion in the Western Region would frown against such a coalition. Moreover, it was obvious that if the Alliance agreed to a coalition with the Action Group, then there might be a crisis within the Party with the Westerners probably breaking away. . . . The other school agreed that a coalition between the Alliance with the N.P.C. would also produce an efficient, but with it, a stable Government: yet a strong body of influential opinion severely criticized such a coalition. Warnings were given that the N.E.P.U. might feel frustrated in view of its traditional struggle with the N.P.C. It was feared that this might create a schism in the Alliance.'

Sklar then adds a passage stating the outcome of these deliberations, partly in his own words and partly in those of the *Daily Times*, as follows:

Eventually, it was decided that in view of the past hostility of the Action Group to the N.C.N.C., the entrenchment of Fundamental Human Rights in the Constitution, which the courts were bound to protect, and the cordial personal relationships obtaining between leaders of the N.P.C. and N.C.N.C., 'the N.E.P.U. leaders should be persuaded to modify their attitude and give the N.C.N.C. a fair chance to work out a *modus vivendi* for the three parties, namely: N.P.C., N.C.N.C., and N.E.P.U. in the interest of national solidarity.'

The *Daily Times* quotation was from its issue of 23 December 1959. In addition to these, Dr Eme Awa, then a tutor in the Extra-Mural Department of the University of Ibadan, and Kenneth Post (cited often above), wrote articles in the university magazine, *Ibadan* (issue of March 1960) briefly mentioning aspects of the post-election alignments.

Post, later in his book (*The Nigerian Federal Election*, page 441), emphasized the point he had made in his article, namely that 'the N.C.N.C. had also realized the importance of the North, and its reaction was to seek an understanding with its ally's enemy'. He agreed that this meant the Federation being put into the hands of a coalition of strange bedfellows, the Northern People's Congress and the N.C.N.C., who were 'apparently' united only in order to keep the Action Group from the seats of power. But Post was also of the opinion that '*nevertheless, it may have saved Nigeria from a great constitutional crisis on the eve of independence'.* (Author's italics.)

Lastly, the words and actions of the northern leaders them-selves are important in the assessment of the situation, as it stood at that juncture. When it became clear that the N.P.C. had won a plurality in the election, Sir James Robertson, the Governor-General, sent for Alhaji Sir Abubakar and invited him to form a government. The Prime Minister came down at once from the north – accompanied by the Sardauna of Sokoto, Premier and Strongman of the North Region and President of the N.P.C., who thus added more weight to the northern dele-gation. Sir Abubakar not only accepted the Governor-General's invitation to form a Federal, Independent Government, but immediately afterwards held a Press Conference at which he laid down the decisive terms on which he was going to take office again.

First, he was not going to form a 'national government', with all parties represented. Secondly, he would not, even in a coalition of two parties, step down for a new Prime Minister from the other party. Thirdly, the N.P.C. would go into opposition, if the two southern parties should reach an agreement to form a coalition at the centre. But on the Prime Ministership, said Sir Abubakar later, 'We certainly cannot compromise.' (*West Africa*, 19 December 1959, page 1115.)

Does it still seriously occur to anyone that Zik was in any position to apply 'certain pressure tactics' against the northern leaders in an attempt to wrest the Prime Ministership from Balewa? What kind of pressure, that would not also have pressed the situation into an explosion, at just the point in Nigerian history when such an explosion would have spelt doom to inde-pendence and to hopes of future unity? And would anyone care to revive the debate by bringing up the matter of later develop-ments and new party alignments? ...

Perhaps Zik had the ambition of ending his public career as Head of State – probably some day as President of Nigeria; perhaps he was tired of politics, for which he had always said he had no ambition. If so, *the decision and the choice happened to have coincided with the fact that in 1960 he could not have insisted on becoming Prime Minister and also kept the Federation intact.* Of course at that point he could have retired from public life altogether there and then, in frustration and bitterness. Instead, he chose a role to which he could bring prestige and dignity. Also a tranquillizing effect for the crucial time-being.

Chapter 26

Azikiwe's Other Nigeria

The Nigeria whose pre-colonial history is summarized, all too inadequately, in Chapter 4, was the Nigeria into which Nnamdi Azikiwe had been born: the Nigeria he met and in whose creation or development he had had no hand. The Nigeria he leaves behind when the time comes will be a vastly changed country, and some part at least of the change will have been due to Zik. Specifically, some of the change will have been due to the anti-colonialist drive of the first ten to twelve years following Azikiwe's return home, behind which drive he was himself, as we have seen, the main force.

Before 1937 it was Zik's predecessors who were laying some of the foundations for a new political and social superstructure in Nigeria, and after 1947 he was only one – though perhaps still the outstanding one – of many leaders sharing in the burden of construction. But in the intervening years between the two, Azikiwe had unquestionably made the greatest single effort of labour to the project. No other record could approach his for that period. And if to it we add the years, 1934–7, of his stirring impact on the whole of English-speaking West Africa from his base of operations in Accra, we have a fair view of the Azikiwe contribution to nation-building in contemporary Africa.

The building of Nigeria, that stage of it which thus involved Zik, was never completed in his day – how could it be? – and today it is threatened by fearful contending claims among its owners and workmen. ... In this, our last chapter, we shall look at some of the facts, examine some of the prospects, and speculate on some of the threats which make Azikiwe's Nigeria a giant both of hope and despair, in modern, revolutionary Africa. We shall also, of course, in the process attempt to place in proper focus Zik's present and possible future role in the drama of his country.

The Recent Past

The closing days of 1959 had witnessed in Nigeria a short, sharp play for power among the major parties and their leaders; the opening days of 1965, exactly five years later, saw the country poised on the brink of political disaster, and saved eventually only by a compromise no less tentative but much more tremulous by far than that of 1959–60. On each occasion Nnamdi Azikiwe was the key figure among all the actors in the deadly drama; on each occasion his decisive moves saved the Union for the time-being; and on each occasion these moves were questioned almost as much as they were praised by sections among the watching millions. We know about the 1959–60 crisis; let us now at least seek some understanding of that of early 1965. For this purpose a summary of the main events is necessary at the beginning.

An election for a new Federal Parliament was due at the end of 1964 or early in 1965, and was eventually held on 30 December. But it was a disputed election. President Azikiwe himself had asked that it be postponed for six months (for reasons to be given presently), and the East Region had boycotted it, threatening, moreover, to secede – dreaded word – from the Federation.

The Prime Minister's new coalition of parties, the Nigerian National Alliance, having won what the *Daily Times* described as 'the half and half election', a constitutional crisis developed rapidly when President Azikiwe, suiting his action to his word, at first refused to invite Alhaji Sir Abubakar to form the next Government. After days of negotiations and conferences behind guarded doors, in which many of the highest in the land took part and which much of the world watched with interest or anxiety, the President and the Prime Minister announced that they had at last struck a compromise.

Dr Azikiwe had agreed to the formation of a Government under Alhaji Sir Abubakar on the basis of the results of the election already held, and on the following points of agreement, stated by Dr Azikiwe himself:

1. 'A belief in the unity of the Federation', with 'equal opportunity' and freedom from oppression for every citizen,

2. 'A strict observance of the Constitution until ... amended according to law and the will of the people',

3. The 'hope' that 'in those constituencies where elections have not been held arrangements [would] be made to hold them as soon as possible',

4. Agreement that steps would be taken 'within a short time to review the Constitution and the machinery for elections in the Federation', and

5. The immediate formation by Alhaji Abubakar of a 'broad-based national government'. (The word 'national' was soon in dispute and later disappeared altogether or lost significance.)

(*Daily Times*, 5 January 1965)

Before this agreement between the Head of State and the Head of Government was reached the fate of the Federation had seemed to hang on no more than a flimsy string. How serious the position was could be gleaned from the opposing coalition-party of the East Region and parts of the West (the United Progressive Grand Alliance – 'U.P.G.A.') on 30 December welcoming a 'suggestion' of the Sarduana of Sokoto that the President should call a conference for the breaking up of the Federation and the dividing of assets! Reports of violence and sabotage were widespread. Troop movements were reported, or expected, at strategic points, and certainly the official residences of the President (State House) and the Prime Minister were heavily guarded by armed soldiers and police. Then, on 4 January, at the height of the tension, the State House settlement was announced, to the relief of most people at home and abroad. President Johnson led those who sent personal congratulations to Dr Azikiwe and Sir Abubakar.

What was all the trouble about? To answer this question fully we shall here return to the story of Azikiwe's Nigeria, where we had left it in Chapter 4 with the introduction of the Ibadan historian, Professor J. F. Ade Ajayi.

Excercises in Unification

Dr Ajayi had been asked to give a series of broadcasts on the eve of Nigerian independence in 1960, and had taken as his theme Nigeria's national unification, explaining that he considered this to be the most important for the occasion. In four talks* he gave

* Published later as *Milestones in Nigerian History* in 1962, by the University of Ibadan.

the history of what he judged to be the four factors – corresponding to four successive periods as well as phases – towards unification in Nigeria which had occured at their various points in time-past, during more than a century and a half.

The first factor was *Islam*, beginning with Shehu Usuman dan Fodio's *jihad*, 1804–onwards, which resulted in a firmly established and territorially extensive empire. Islam, says Ajayi, was 'a unifying factor in a number of ways':

It brought a large number of Nigerians, irrespective of ethnic origins, under the influence of the same religious and cultural ideas. It encouraged the spread of a common pattern of education in Koranic schools and a common literary language in Arabic, this facilitating inter-group movement and understanding. It was also under its influence that the Fulani united most of Northern Nigeria into a single empire.

The second factor of unification was *Christianity*. The coming of the missionaries and the intensification of their proselytizing, more especially of their educational efforts, during the decades after 1820, was responsible for the gradual creation of a fairly homogeneous class of educated Africans, both in Nigeria and, particularly, in and from Sierra Leone. For instance, the influence on his generation of an outstanding product of this period and this process, Bishop Ajayi Crowther (the first West African bishop), was considerable.

British colonial policy and administration comes third* in chronological order among Ajayi's factors of unification. This British interest, at first connected with the Abolition movement, was, by the time of the annexation of Lagos in 1861, mainly concerned in the commercial activities of English traders. Professor Diké notes how Englishmen on the Nigerian coast were in fact only foreigners in status up to as late as 1851 when they captured Lagos from the European slavers. British 'consular power', in

---

* Kalu Ezera, in his *Constitutional Development in Nigeria*, 1960, C.U.P. (p. 15), states that 'the first step in the process of unification in Nigeria was taken in 1906 when Lagos and Southern Nigeria, hitherto separate colonies were merged under the name of "the Colony and Protectorate of Nigeria".' But this kind of traditional, European-biased, *administrative* view of African history is now under vigorous challenge by African historians like Ajayi.

Diké's phrase, began to rise only in that year, on the coast. Some sixty years later, however, Lugard was able, on the strength of its development into the interior and up north, to unite the two 'halves' of the country under one central administration. This was the important contribution made by the British. But it was third in time to the other two, and lagged behind the Christian missions in purpose and intention. Moreover, it never succeeded in uniting north and south in spirit, though it did so in law. To this third factor, nevertheless, Ajayi gives the credit that 'for the first time [it] brought the whole country under one administration, established the boundaries, provided the railways and the rudiments of a modern system of communication, an increasingly unified civil service, new cosmopolitan urban centres, and other facilities for inter-group communication in social and economic affairs.

Dr Ajayi's last factor of unification is, of course, *Nationalism*. This movement, beginning its final phase in the years after the Second World War, reached its apogee in 1959. From the sowings of twenty years or less came the full harvest of Independence in October 1960. The very next month Azikiwe was made first African Governor-General. Three years later, exactly, Nigeria became, like India, Pakistan, and Ghana, an independent Republic within the British Commonwealth. Its first native-born Governor-General became its first President.

Antecedents of Fate

That in summary, was Ajayi's account, and it lacked little in historical validity. The only trouble is that it was set down in greater optimism than the events and trends of the recent past have justified. But who could blame Dr Ajayi? He, like millions of others both in and out of Nigeria at the time, could have entertained no other sentiments towards the new Federation than those of optimism and goodwill. He could have done nothing more suitable or more natural, even for a professional historian, than to emphasize the positive features of the new nation-in-the-making. Prophets of doom on such an occasion would have been as out of place as mourners at a wedding, and much more wretched to boot.

But after the flood of happiness had subsided in 1960, the

visiting thousands gone back home to the ends of the earth, and the decorations taken down, the cracks and fissures began to show. Indeed another and a different kind of flood took the place of the one just past. For now the realities of statehood, and the new politics – the politics of independence – suddenly appeared, and most brutally demanded simultaneous attention. Within a year of independence, internal affairs: party, ethnic, regional, economic, and others, were engulfing every leader, official and unofficial; and external relations were meaning not merely the establishment of diplomatic relations, the opening of embassies and consulates abroad, and the receiving of foreign representatives at home, but, much more, the formulation of a national policy towards the cold war between East and West, the taking of a prominent stand on Pan-Africanism, the suturing of ruptured relations with neighbouring Ghana, together with many other immediate, non-postponable tasks of independence. And these problems tested severely the relations among Nigeria's leaders, with their still strong regional and ethnic attachments.

Furthermore, in 1962 the West Region exploded with alarming reverberations, bringing in its train the splitting of the Action Group into two factions, a confused constitutional situation, a distressing commission of enquiry – the Coker Commission – into administrative and financial matters in the Region, and the near-disintegration of that area in these matters. That same year the first of two explosive post-Independence census counts was taken for the whole country, the repercussions of which form the major feature of our consideration of the 'antecedents of fate'.

The first census and its troubles were followed by a re-take of the count in 1963, and this resulted in an even greater upset of the body politic, casting its evil spell forward and poisoning the atmosphere effectively until the election of 1964 brought the situation to a head. To add to the immense strain of this period, we had the drama and tragedy of the Awolowo trials and imprisonment, beginning in 1963 and stretching, with spasmodic sadness, into 1964.... It was a catalogue of turmoil, profoundly shaking for a new state, and posing for Nigeria the question how much unity the Fulani, the Christians, the British colonialists, or the African nationalists themselves had been able to promote among the various groups after all?

Of these many antecedents to the Nigerian crisis of December–January 1964–5, the most threatening were the census episodes of 1962–3 and 1963–4. *Africa Diary* of 22–28 December 1962 (pp. 918–19), taking its material from the *West African Pilot*, *News from Nigeria*, and the *Times* (London) made the following report, in part, on the position:

The Nigerian national census which took place in May this year became a matter of controversy in the first fortnight of December because of its significance in federal parliamentary representation. At a national executive meeting of the Enugu … (N.C.N.C.), on 5 December, concern was expressed over the delay in the release of figures, about the doubts of wrong figures in the Western region and about the recount in Benue province.

The Federal Economic Development Minister, Mr Waziri Ibrahim, said in the Parliament on 5 December that the delay was due partly to figures for the region arriving late in Lagos and partly to errors in the figures. …

The Minister said that he had decided that the figures should be verified and checked before publication. Verification would be carried out by each regional government; the north had completed this, but it was not started in the east and west.

The Eastern Nigerian Economic Development Minister, Mr Okeke, asserted that any attempt to impose new population figures on the country under the camouflage of verification would be resisted. …

He said the census figures were very important to Nigerian unity, and further delay would affect the 1964 federal elections as electoral registers would be compiled from the current census figures.

The Action Group 'called on Mr Ibrahim to resign because of the "inept way he has handled the census affair"', further reported *Africa Diary*. On 7 December 1962 both the A.G. and the N.C.N.C. withdrew from the House of Representatives during a debate on the census in which there had been heated exchanges, the Prime Minister being forced to censure both the 'walk-out' members and his own Minister for the scenes they had created. …

In the end, according to a report from the *West African Pilot*:

The Prime Minister, Alhaji Sir Abubakar Tafawa Balewa, the Regional Premiers – Alhaji Sir Ahmadu Bello (North), Dr. M. I. Okpara (East), and Chief S. L. Akintola (West) – held a meeting on 19

February, at the Prime Minister's residence in Lagos on the issue of the national census.

After consultations and in view of the loss of confidence in the figures, the Federal Government decided to nullify the results of the census. ...

The figures were later reported by Premier Akintola to have been, in round figures:

North Region 30,200,000 (as against 18 million in 1952)
East Region 12,500,000 (8,500,000)
West Region 10,500,000 (6,500,000)
Total 53,200,000 ... (app.)

In other words, according to Akintola's figures the population of Nigeria had increased by some 20,000,000 in eight to nine years, or about 62% over the period, or nearly 8% per year, a rate held to be virtually impossible under any circumstances. In fact the West Regional Premier's figures were unaccountable, since the 'official' figures were eventually stated to be twenty-two, twelve, and nine million respectively. Even so, the south was alarmed at the seemingly increased disparity in absolute numbers between north and south which even the 'official' figures represented.

At enormous cost to the national exchequer a new census was ordered for 1963, and this was carried out in November of that year. It made matters worse. The totals reported now justified Premier Akintola's 1962 projections:

North Region 29,777,986
East „ 12,388,646
West „ 10,278,500
Middle West Region 2,533,337
Lagos Region 675,352
Total 55,653,821

The reaction of the south to this new blow was one of outrage not unconnected with genuine fear. Now the north was said to have a large absolute population majority over all other areas of Nigeria combined; now, said the south, the north will rule and *dominate* the country for ever! Immediately there arose a general affray of challenge and counter-challenge, charge and denial. The Eastern Nigerian Government, through their Premier, Dr Okpara, said they 'completely rejected' the results announced, as disclosing 'inflation . . . of . . . astronomical proportions' which made the figures 'worse than useless'.

University students from Ibadan attempted a 'march' on Lagos by lorry. (They were turned back by police only a few miles from the capital, after tear-gas had been used.) Students of the Nigeria University at Nsukka staged demonstrations; indeed a deputation from that institution handed a 'petition of protest' to Sir Abubakar in Lagos. Chief Dennis Osadebay, Premier of the new Mid-West Region, also rejected the census, describing its declared results as 'the most stupendous joke of our age' (*Africa Diary* p. 1664, March 1964). The N.C.N.C. did likewise – even that section of it which then shared government with Chief Akintola's U.P.P. in the west.

In Kaduna meanwhile, according to the local press of the week of 21–7 March (*West African Pilot* and *Daily Times* among the leading papers), the Sardauna of Sokoto and leader of the N.P.C., Sir Ahmadu Bello, was warning the rest of the country of his readiness for a 'complete showdown': 'my people, my government, and my party', he was directly quoted as saying, 'are fully prepared at any hour of the day for any eventuality and would meet any challenge.' But Sir Ahmadu added: 'I warn all Nigerians that the present situation calls for calm and forethought.' (The N.P.C. and Chief Akintola's West Region Government had alone accepted the census figures at sight.)

Some moderating voices, however, were also heard. Mr F. S. McEwen, N.C.N.C. National Secretary, made a statement affirming the confidence of the party's Central Executive in the country's leaders, and their 'unshaken belief' that it was not impossible for the leaders to arrive at a 'mutual agreement acceptable to the nation.' President Azikiwe himself also issued statements in which he appealed for calm, describing the census affair as 'delicate and explosive'. He pointed out that in rejecting the results, Eastern Nigeria had made serious allegations against the conduct of the census which, if not carefully handled, might plunge the nation into disaster.

In the end a 'stalemate' developed over the situation. And the main reason for this could not have been other than the enormous frustration of spirit which even the contemplation of a second cancellation of the census and a third count of the population engendered in all concerned. But though they were thus forced to abandon any further hopes of ever seeing a redressing of the imbalance of which they considered themselves to be the victims, neither could the southerners abandon their frustration or their apprehensions for the future; the north, on the other hand, was in no way shy of the advantages which the situation seemed to promise. Thus as the date for new elections approached, Nigeria was a long way off from the ideal of unity and corporate goodwill so hopefully presumed by Professor Ajayı.

Alternatives to Disaster

Indeed as the election approached, that hope of unity receded steadily and by mid-December Nigeria was facing the conditions which led the President first to suggest a postponement of the election and then to withhold his constitutional prerogative of summoning to office the leader of the government-party-apparent. Dr Azikiwe described the dangers of the situation, and the causes of his disturbance of spirit, in a radio broadcast to the whole country on 10 December 1964. Said he, in part:

I am not quite happy at the political turn of events in our embryo Republic. The way and manner our electioneering campaign is being conducted leaves much to be desired. The situation in some parts of the country is confusing and it would appear that certain political parties are preventing their opponents from having the opportunity conveniently to explain their party policies and programmes.

In recent weeks, hundreds of telegrams and letters from different parts of our Federation have been received by me in the State House, pleading that I should use my good offices to ensure a free and fair election. The allegations contained in these messages are incredible and challenging, because they point to what appears to be a deliberate attempt to flout the provisions of our Constitution. ...

Dr Azikiwe proceeded to give details of some of the allegations made to him directly, or indirectly through many sources public and private (as he emphasized verbally before and after the broadcast):

There have been complaints about denial of the most elementary courtesies to political leaders campaigning in Regions other than their own. It is said that accommodation was refused them in public hotels and rest houses, food and victuals denied them in restaurants and catering establishments, shelter refused them in public buildings during rain storms, and road barriers used to blockade the entrance to towns where they intended to campaign. Indeed, these alleged acts of intolerance distort the image of our traditional hospitality as a nation.

Charges have been made also that freedom of expression has been denied citizens of Nigeria because they dared to criticize their Ministers, (who in reality are their servants) and had the courage to denounce the policies and activities of their governments. If these charges are true, then they reflect adversely on our reputation as a democratic country. No Nigerian office holder is sacrosanct and none can be exempted from public criticism lawfully made by Nigerian citizens. In fact, that is one reason why they are well paid by the taxpayers.

Permits to hold public meetings are said to have been denied Nigerian citizens on the flimsiest pretext that such meetings would generate disorder and disturb the public peace. Within reason, no responsible citizen would object to the law enforcement agencies taking reasonable precautions to avoid public disorder. But it is generally known that during the period of elections, no responsible Government would encourage its instruments to deprive its citizens of this valuable fundamental right. Not if such elections are to be free and fair.

Moreover, the fact that during the period of electioneering campaign our governments had transferred the power of granting permits for public meetings and processions and demonstrations from the Police to the Local Authorities, has intensified the suspicion that the police power is being subverted for political ends, since the Local Authorities are constituted by politicians who have a stake in their survival as the party in power.

Next the President spoke about the resurgent menace of tribalism and the consequent threat to unity in the Republic:

Another phenomenon of contemporary Nigerian politics is the publication by our political parties of pamphlets which incite tribe against tribe and raise disaffection among our multi-national communities, contrary to our criminal laws. To villify any particular community in writing is capable of causing upheavals, but to advocate the extermination of any Nigerian community by a combination of other Nigerian communities is to invite repercussions which can definitely strain the resources of our security organization.

The right of any person or party to publish political pamphlets and air its views and also criticize its opponents is guaranteed under our Constitution. But no person or political party is entitled to publish any pamphlets which can be calculated to undermine our constituted authority by inciting the communities of this country to annihilate one another.

Whether our beloved Nigeria will continue to remain united as one country or will become disintegrated into minute principalities depends now upon two factors: whether our politicians would desist from inciting our communities to liquidate themselves, and whether our politicians would cooperate so that the law-abiding elements in this colossus of Africa will experience a free and fair election? Which reminds me of a favourite couplet, which I pass on to our politicians:

> 'Sir, there's the marble, there's the chisel
> Take it, work it to thy will.'

Should our political leaders, after bearing all the above factors in mind, prefer to crucify the unity of this country on the Golgotha of their inordinate ambition for naked power, then hundreds and thousands of Nigerian patriots, who sacrificed dearly for its unity and its freedom, must take note and pass this doleful information to posterity. In which case, it would be an irony of history that the liquidation of our national unity occurred after we had become free from a political bondage that lasted almost a century.

It was near the end of December, a few days before the date fixed for the election (the 30th), that the differences between President Azikiwe and Prime Minister Balewa developed into a crisis. The principle points of disagreement concerned (a) the alleged incidents of electoral irregularities and violations in some parts of the Federation, and (b) the desirability and legality, or otherwise, of postponing the election. The two leaders held completely opposed views on both matters.

Two speeches prepared for radio delivery by Dr Azikiwe and Alhaji Abubakar at the height of the crisis were hastily withdrawn before delivery but published later in the press, in circumstances of inadvertence when eleventh-hour and successful efforts at compromise were being made. From these speeches some crucial passages were highlighted in the press to show the public how close a call the young Republic had had:

PRESIDENT AZIKIWE: I have, therefore, decided to take steps in the name of Nigerian unity to arrest a situation which is rapidly deteriorating. I find it extremely awkward to exercise the power to call upon any person to form a Government. True, the Constitution is clear on this issue, *but my decision is that I will not exercise such a power and I would rather resign.* This should release my conscience from the chains of power politics.

*

My association with Alhaji Abubakar Tafawa Balewa has been a happy one.

Since 1960, in a spirit of understanding and compromise, we both developed implicit confidence in each other's good faith in the future of this Republic.

But the undercurrents of partisan politics would appear to have made it extremely difficult for any person in our predicament to have a free hand in serving this nation according to the dictate of conscience within the law.

PRIME MINISTER BALEWA: I have been working closely with Dr Azikiwe as the President of the Republic for the last four years. He has always treated me with courtesy. *Knowing of his desire for the unity of this country, I was very concerned to see him go.**

The disagreement between me and the President was not a personal one. It was a disagreement on principles.

I think that, in order to avoid bloodshed, for which I cannot accept any responsibility because it is not for a cause which I think is right, I would humbly suggest that we have a conference of the representatives of all the Governments in the Federation so as to decide among ourselves what the future of our country should be.

That was as close as it got, and it was probably a unique occasion and situation. At the eleventh hour the descent was halted. The President yielded to the pressure both of overwhelming legal and constitutional logic, and of his own patriotic obligations as he felt them. (Once more, however, voices were heard accusing him of capitulation, where, they said, firmness on his original stand could have forced upon the warring parties a realistic and sober approach to the fateful problems of the country, *without bloodshed*.) The Prime Minister for his part seems to have succeeded in resisting pressures arguing for another kind of settlement, in place of which he based his whole approach to the crisis

*Author's italics. This was obviously to have been the 'end'. The prematurity of the broadcasts, and the reasons for their withdrawal, can now be fully appreciated. But the speeches were later published in full because the President's had already been scooped by one local and several papers of the world press.

, solely on his belief in 'our Constitution and our laws as they are now, until we change them.'

There is no question that what Nigeria faced at the end of 1964 and the beginning of 1965 were a set of alternatives of which the majority were alternatives of disaster, and only one offered a truce from disaster : the one chosen by Zik and Balewa – advised, be it emphasized, by most of the leaders of the country : Regional Governors and Premiers, the Chief Justices, the Attorney-General, Solicitors-General, Federal Ministers, and others of their fellow-citizens high and low.

The other alternatives seemed to them to offer : civil war, a break-up of the Federation, with or without bloodshed, an invitation to arbitrators like the United Nations (already overburdened with intractable problems elsewhere), an invitation, worse still, to interference by international adventurers only too ready to discover new fields of intrigue and political spoils, or, at the very least, an uneasy arrangement permanently bedevilled by frontier difficulties, trade wars, ethnic conflicts, and worse.

The Arguments for Unity

Political strategists would tend to hold generally that political threats and ultimata are powerful weapons against the opponent, *as long as they can remain threats and ultimata.* The moment they are carried out or have to be withdrawn they are not only themselves immediately spent and thenceforth powerless but also leave their user weaker and his adversaries stronger.

This is how critics see the action in Eastern Nigeria, for instance, where the boycotting of the 1964 election seems to have brought them no gain but only confusion and reversals. And this is how they view Dr Azikiwe's 'withdrawal' of his threat to resign rather than go against his feeling that many of his fellow citizens had suffered gross interference with their constitutional rights. These critics consider not only that Dr Azikiwe's action was damaging to himself personally but that, as in the case of the 'Zikist' episode in 1951, he had thus let down an expectant following, at the same time as again abandoning a radical and dynamic line.

The argument, as a purely philosophical exercise, or in a moralistic sense alone, is valid: one should not let one's friends down least of all through a moral act which is not only unilateral but also repugnant to the cause. But this is only one-half of the question. An act, says Sir David Ross, 'may be wrong in some respect and yet, in its totality, the most right of all the acts open to us, and then we *are* bound to do it. . . .'*

In this case, the President's friends were the whole nation the 'totality' of his conception of duty, so to speak – apart from his still ideologically-committed partisans, his critics, and even his hitherto large personal following in the east. He was bound to act in and for that totality. Secondly, though the compromise was no more than that – no more, that is, than a truce – yet it seemed to offer the only chance of peaceful negotiations towards a better union. For the arguments in favour of Nigeria staying together as a unit are many and strong, the arguments against a break-up of the Federation equally so. These can be stated briefly, and on their most relevant points alone.

First, there is the political argument for unity. Larger national states are more viable, more powerful, more influential, more nearly self-sufficient, than smaller ones. Especially for Africa at this time, too, they are vital for all intra-African purposes, including national self-defence and inter-continental security, if possible under the aegis of the Organization of African Unity. With a population now presumably accepted at over fifty-five millions, Nigeria offers the greatest single future challenge to possible aggression against Africa from the outside. (One recognizes, of course, that in case of nuclear war nothing will avail anyone anything; *all* will perish thoroughly!) In short, both internally and externally the size of Nigeria's territory and population is a great asset not to be thrown away for misconceived reasons.

The economic argument for unity in Nigeria is even stronger. The progressive mobilization of her immense man-power resources for efficient production can alone harness the country's economic potential and gradually overcome the crippling under-production from which the whole continent suffers. The cotton and cattle lands of the north, cocoa and timber forests of the west, and vegetable and mineral-oil soils of the east, in combined

* *Foundations of Ethics*, Oxford, 1939, p. 84.

production under steadily improving conditions can gradually force a break-through to increased national wealth and higher standards of living.

Africa has upwards of 240,000,000 inhabitants, but (according to statistics offered by the Economic Commission for Africa in Addis Ababa) she accounts for the appallingly low rate of only 7 per cent of total world production – equal to the annual production of not-large or over-prosperous Italy, and to only half of Britain's! Her soil, over vast areas, is constantly reported by even her best friends to be uniformly poor in composition. Her man-power is undernourished, uneducated in the main, and technically untrained. Her transport and communication facilities are largely non-existant, or wholly primitive. She is still suffering, in the words of Elliot J. Berg,* from the colonial heritage of paternalism in politics and economics.

Worst of all is the disability which the continent suffers from the fact that her economic life, in the main, is controlled from the outside. Both Berg and a fellow-contributor to the same book, Andrew M. Kamarch ('The African Economy and International Trade', p. 168 of *The U.S. and Africa*), record this brutal fact:

BERG: The 'commanding heights' in the money economy, then, are occupied by expatriate organizations even in peasant-producer countries, while in the mining and European agricultural economies the capital and management of the basic production units are also non-African in origin.

KAMARCH: Since African economies are dependent upon the export and import trade, economic conditions in Africa are shaped by the forces of the outside world. What happens in the West determines whether prosperity or depression will be the order of the day: the Africans have precious little to say about it themselves.

And we know that before, during, and since the Geneva World Trade Conference of 1963–4 the despairing cry – even of those whose tears are the tears of a crocodile – has been: 'The rich nations are getting richer, and the poor ones are getting poorer' – in the sense of the gap steadily widening between rich and poor.

* 'The Character and Prospects of African Economics', in *The U.S. and Africa*, New York, Praeger, 1963, p. 126.

The way for Nigeria to try to meet these prostrating economic facts of African life, in her own case at any rate, is not to reject what advantageous factors of viability she possesses but to cling to them; not to abandon, that is, the advantages of a large territory with great soil-improvement possibilities, a large population with immense mobilization potentials, and a diversified, rotating, self-nourishing supply of economic products.

Consider, in the alternative, the utter waste of time and talent that would have to go into the processes and procedures of dismantlement of the Federation and Republic! With the best will in the world and to avoid the risk of civil war, it would require years of enervating and expensive negotiation just to divide the assets, determine and delimit boundaries, settle questions of waterways and outlets, agree on the exchange and resettlement of populations in accordance with ethnic identification. . . . The list is endless, the possibilities of conflict better imagined than projected.

These were some of the considerations that went into the decision of the Prime Minister and the President to compose their differences and save the Federation. What of the future for Zik and this, his other Nigeria?

Epilogue

Zik and the Future of Nigeria

To give any reasonable consideration to the question of future possibilities for Dr Azikiwe, it is first necessary to ponder over the many other elements of his life, apart from all that has gone before. Even then, with most of the facts laid out before us, it would be easier to speculate upon than to predict exactly the next major changes in his career.

We have not so far said or seen much of the Azikiwe family life, obviously a principal element. This is partly because it has been in truth a private life, and partly that the family has not often stayed together as a unit for long periods of time. The stately Mrs Azikiwe has, when at home, appeared with her husband on most ceremonial occasions during his tenure of high public office; and the children – three boys and a girl – have been seen by many people when they have been with their parents. But much of the time they have been at school away from their father or in boarding schools away from both parents. Besides, during the mid-1950s Flora Azikiwe herself was in the U.S.A. adding to her education. (She followed in the trail of her husband by going first to Storer and then to Howard in Washington, from the latter of which she took a Bachelor's degree in 1955.)

The 1950s also marked a period during which the marriage – like the rest of the '99 per cent of them' – had its series of trying ups and downs. Both Zik and his wife are spirited individualists of the volatile Ibo blood and can summon up every now and then moods and mutual reactions not exactly designed for 'peace in their time'. But the worst period passed, and what with that and the necessity of setting a good national example, the Azikiwe family life has since been, most of the time, a quiet, unobtrusive one. The encompassing preoccupation of Zik with public affairs is of course another factor to be kept in mind in this connexion.

The children, Chukwuma Bamidele ('Chuma'), born February 1940, Chukwuemeka Nwabufo Ayo (June 1941), Nwachukwu

Abiodun (December 1944), and Ngozichukwu Obiozo (October 1946), both by accident and by choice, are all, presumably, destined to take their higher education, like their parents before them, outside Nigeria and mostly in America.

The accident arises from the fact that the two oldest boys were ready for college before the opening of the Nsukka university of which their father is in effect the founder; and since Zik continues to prefer the rugged, multi-lineal approach of the American system of education, he chose to send them to the United States. The third boy – thought by the rest in 1964 to be 'the brains of the family' – has gone the same way, making the choice himself because of the fact that the branch of chemistry in which he was interested was not yet being offered at Nsukka. The girl – 'Ngozi' – had to be sent off to England to strengthen her secondary school foundations before embarking upon a possible academic career also.

Dr Azikiwe thus has no intractable family problems to consume his time and energies on the one hand, though, on the other, his public responsibilities of course do. His family aside, therefore, it is possible to catalogue the major interests and activities which have and will increasingly continue to have a bearing on the President's future choices.

There is no doubt at all in the minds of those who know him that if Nnamdi Azikiwe had not become a nationalist-politician and public servant by sheer force of necessity – as well as by the dictates of one-half of his psyche – he would have loved most to belong to the world of books, lectures, and the academic life. In short, Zik exhibits that combination of 'martial' temperament with intellectualism (or at any rate with literary ambitions) so characteristic of so many historical figures: Caesar writing the accounts of his own great campaigns in Gaul; Napoleon codifying the laws in a famous document and producing many other literary works of quality; Churchill, the soldier-politician-war leader, not only making great speeches but writing national and war histories as well – the list is very long. And in the revolutionary Africa of today examples of this *genre* of man are not lacking: Prime Minister Jomo Kenyatta of Kenya is the well known author of *Facing Mount Kenya*; President Leopold Senghor of Senegal is an established poet-philosopher; President

Nkrumah of Ghana is the author of several books (including his autobiography and the recent *Consciencism*, a philosophical-nationalist treatise); and President Nyerere of Tanzania, who combines intellectualism with a true literary flair, has, among other accomplishments, translated *Julius Caesar* into Swahili.

Zik is an enthusiastic member of this fraternity. The boyish delight with which he dons hood and gown every now and then to visit some college or university to deliver an official address or receive an honorary degree, shyly identifying himself with students or hoping, in effect, that the academic body would condescend to admit him into their company – these are just the outward signs of his deep inner state of happiness in academia; the real, concrete facts of his attachment to this vital world are quite staggering.

We have already seen how much Zik has written and published himself. His private library, that section of it which he is enlarging for the University of Nigeria, and its Africana section – each of these must be either the outstanding private collection of its kind in Africa, or unique in some way. The Africana section, for example, features such items as many rare books of great value, rows of bound volumes of Nigerian and Gold Coast (Ghana) newspapers of both this and the nineteenth century, and a large number of unpublished M.A. theses and Ph.D. dissertations by Nigerian graduates. Zik keeps in close touch with this wide range of materials in his own library as well as with the book world in general.

Secondly in this connexion, Zik is not only almost nervous in his concern to see this kind of material quickly made available to the youth of Africa, but he wants to write much more of it himself while he is still mentally and physically vigorous. He is anxious to encourage other Africans, moreover, to write more and more about and for themselves, and to help publish and publicize such material personally : as is well known, he has for many years had a small publishing company among his business enterprises, and for almost as long has been working on a collection of modern African poetry for an anthology.

Zik has given ample proof of his awareness that the literary and intellectual productivity he dreams about requires as foundation both a realistic expansion of educational facilities and the

provision of special individual opportunities. He has done so by
his promotion of free primary education – as a start – in his East
Region, at a time when this looked like vain, senseless ambition;
by his sponsorship of the establishment of the University of
Nigeria at Nsukka, for which he will probably be remembered
best and longest; and by the provision, out of his own pocket, of
numerous scholarships* of all kinds for school children as well as
college students – a fact less well known than others about him.

Libraries, sponsored publications, and scholarships, however,
are but a small part of the vision. What Zik was always interested
in are the possibilities of large-scale philanthropy, involving com-
plicated endowment schemes, trusts, and the like. Accordingly,
he has for some years now been engaged on preparations for the
setting up of a trust organization, or foundation, which would
eventually assume responsibility for managing the business of his
philanthropic enterprises. Even so, Zik needs more time than he
can now find, to devise with his advisers a suitable organization
or framework for what he has in mind.

The last of his major interests outside of his present national
position is of course the journalistic enterprise which first brought
Zik fame and power. He would like to see the *West African Pilot*,
in particular, resuscitated and restored to its pristine place of influence, at a time when influence for the constructive good of the
Nigerian community needs to be exerted more than ever before.
The *Pilot* apart, there are the other papers of the original chain:
those among them which are not already dead are almost mere
skin and bones just now. They have no flesh on them. The spirit
to fight for further progress of further change is still alive in them
but very dormant. . . . If Zik were not a public servant he could
bring this press to vibrant life again.

But against these admittedly 'Nigerian perspectives' – to bor-
row the title of Thomas Hodgkin's anthology – stands Nigeria
herself, with her unexpired claims on the time and attention of
Nnamdi Azikiwe. What was the relationship between these two,
at the end of our story?

* 'Dr Azikiwe has donated £5,300 to the University of Nsukka, in the
form of 6,000 books for the University library and £3,000 sterling as
scholarships tenable at the University.' (*West Africa*, 2 December 1961,
p. 1340.)

At the time of writing these last few paragraphs (February 1965) the position in Azikiwe's other Nigeria was far from settled, and could well erupt again into political conflict, if not worse. But there was ample reason for the belief that the overwhelming arguments against rashness leading to catastrophic possibilities would suffice to keep the truce, while the 'city fathers' sought the ways of permanent peace.

The single most important way to 'permanent peace' in Nigeria in early 1965 was a reconsideration and review of the then existing Federal Constitution. Many Nigerians of knowledge and patriotic anxiety had long held that the country could never keep the Federation intact nor move forward from that point under the existing basic law of the land. They complained about its way of distribution of powers among the Federal organs of government and between the Centre and the Regions, about the haziness of the executive arrangements, about certain vital aspects of the defined rights of the citizen, about the status of the law enforcement agencies and of lower courts in the Regions, and about many other points.

Among the complainants was Nnamdi Azikiwe. At the beginning of 1965 he was of the opinion that he would happily serve out his full Presidential term of five years from 1 October 1963, if all Nigerian leaders agreed (a) to uphold and keep the Federal union intact, and (b) to review the 1960 Constitution, in a Constituent Assembly properly called for that purpose. But if the people did not desire to continue in a federation, then a federation, he said, would not work, and in that case he would retire to his part of the country and to his other interests.

Zik's own ideas of main features in a new Federal Constitution included a Federal Republic of four Regions, twenty States, and ninety-four Provinces, with

1. A *President* elected by popular vote (instead of the existing parliamentary election) to hold office for five years;

2. Four *Vice-Presidents* elected by popular vote to represent the existing Regions for five years each;

3. *Regional Governors* and *Premiers*, *Federal Ministers*, and *corporate* Executive, Judicial, and Legislative bodies, etc.;

4. A *Privy Council*; and

5. Four principal *Councils*, viz. Economic, International Relations, Production, and Social.

If the four Regions could not agree to live together under one flag and one government, Zik hoped that they would at least agree to go their separate ways in peace, each to test their own economic viability as to *natural resources and export facilities*, each to try out their own powers of survival.

And whatever were the choices made at such future deliberations as all were envisaging, Zik had one more hope: that the frightening possibilities of January 1965 in Nigeria might be transmuted only into vivid memories – no worse – in the minds of those who had felt their awful nearness at the time.

More than that his biographer could not wish for Azikiwe's Nigeria.

THE END

Appendix A: The Zik Letters

NOTE: We have spoken in our preface about 'honest imperfections and enthusiastic exaggerations in language' to be found in this correspondence. But readers will very probably be ready to conclude that half the trouble was due simply to typographical errors and one or two instances of wrong usage which were just never 'proofed' by their author.

c/o P.O. Box 7
Calabar, Nigeria
31 July 1925

Prince C. Anazonwu
P.O. Box 22
Onitsha

My dear Cousin,

I am grateful to you of your letter which was handed to me yesterday. I am really surprised that you should have taken such an hostile attitude against me, for if my memory serves me right it is quite about two months that my letter was detained.

The rumour of my having gone to England for legal studies with Honourable G. Graham Paul is nothing but concoctions of fabricated mendacities which to all intents and purposes are solely to mislead you people at Home. It is a fact that I have the ambition to study further but it is not true that I intend following any Honourable man, for the apparent lack of cohesion between me and my financial backer shows clearly that the matter is still *sub judice*.

I am quite well and I think I can say most emphatically that I am as strong as a nine-pence loaf of bread for I always keep my head above the water. How is your Mam, I hope that she is well as well as my own lovely mother. I hope to hear from you as early as possible giving preference to the political situation of Onitsha as regards the installation of telephone and metalling of roads which were approved at the last Legislative Assembly.

There are no news at present at Calabar but I can assure you that the Legal Servants' Association founded by me here is growing to become a very powerful organization in Nigeria. We have as our Patrons, Their Honours Messrs Justices Webber and Maxwell and the membership is restricted to Legal servants only.

I am pleased to hear that Mr L. Anyogu is now the responsible official of the Onitsha Literary Club. I am also very glad to hear that he is discharging his official duties in the Club well and I trust that he will in reality understand his great position of trust, as one of the most important factors underlying the success and foundation of the Club is the uniting together of the vast multifarious members of various denominations at Onitsha so that they may understand one another mutually. I hope therefore that nothing unpolitic will disturb or harrangue the progress of the Club. When I have the opportunity I shall communicate with Mr Anyogu so as to congratulate him for his endeavours in striving to unite the masses of Christians at Onitsha who are diametrically opposite with their various doctrines, dogmas, and orthodoxies.

I now stay at Garden Street with a boy of my own as my father is due to retire on pension very soon. Do not be surprised any more if you hear perchance that I have set sail for the Atlantic or Pacific Continents but rest assure your conscience that I shall communicate with you e'en though I am in the Antarctic Regions.

Good bye. I beg to close.

Very affectionately yours,

Ben N. Azikiwe

Box 92
Howard University
Washington, D.C.
16 June 1928

Dr T. J. Jones
Ed: Director
Phelps-Stokes Fund
101 Park Avenue
New York, N. Y.

Dear Dr Jones:

With further reference to my letter of 21 May to which you acknowledged, stating that the matter will be brought to the attention of the Trustees of the Phelps-Stokes Fund at their 6 June meeting. Vide yours dated 25 May, I take this opportunity to further explain my case and to ask for a 'scholarship-loan' in the event of there being no possibility of an aid forthcoming.

Dr Jones, I am from Nigeria, B. West Africa. I am 23 and a half years old. In 1920 when you and the late Dr J. E. Kwegyir Aggrey visited Lagos, *en route* to South Africa, under the auspices of the Phelps-Stokes Educational Commission to Africa, I happened to be among the congregation at Tinubu Church. Dr Aggrey's appeal moved me and since then I have doggedly plodded along and plugged my way ruggedly to America.

My aim in life is to be an Educator and a Philanthropist. My parents cannot afford to educate me beyond the high school. I am incumbent on my own individual resources. It is my ambition to specialize in the Administrative and Psychological branches of the field of education, majoring in the newer philosophy of education as propounded by Dewey *et alia*, rather than the servile idea of the principles of teaching as it obtains in Africa today. That this is one of the needs of Africa now is obvious. I have therefore decided to be among those who will take up the mantle left by the immortal Aggrey.

My ambition could be realized in three ways after graduation. The first is by entering the British Colonial Service in the department of education as Dr Aggrey did. The second is by affiliating myself with a missionary organization (altho I hardly know any of them now) and the third is by independently establishing a school of my own, organizing its curriculum etc. in the light of the knowledge I have obtained in the United States. The first and second may be feasible but for financial reasons, the third, meanwhile, seems to be chimerical.

I am therefore training myself to be a specialized teacher who will help in the solution of the educational problems confronting all who are interested in the amelioration of Africa.

I entered this great nation in 2 October 1925 and matriculated at Storer College, Harpers Ferry, W. Va. Having spent two years there, I had to move to Pittsburgh, Pa. so as to earn money for the completion of my education. Inability to secure permanent employment coupled with financial troubles prevented my returning to school in the fall of 1927. For nine months I was out of school, and the Immigration authorities threatened to deport me. Certain friends came to my rescue and I was able to enter Howard University in the past spring quarter.

This is my problem. In this country, education, to a large extent, means money. It means constant supply of funds to meet the demands of college life. Tuition must be prepaid. Boarding and lodging must be paid for in advance. Unlike Africa, America is an arithmetical environment, where one speaks with dollars and cents. Realizing this, you can visualize my position.

I really want to finish my studies. I have made a fair percentage of average since my stay in this country. I also realize that staying out of school for any unusual period means immediate deportation. It is always difficult to land a good job which will yield a substantial income to enable one to carry on and complete his college training.

Dr Jones, I have proven to you that I am deeply inspired to serve Africa. I have also shown you what I intend to do after obtaining my degrees. And I have made it plain to you that I needed funds to enable me to steer my way along. The question at issue, will now be introduced in the next paragraph which is the main subject of this letter.

It will cost me approximately $1606.00 to obtain my A.B. degree in a Negro College and do one year graduate work either at Harvard or Columbia. During the summer vacations I could earn enough money to take care of my personal expenses including cost of books. Under this circumstance may I humbly and respectfully request thru you to the Phelps-Stokes Fund, that I be loaned the said $1606.00, *ut supra*, payable after obtaining my Master's degree and returning to my homeland and having been actually engaged in the 'field' for active service among my rather unfortunate people. This request of mine is based on the assumption that I cannot ask for a gift of $1606.00 when I am ablebodied and can work to repay it and indirectly help future students who might need such aid. I really will work to repay it in full plus the accumulated interest that might accrue, according to the terms of the transaction, if it is granted.

The world today needs men who can be trusted. I am therefore submitting the names of the following gentlemen as references. They, in reality, know nothing of the subject matter of this correspondence, and so might be in position to give you a first hand information, and probably a better perspective relative to my needs. They are:

Dr J. Stanley Durkee, Plymouth Church, Brooklyn, N. Y.

Dr A. M. Lamb, The Manse, Cheswell, Pa.

Dr H. T. McDonald, Harpers Ferry, W. Va.

Dr Alain L. Locke, Howard University, Washington, D.C.

I understand that Dr Locke will be away this summer and that Dr Lamb, who is a Presbyterian minister, is making a tour of Egypt and the Holy Land. He is leaving the United States by 5 July, and will be back in September.

It is my aim to graduate from Howard University or any other college and do graduate work either at Harvard or Columbia. But should you rule otherwise, I shall not object, for after all, it will be for the ultimate good of Africa and humanity.

To assure you of my earnestness and sincerity of purpose, I may submit that in the event of the 'loan and scholarship' being approved, that it be credited to my account at Howard and be drawn only by authorized officials when needed.

Attached to this letter are eight appendices, which are mostly of an informative nature. They will attempt to show you what I have done both in my school work and in the extra-intra curricula activities, and also what I want to do. If they prove satisfactory enough to support my request and warrant your approval, I shall feel that they have served their purposes. Will you please, after perusal, return those marked V, VI, VII and VIII. Thanks.

With the hope that this letter will serve to bind us closer and that it will open a way for me to materialize my honorable ambitions and legitimate aspirations in the land of the brave and of the free, rather than be forced to be out of school again and stand a chance of facing absolute deportation, and be like a flower born to blush unseen and waste its sweetness on the desert air. I pray that the Lord may help me so that I may return to Africa with the golden fleece, and propagate from the Zambesi to the Nile, yea! from the Nile to the Congo, the new learning, the recent philosophy of education, that education itself is life and not necessarily a preparation for life.

Very sincerely yours,
Ben N. Azikiwe

NOTE: The results of this remarkable 'say-it-all' letter – similar in tone and intention to many others from foreign students to such American philanthropic bodies over many years –themselves make up part of the story of Zik's U.S. career and subsequent choice of profession.

Dr Jones could not grant his request immediately or in the main, but advised Zik to persevere with his courses in education, with the promise of later assistance in seeking an education job in Africa. This Zik did, adding educational psychology, measurements, etc., to this branch of his studies. On first graduation Dr Jones did help him to look for a suitable job in Africa: Liberia, Gold Coast, Nigeria, Sierra Leone, – with the governments, schools, missions – all to no avail. He could not get a single acceptable offer, and it was at this point that Phelps-Stokes gave him the small grants through which he was able to take his summer courses in journalism at Columbia University.

This letter – but not the facts concerning it – was kindly made available to the author by Professor St Clair Drake, of Roosevelt University, Chicago. (See page 10.)

P.O. Box 92
Howard University
Washington, D.C.
24 December 1928

Mr C. O. Anazonwu
P.O. Box 22
Onitsha, Nigeria

My dear Cousin,

In one of my letters to you, presumably dated 31 July 1925, I stated in the second to the last paragraph the following:

'Do not be surprised any more if you hear perchance that I have set sail for the Atlantic or Pacific Continents but rest assure your conscience that I shall communicate with you e'en though I am in the Antarctic Regions.'

This statement still goes and it still holds true to fact *à mon avis*. I told you that wherever I was I shall write and as I have a spare time today, I think it highly essential to write and express to you my feelings anent to my stay in this part of the world.

The United States so far is a good country but with the complex material civilization that had encroached upon its ideals of manhood, she is materially inclined and less spiritual from the philosophic standpoint. She is the home of billionaires, yet the worst type of crime, (viz. – lynching, a most brutal crime yet perpetrated on mankind, savage in its ideal and barbaric in its operation is being committed daily by the numerous thugs and swindlers who pry and ply on innocent strangers and less virile of the citizens of America).

I am not at all harboring in my mind a juridical enquiry into the ethical conception of the United States as a sovereign state worthy of the respect accorded a foreign nation according to International Law and usages, but I think that the Negro today in the United States is worse off there than anywhere else. I say this with knowledge of the South African fiasco. Anyhow conditions are changing and we scholars of the science of humanics are anxiously awaiting with bated breath to see whether the theory of Social Darwinism shall supercede over the philosophy of Hobbes and Locke in respect to the Social Contract theory of society. Let us hope that the time will come when the precepts of Christianity that is being unethically and unmorally imposed on the already religious African, will be practised wholeheartedly to the very letter of the Decalogue. The United States once more, I say, is the place for the socio-economically minded person and not the usual humanic type of the average African: everything here is business. Here is an arithmetical country. The language is interpreted in dollars and cents. Do you get that?

You will realize that this modern age is an age of materialism, an age where economics is playing a great fundamental part in the moulding of nations and men. Be well advised and take it from me that the problem that will confront the African tomorrow will be largely a socionomic one. We are therefore trying to find out how we can aid in making this world safe for democracy under our different governments. This can only be done by mutual collaboration and international goodwill and fellowship.

Are you still teaching? I am just wondering what you are doing now, since teaching does not pay here, where they are paid up to fifty pounds a month (small salary); how much more in the homeland!

I cannot write a very long letter, but suffice is it to say that I always remember my friends, and I never slight anyone. In my bosom reigns the open sesame of democracy. If even I have not written ere this, please let the spirit which prompted my writing this, or even let the Yuletide spirit banish all your hynogogic opinions of my sincerity.

While the sun shines and roses bloom in Africa (the land where the sun shines and palm trees grow), and the snow falls here blanketting the earth with white flakes, and the blizzards hum their sonorous sounds in adoration to their Maker, I rest my pen, wishing you and the family a merry Christmas and a Happy Prosperous New Year.

> Believe me to be,
> Cordially yours,
> Ben N. Azikiwe

> Lincoln University
> Pennsylvania, U.S.A.
> 8 January 1930

Dearest Cousin,

Thanks for your letter dated November – but mailed 30 November! How come you to try to 'slip something on me'? Oh Mi gosh – Boy, I am one hard nut to crack. I got you that time. Didn't I?

I was surprised to learn of your attitude toward my silence. But, considering the fact that you do not realize what it is to be in a college here, I will readily overlook your critical remarks. Very few of my correspondents understand. But I have to spend up to twelve hours in the library daily digging out materials that might be of some value to human knowledge.

Thanks for your information regarding Onitsha and the educational problem now facing Nigeria. I have no comments to make pro or con.

Perhaps on my return I will take the matter up thru an international channel to establish the plausibility of the theory that a state is responsible for the primary education of its subjects.

I am afraid no one understands what an enigma I am. Some are under the probable idea that I am studying law. Others say education. Some say mission work. Some say engineering. Well I have, since coming here, renounced any profession that has as its objective personal gain. My outlook on life has widened. I am not interested in pettifoggism and other external economics of ribaldry. I am more interested in the world politic.

I have therefore limited my research specialization to modern and comparative jurisprudence on the one hand and Scientific Journalism and 'Humanics' on the other. I am in training for the journalistic profession. I mean the 'Scientifically trained' type and not the mediocre type that now speckle West Africa. My field is toward a better understanding between the people and their 'protectors'. It is my aim as a Statesman to establish the idea that a subject people has an inherent inalienable right which colonists must respect. This will revolutionize Colonial diplomacy. I neither condone nor do I condemn petty partisan politics nor even radicalism. But my magazines and newspapers will come with a 'Locarno Spirit' for preserving the territorial integrity of the indigenous African. The time has come in the evolution of thought where the ruler and the governed should meet on a common ground based on peace and goodwill.

My theses for the M.A. and M.Sc. are in the making and perhaps soon I will be thru. Nevertheless I plan to be home by December 1930 or a few months later.

I am not sure if you will like the pictures I enclose herewith. Nevertheless they are the best I have at the present.

It is too cold out here now. But a sedentary life as I lead while communing with the ghosts of literateurs of antiquity seems to make me unmindful of the frigidity of the weather.

Keep fit and always write me. Tell me all about home.

I am glad to learn that you are still with the mission. Stick fast to them. The future has some good in store. Who knows may be tomorrow you'll occupy an editorial or reportorial position in one of our chain newspaper organizations in Nigeria. I like your English. Brush up the facts that you read in the foreign papers. The future lies in the hands of youth. It is youth like you and I that will actuate the neuro-mechanism of man to scale the heights of liberty. While I rest my pen, I remain

Your sincerest friend,

Ben N. Azikiwe

Benjamin N. Azikiwe
Lincoln University
Pennsylvania
11 March 1931

My Dear Cousin,

Thanks a whole lot for your very kind letter of recent date. I have been so busy with professorial duties that it was impossible to reply at once. However I may say that with this mail, under separate cover, I am returning to you the four educational bulletins you were kind enough to loan me last spring.

I enjoyed some of the [words blotted out here] the one dealing with the mentality of the African. Additionally I am deeply interested in that phase of modern educational philosophy, as I recall taking a course – Mental Measurements – in the summer, in the quest to ascertain whether the mentality of the Negro is inferior or superior to that of other races. Admittedly Dr Loram is a fairly brilliant student of Afro-Dutch mental ability, yet he reveals the usual weakness of psychologists without an adequate socio-anthropological background of the subjects examined. Without taking into consideration the vituperations of certain American and British pseudo-psychologists on the mental incompatibility of the African Negro, it is plain from the reference to works of Oldham and Kidd, not to mention such authorities in sociology as Dorsey, Heuter, Hooten of Harvard and Woodson, that all such intelligence tests are the bunk, because they have no definitive value in the objective correlations of mental measurements. I am glad that the author of the article did not fall into the same blunder that Loram made. Of course Loram is too theoretical and prejudiced for us to accept his conclusions at their face value. We must not forget that to accept the postulated thesis of any authority, certain lines of demarcation have to be drawn. In order to regard the thesis of Loram on the mental inferiority of the African to Europeans and Indians, one must question firstly the validity of his method, procedure and standard situations; secondly whether he is a biassed investigator or not. In the first instance, he admits that the situation, and otherwise of the three races is not the same, therefore it is not a standard situation, and his test therefore is lacking in objectivity because it is not a standard one. In the second instance Dr Loram is a product of the prejudiced union of Herzog's South Africa. He is used to the racial philosophy of the Boers (i.e. Boors to use the correct terminology) who are arrogantly decentralized so far as their 'superiority' to the Zulus, Kaffirs and Hottentots is concerned. He is therefore prejudiced, because he did not at the outset accept the universal theorem on the equality of man. Outside of these brief remarks, I like Loram's treatment, although it is not wholly a scientific one. With reference to my idea of these 'intelligence tests' I may say that much could be written on them. The Alpha test of the U.S.A. army, and even the Simon-Binet tests and the Terman standardized tests show a lack of congruity in one respect or the other. Please write soon. Best of wishes,

Ever sincerely yours,
Ben N. Azikiwe

Ben N. Azikiwe, M.A., M.Sc.   9 February 1933
Instructor in Political Science
Lincoln University
Pennsylvania

Dearest Cousin,

Yes, you have every reason to be angry with me. And the joke of it all is that not only you, but about a score of my friends are wondering at my curious silence. I have no valid explanation to make save one – those four or five letters after my name explain the whole mystery in a nutshell! It is not an easy task to be both a professor and a post-graduate student. M.A. is a hard nut to crack and to attempt it plus an M.Sc. makes the nut harder to crack. I have succeeded in cracking both. And I can now write my friends as fast as they can write!

How are you progressing? I suppose Onitsha will have changed by the time I return home. Well I am eagerly hoping to see the home folks once more. I am not definite but my plans call for a cessation of studies *ad interim*, so I may have to get home by this summer.

*

Thanks for your comments on my articles. I am afraid you flatter me when you say that my thinking is deep. Personally, I would rather believe that I am still learning to think. The deep thinkers surround me now in a host of imperishable thoughts preserved in books!

As soon as it is possible I will send you some postal cards and papers. Meanwhile let me say that it is true that I left home with the intention of embracing the law as a profession. However, the longer I stay here and the more I know, I have come to realize that a wider field of creative scholarship is at the end of the rainbow's trail. This has tended to curb my ambition in law even though I hold a Certificate in Law. For the last four years I have been studying the technique of Journalism and that is the Profession I have been preparing myself and specializing in. If the field is not prospective in Onitsha or Enugu, I might have to go to Lagos or Calabar. But as far as I am concerned my interest is not in the 'commoner' professions with mercenary considerations. I am writing a book on Onitsha history and the field of Journalism offers me a better scope to utilize my academic background. My legal training will help me to keep out of libellous troubles which otherwise I would commit without a legal education. When I was home I was fascinated with wigs and gowns. But for the last seven years and four months I feel that the challenge of the Caucasoid world to the Negroid World is creative scholarship. I would not mind writing books on Law and Procedure. That is a good field – legal *scholarship*, but practising law has its fascination all right – for the uninitiated – but when you drink of the Pierian Springs, and you drink it deeply – you will see the scales off your eyes. I will stop over in London and encourage Messrs Egbuna and Mbanefo* to continue in their ambitions so that Onitsha may have its own quota. But now, I am not only an Onitsha man, but I am an African. My task is to aid in the reconstruction of the mind of Young Africa to a nobler destiny, that is to let them *think* of the future of the darker races.

Please let me know how many newspapers are published in Onitsha or Enugu now. According to information to date, there is only one paper in the Onitsha and Owerri Provinces, and that is the *Dawn* of Port Harcourt. The field ought to be prospective. If my studies in Journalism mean a thing, there is not a *modern* newspaper in Nigeria today, the Nigerian *Daily Times* notwithstanding! Do you think I am too radical? I hope not. It is just an attempt to show you the difference between staying abroad for three or four years and get at the surface of things, and staying longer and digging deeper into the furrows beneath the surface. Yes. The tap root of a thing is the thing itself.

My teaching is a success so far. If I did not swear that I shall return to serve my folks in Africa, I think that I have a better chance today to make a name in the world of scholarship. If I would make here my home, my promotion would be plain. But since I refuse to do so, I am just working on a part-time basis and I receive a mere pittance for my services – about three hundred pounds a year on the basis of recent English exchange since Britain fell off the Gold Standard. If I were an American, and working full-time, I would be worth twice or thrice that amount. And that is being too modest too!

How is the Onitsha Literary Club? I hope that it has not died a natural death. If it has, then it shall be resurrected from its present state of suspended animation!

Affectionately yours,
Ben N. Azikiwe

* Both did qualify as barristers, and the latter is at this date Sir Louis Mbanefo, Chief Justice of the East Region.

26 May 1934

Ben N. Azikiwe, M.A., M.Sc.
Head of Department of
History and Political Science
Lincoln University
Pennsylvania

C. O. Anazonwu, Esq.
P.O. Box 86
Onitsha, Nigeria

My dear Cousin,

I have not replied to your letter of some time ago due to academic duties. I am sure you do realize the tremendous tasks before me, much more to find time for writing letters.

To an extent, I feel that I have accomplished my objective in the New World. At least, the first stage of my educational venture has been successful. Probably the scene ought to shift to the Old World – Africa – for the practical application of my training.

I appreciate your information regarding the conditions in Onitsha, particularly in the field of journalism. They are not as bad as in certain rural communities either on the American continent or in Europe. They could be remedied. Truly, success is born out of disappointments. My experiences in America vindicate such a conclusion.

I will sail from the United States by July or August. I may stay in England for a few weeks so as to correct the proofs of my new book on Liberia. Then I will return to Onitsha for few months' relaxation. I have two appointments in view: one in Liberia and one in the Gold Coast. The salary and conditions are as lucrative as in the other learned professions.

Here's hoping that it will not be long before we shall see each other once more. With personal regards to all.

Ever yours,

Ben

Appendix B: W.A.S.U. and the N.C.N.C. Deputation

(a) Notice of Official Reception
(b) Programme of Public Meeting
(c) The *Wasu Magazine* Editorial
(d) Members of the Historic Wasu Executive of 1947
(e) Notes on (d)

(*a*)
PROGRAMME

RECEPTION OF N.C.N.C. DELEGATES

arranged by

THE WEST AFRICAN STUDENTS UNION

AFRICA HOUSE,

1, SOUTH VILLAS,

N.W. 1

JULY 30th, 1947

PUBLIC MEETING AND

INFORMAL DINNER PARTY

Admit bearer   *1/6d.*

(*b*)
PUBLIC MEETING

at

CONWAY HALL, RED LION SQUARE, W.C.1

JULY 30th, 1947

4.00 p.m. Chairman's Opening Remarks
4.15 p.m. What is the National Council of Nigeria and the Cameroons?
By *Prince A. Adedoyin*, B.L., Sec. N.C.N.C.;
Elected Member of the Legislative Council of Nigeria and the Cameroons.
4.30 p.m. Greetings from the Women of Nigeria
By *Mrs F. Ransome-Kuti*, Educationist; President, Abeokuta Women's Union.

4.35 p.m. Greetings from the People of Northern Nigeria
By *Mallam Bukar Dipcharima*, Businessman; former Member of Maiduguri Town Council.

4.40 p.m. Greetings from the People of South-Western Nigeria
By *Dr Al. H. Abu Olorun-Nimbe*, Medical Practitioner; Treasurer, N.C.N.C.; Elected Member of the Leg. Co., Nigeria.

4.45 p.m. Greetings from the People of South-Eastern Nigeria
By *Chief Nyong Essien*, former President, Ibibio Union; Nominated Member of the Leg. Co., Nigeria.

4.50 p.m. Greetings from the People of the Cameroons
By *P. M. Kale*, Educationist; President, Cameroons Youth League.

4.55 p.m. The Purpose of the Delegation
By *Dr N. Azikiwe*, Journalist and Newspaper Proprietor; President, N.C.N.C.; Elected Member of the Leg. Co., Nigeria.

6.00 p.m. A Voice from Britain: *Rev. R. Sorensen*, M.P.*

6.10 p.m. Comments and Questions.

6.50 p.m. Vote of Thanks.

7.00 p.m. Closure

7.30 p.m. Informal Dinner Party at Bonnington Hotel, Southampton Row, W.C.1.

Charge 7/6d. each

(c) *Wasu Magazine Editorial*

ANOTHER DELEGATION COMES AND GOES

Like all serious students everywhere, we owe a duty to ourselves to face facts squarely, to make certain assessments objectively, and to state certain findings truthfully, even if the truth hurts quite often. The National Council of Nigeria and the Cameroons delegation which arrived in England last June and left in September did not accomplish much. In the nature of the circumstances and the situation it could not accomplish much. The sum total of what the delegation actually did can be put down in a few words: they did see the Colonial Secretary; they spoke to scattered groups of the British public; they presented phases of their case in sections of the British press; and they circularized a lot of individuals and organizations with a complete statement of that case.

No doubt it is possible, even reasonable, for the optimists to hope and believe that the delegation came to England as a farmer goes to a freshly prepared field with seed, knowing that in due time his depen-

* Now Lord Sorensen of Leyton, long-time Chairman of the Board of W.A.S.U.

dents and hired hands will reap the harvest of his labours. They may protest, and with some justification, that it has happened before in the political and economic history of West Africa. Delegations have come to Downing Street, they will say, and been turned down flat regarding their major demands, only to see those same demands more or less met in one, two, or ten years afterwards. They will name the Gold Coast Aborigines Society lands deputation of 1898, the West African National Congress deputation of 1920, and the Gold Coast and Nigeria Cocoa delegation of 1945, as cases in point. They will say these bodies scored victories, either immediately or long afterwards.

So let it be. We do not contest the point. But we are entitled to our opinion in the matter, as in all matters affecting the present and future of our country and our people. And we say that the day of such delegations and deputations is long past. The game of politics is played, or should be played, *on the spot*. Presentation abroad of one's case, when it can be heard at home more effectively, is an outmoded form of social waste. If we have the means, the ends to be sought should be a following – educated to the cause, devoted to its leaders, overwhelming when it strikes. A delegation is not an end to be sought. Not even its results.

The glamour and romance implied – for Africans – in the decision 'to send a delegation to England', like the glamour and romance implied in the decision 'to take our case to the Privy Council', regardless of cost, is the kind of mental slavery from which it is high time to release our people. The time, trouble, and expense involved in most of these prestige-expeditions are not anywhere nearly justified by the practical results.

If we have the leaders and the following, we need never again come to see Creech Jones. Creech Jones will come to see us. For power understands only the language of power. That is the lesson of contemporary political history that we ought to be learning by now.

(d) *Members of Wasu Executive 1947*

Among these were the following:
G. K. Amachree, who was the General Secretary; M. Odesanya, Financial Secretary; J. E. Appiah, Liaison Officer responsible for inter-organizational relations; B. Akpata, Study Group Leader; and R. B. P. Botsio, Acting Warden of the Wasu Hostel.

There were two ordinary members of the Committee, listed as: F. N. Nkrumah and B. O. Alakija

The Editorial Board of the Union's official organ (the *Wasu Magazine*) was composed of the following:

Kankam Boadu (Chairman), M. Odesanya, A. Ejiwumi, O. Asika, K. A. B. Jones-Quartey

The Union's Business and Advertising Manager was Harold L. Walker, of Fleet Street, London (since retired).

(e) *Notes on Executive Members*

Godfrey Amachree: studied law, returned to Nigeria and became Solicitor-General; subsequently went as an Under-Secretary to the U.N. and Special Adviser to the Secretary-General.

'Mike' Odesanya: became a barrister of the Supreme Court of Nigeria.

'Joe' Appiah: of Ghana, studied law and married Peggy, daughter of the late Sir Stafford Cripps, Chancellor of the Exchequer in the post-War Cabinet of Clement Attlee.

Bankole Akpata: of Nigeria, became a Senior Lecturer at the Kwame Nkrumah Ideological Institute in Ghana.

Kojo Botsio: a founder-member of the C.P.P. in Ghana, and Minister (at the time of going to press) of Foreign Affairs.

F. N. Nkrumah: founded the C.P.P. and became Osagyefo the President of Ghana.

B. O. Alakija: returned to Nigeria in one of the professions.

F. Kankam Boadu: was for a time Deputy Managing Director of the Ghana Cocoa Purchasing Company in London. (See also page 187).

A. Ejiwumi: of Abeokuta and Lagos, studied industrial chemistry.

O. Asika: from Nigeria, studied law.

Soas Jones-Quartey: started work under Zik in Accra, was of the cited editorial opinion of the *Wasu Magazine* in 1947, and, at the time of going to press with this book, was engaged on a biography of Nnamdi Azikiwe.

Appendix C

Statement by N.C.N.C. representative, Magnus Williams, Esq., at meeting of fifth Pan-African Congress (organized in Manchester in October 1945 by late George Padmore, Kwame Nkrumah, and Jomo Kenyatta, and held under chairmanship of late W. E. B. Du Bois.) Williams' statement illustrates general mood of African Peoples in 1945, the year of the end of the Second World War and of first notices of Richards constitutional proposals in Nigeria:

MR MAGNUS WILLIAMS, The National Council of Nigeria and the Cameroons: The Colonial Office has always told us by words and implication that there is a happy land; and we have always answered 'far, far away'. We have come to this Congress to decide and enforce the means by which we shall make that happy land our own. The Colonial Office is an instrument of oppression and we must do our best to abolish that office. When the war came, with its clash of interests between imperialists, the Nigerian Government vested the mineral wealth in the Crown, and the Government of Britain says that every mineral in the Nigerian ground must come to them. While the people of Nigeria are contributing to the revenue of the country, the sons and daughters of the rulers reap the benefits. We must do our best to right these wrongs.

From *A History of the Pan-African Congress*, ed. George Padmore, London, 1947 and 1963, p. 35.

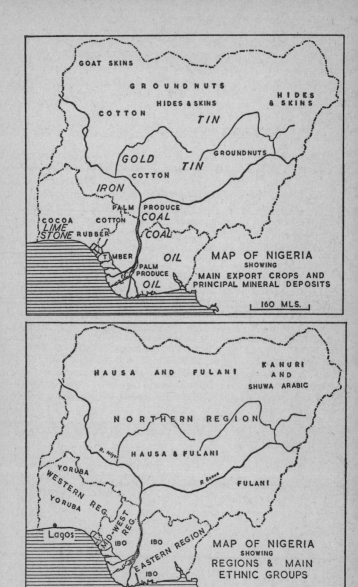

GOAT SKINS

G R O U N D N U T S

HIDES & SKINS

H I D E S
& SKINS

COTTON

TIN

GOLD

TIN

GROUNDNUTS

COTTON

IRON

PALM PRODUCE

COAL

COCOA
LIME
STONE

COTTON

RUBBER

COAL

TIMBER

OIL

PALM
PRODUCE

OIL

MAP OF NIGERIA
SHOWING
MAIN EXPORT CROPS AND
PRINCIPAL MINERAL DEPOSITS

160 MLS.

HAUSA AND FULANI

KANURI
AND
SHUWA ARABIC

N O R T H E R N   R E G I O N

HAUSA & FULANI

R. Niger

YORUBA

WESTERN REG.

R Benue

FULANI

YORUBA

MID-WEST REG.

Lagos

IBO

IBO

EASTERN REGION

IBO

MAP OF NIGERIA
SHOWING
REGIONS & MAIN
ETHNIC GROUPS

IBO

160 MLS.

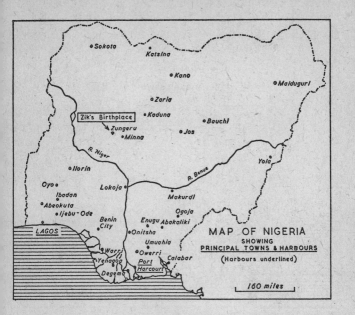

MAP OF NIGERIA
SHOWING
PRINCIPAL TOWNS & HARBOURS
(Harbours underlined)

160 miles

Index